Librarians in Fiction

Librarians in Fiction

A Critical Bibliography

by
GRANT BURNS

McFarland & Company, Inc., Publishers
Jefferson, North Carolina and London

"To librarians everywhere."

British Library Cataloguing-in-Publication data are available

Library of Congress Cataloguing-in-Publication Data

Burns, Grant, 1947–
    Librarians in fiction : a critical bibliography / by Grant Burns.
      p.   cm.
    Includes indexes.
    ISBN 0-7864-0499-X (sewn softcover : 50# alkaline paper) ∞
    1. English literature — Bibliography.   2. Librarians in literature —
Bibliography.   3. American literature — Bibliography.   I. Title.
Z2014.L45B87 1998
[PR151.L53]
016.8208'0352092 — dc21   98-10695
                                                                        CIP

Manufactured in the United States of America

McFarland & Company, Inc., Publishers
    Box 611, Jefferson, North Carolina 28640

Contents

Introduction

The members of most professions and occupations are sensitive about how the public sees them. Librarians share this sensitivity. After my 25 years as a library worker (21 of them as a reference librarian), I can attest to that claim personally — and the literature backs me up. An examination of relevant works shows that librarians have been somewhat preoccupied with their image nearly since the inception of the profession.

One of the major vehicles for the development and propagation of images of any group is fiction. Librarians are plentiful in fiction. This should come as no surprise. Practitioners of fiction who are good at their work write about what they have seen. Most of them have seen librarians, often at closer range than has much of the public at large. They tend to spend more time than most in libraries, are usually sympathetic to ideas about the collection, preservation, and dissemination of literature, and, even if they do not know very much about the particulars of library work, recognize that librarians are involved in those activities.

This bibliography has two purposes: first, to explore the images of librarians in fiction originally written in English, or fiction that has appeared in English translation over the last century or so; and second, to lead the reader to good and interesting fiction featuring librarians.

What Fictional Librarians Are Like

Librarians in serious fiction tend to be unhappy and beset with problems. That fact probably says far less about librarians and their image than it does about serious fiction, which after all is not about happiness, but trouble and sorrow. As Tolstoy observed in his famous opening of *Anna Karenina*, "All happy families resemble one another, but each unhappy family is unhappy in its own way." Happiness and harmony allow few openings for fiction; unhappiness and trouble offer an endless supply. If fictional librarians in serious work are troubled, then their trouble is in keeping with the experiences of serious fictional characters in general. They probably should not be regarded as emblematic of real librarians' ill adjustment to life; nor should their fictional creators be accused of indulging in easy stereotyping.

Novelists and short story writers do tend to portray librarians along certain lines, although wild deviations exist. Though too unsystematic to provide proof of any particular theories, the following exercise may indicate something of the way creative writers think of librarians. The positive descriptors below are applied to librarians in novels covered in this bibliography:

adaptable	exotic	respected
alert	friendly	scholarly
attractive	funny	serene
beautiful	gentle	serious
beloved	genuine	shrewd
brisk	good	smart
charming	industrious	striking
clever	intelligent	tactful
composed	kind	tender
decent	knowledgeable	thrifty
devoted	nice-looking	well-built
dignified	observant	well-informed
direct	pretty	wholesome
efficient	professional	wise
elegant	reflective	witty
enthusiastic	resolute	wonderful

As the list above indicates, positive descriptors applied to librarians in fiction are concerned more often than not with issues of intelligence or nurturing ability. Evidently these are the qualities the public looks for in a librarian. Librarians should be smart, and scholarly, as well as tactful and friendly. If they are sometimes pretty or funny, that is merely frosting on the cake. It is more important, in library country, to be well-informed than it is to be well-built.

When fictional librarians are neither smart nor tactful nor friendly, what are they? A list of descriptive words drawn from this bibliography's novels includes the following, which seem to be reasonably representative of the dark side of librarians in fiction.

awkward	devious	emaciated
bald	dirty	exhausted
chunky	disagreeable	feeble
condescending	dreary	florid
cranky	dry	friendless
cruel	dull	frightened
desiccated	dumpy	frustrated

glowering	odd	spinster
hesitant	old maid	stiff
huge	pale	thin
humorless	peculiar	tired
hysterical	portly	tortured
idiotic	possessive	trapped
ill-tempered	red-faced	ungainly
inhuman	repressed	unhealthy
interfering	sad	unlovable
lonely	sexless	unnatural
mincing	sex-starved	unscrupulous
myopic	shapeless	vengeful
narrow	sharp-tongued	waxen
nasty	shy	wilted
nervous	slow	withered
neurotic	sly	wizened

Judging by this list, it is hard to avoid the impression that novelists often suspect librarians of missing out on their fair share of amorous fulfillment. The professional-virgin sharp-tongued desiccated sex-starved shapeless spinster librarian is a caricature that seems so extreme on its face as to be laughable, yet many writers have not been beyond indulging in some variation of it, in an apparent knee-jerk reaction to that old problem of fiction: how to bring a character to life in a believable way. Do novelists and short story writers turn to this stereotype because it sells, or because they, along with the rest of the public, too often accept it as truth?

It is amusing to observe the many ways in which authors relieve librarians of their mortal encumbrances. Librarians in fiction are, among other means of exit, shot, stabbed, strangled, beaten to death with books, rolled over by boulders, and hurled down the library stairs. If librarians serve as symbols of orderliness and the preservation of civilization, their frequent status as targets for fictional homicide may imply some thoughts about writers' and readers' desires to cast away the restraints of civilization. What better way than to pummel a reference librarian with an encyclopedia? So much for your treasured alphabetical order!

Librarians themselves appear in some shocking deviations from the professional norm. True, when fictional librarians go bad, they tend toward crimes of relative gentility, such as swiping rare books. They do, however, on occasion indulge in more spectacular and messier transgressions. The former librarian in Jim Thompson's *The Getaway* (Item 205) has thrown over the literary life for that of the rampaging felon. The librarian antiheroine of Elsa Lewin's *I, Anna* (Item 129) beats her lover to death with a clarinet. The featured librarian in Ernest Raymond's *A Chorus Ending* (Item 182) slays his lover's mother with a hatchet.

Lest we fear that librarians in fiction are running in unfettered villainy, we can take solace in knowing that a veritable army (well, a platoon, anyhow) of librarian sleuths is dogging the evildoers' footsteps, driving the miscreants into the light. Among many other librarian upholders of truth, justice, and civilization are Aurora Teagarden (*Dead Over Heels, Real Murders*, Items 89, 90); Glynis Tryon (*Blackwater Spirits, North Star Conspiracy, Seneca Falls Inheritance*, Items 154–156); Elizabeth Merritt (*A Town of Masks*, Item 42); Gilda Gorham (*The Widening Stain*, Item 13); Jacqueline Kirby (*Die for Love, The Murders of Richard III, The Seventh Sinner*, Items 173–175); and Dewey James (*A Slay at the Races*, Item 160). For every librarian who takes the money and runs, as does Francine Pennypack in Robert Rossner's *The End of Someone Else's Rainbow* (Item 184), there are several who stand with Charles Goodrum's creation, Dr. Edward George (Items 83–85), on the side of integrity, uprightness, and, presumably, returning books on time.

These examples come from popular (or would-be popular) fiction. In more serious fiction, as already noted, librarians struggle with the vicissitudes of existence as do other characters in the same sort of works. These librarians display a wide range of behavior, from emotional paralysis (Augusta Walker's "The Day of the Cipher," Item 324) to courage in the face of inevitable defeat (Mrs. Vickers in Frank Gagliano's *Night of the Dunce*, Item 333.)

In the end, the image of the librarian in fiction is decidedly mixed. One meets many fictional librarians next to whom one would not choose to sit on a long airplane flight; one also meets many who are portrayed as good, hard-working, honest, compassionate, and intelligent people. In spite of those positive portrayals, the cumulative weight of the fictional librarian's representation inclines perceptibly to the negative pole, and the entries in this bibliography, taken as a whole, will demonstrate that leaning. Why is it so? Are librarians not being treated fairly? Do the authors who attempt to portray them not understand them? Do they buy too freely into hoary stereotypes, finding it easier to deal in superficial renderings than in complex investigations? Or can it be (to paraphrase Shakespeare) that the fault, dear colleagues, is not in our authors, but in ourselves? And if not the whole fault, at least a helping of it?

False Leads

Among the challenges encountered in preparing this bibliography were the many dubious leads that appeared in a variety of sources, ranging from other bibliographies to asides in critical articles. Thoroughness is admirable, yet to imply that a novel features a library theme because on a single page the main character returns a book to a library, without any further involvement with the library or its staff, seems a bit of a stretch. Among the large number of possibilities rejected was Henry James's *The Bostonians*. Some benefit no doubt obtains from enduring 464 pages of James's verbiage to discover two pages that mention Miss Catching, the cataloger, even if the benefit is only to be reminded after a 25-year hiatus from that novel how unappealing is every major character in the book. The treatment of Miss Catching, like that of many other librarians in fiction, is so slight and glancing that the novel does not deserve a place in this bibliography. Similarly shunned are items focusing on library workers other than librarians. No one who knows libraries would question the importance of the clerks, paraprofessionals, student assistants, and other nonlibrarian folk who do so much to make libraries work well. The focus of this bibliography is, however, on librarians.

Generic Questions

Aside from examining and ruling out works of false promise, the matter of how to deal with genre fiction presented some concerns. I have included work from the science fiction, horror, mystery, and thriller ghettos but have omitted work intended chiefly for children and adolescents; my interest is in literature for adults. Although, presumably, the genres of romance and what has come to be known, alas, as Christian fiction are aimed at an adult audience, they are also missing from this bibliography. It will take a stronger constitution and a braver soul than mine to assay those territories.

The notion of genre fiction is not altogether well founded. In an ultimate sense, there are only two kinds of fiction: good and bad, with the various shadings of those qualities in between. Many works of science fiction and mystery are better written than many examples of "serious" fiction. The two major sections of this bibliography, then, are in straightforward alphabetical order, by author. Mysteries and science fiction rub shoulders with mainstream and literary fiction, as if they actually belonged in the same house. It is hard to ignore ingrained ideas about separation of fiction into types, but I would prefer not to reinforce those artificial barriers further than my own prejudices and indoctrination lead me. So, no, there is not a separate chapter for mysteries.

The bibliography veers away from fiction only to the extent that it includes a short section on theatrical works featuring librarians as characters. It does not veer far enough in this direction to cover musicals. Thus Marian the librarian does not grace these pages, nor do librarians from film or television. Those last two categories are ripe fruit for someone else's investigation. In the film category, any intrepid researcher might well want to begin with William H. King's master's thesis, *The Celluloid Librarian: The Portrayal of Librarians in Motion Pictures* (Univ. of North Carolina at Chapel Hill, 1990). *Drôles de Bibliothèques*, an excellent book by Anne-Marie Chaintreau and Renée Lemaître (Item 344), would also be useful for cinema enthusiasts — or even for movie buffs.

Most of the entries in this bibliography are more like reviews than annotations. By spending some time on plot summary and character description, I hope to encourage reading of the original work. A bare-bones annotation is unlikely to accomplish that objective. The "Bibliographer's Choice" list toward the end of this book is a further effort to lead readers to the original work. Here are noted a number of works that stand out from the pack for a variety of reasons. It is a list based on personal reactions, of course; many good works have been omitted. Nevertheless, if one has doubts about where to begin reading the adventures of fictional librarians, "Bibliographer's Choice" should help.

As for completeness, it is pleasant to think that one has done an unflaggingly thorough job of unearthing citations to the literature that forms the quarry of the moment. Bibliographies are like poems, however, in the sense that they are never finished. There is always the novel or the story that has somehow escaped the net, evaded the beating of the bushes, or flown under the radar of the bibliographer's search. My hope is that the escapees and oversights are few. Still lurking in my files are leads for a handful of potential items that I was unable to obtain for review. It is unlikely that the absence of any of those items will prove an unspeakable loss. One never knows, of course. That is part of the bibliographer's curse.

Speaking of obtaining books, I must acknowledge my colleague Terry Swier's assistance in retrieving often obscure materials. She is the head of the interlibrary lending office at the University of Michigan–Flint's Thompson Library, and she graciously handled my many requests herself. "Just a few more," I said to her time and again. I also want to acknowledge the help of my wife, Stephanie, for her tireless preliminary perusal of novels that offered only a vague hope of actual focus on librarians. Her identification of novels that did, in fact, feature librarians was of great assistance and freed me from pursuing many dead ends. A final bow is due those bibliographers, indexers, and researchers whose previous work on the question of librarians in fiction made my task possible. I may quibble about nonexistent or misleading annotations on the part of some of my predecessors, but their labors were indispensable, and their task was often more daunting than mine.

Citation Notes

The edition used as the text for this bibliography appears first in each entry. Citations for novels generally note both original United States and British editions, when identifiable. When a novel's first publication was not in the United States, information on the non–United States edition usually completes the citation, except, of course, for occasions when the foreign publication provided the review text. No attempt has been made to list every edition of widely published and frequently reissued works; for these, the phrases "many editions" or "other editions" will give some indication of their availability.

Citations for short stories also begin with the text consulted for the bibliography. When other sources were ascertainable, one or more are usually noted in addition to that used for the review. Further sources are indicated by the phrases "many sources" or "other sources." Original periodical publication information, if ascertainable even in part, completes the short story citations. If it has been determined that a story first appeared in the volume cited, with no previous publication in a periodical, that fact is noted by the words "first publication."

Apologies are in order, perhaps, for attenuated periodical citations. Anthology editors habitually refuse to give complete citations for stories included in their compilations; many stories tenaciously resist efforts to pin down their place of first publication. In what seems an act of perverse oversight, collections of stories by a single author also very commonly omit previous publication details. It is probably a vain hope that editors and authors would begin to rectify this thorn in the bibliographer's (and reader's) side. Nevertheless, in the belief that a little information in this regard is superior to none, I have shared what I was able to find.

One of the great pleasures in preparing such a bibliography is the discovery of authors and work one has previously overlooked or of which one has been wholly ignorant. This discovery is especially rewarding when it involves writers from past decades who have faded, if not disappeared altogether, from public recognition. In our commonplace compulsion to keep up with the current, we often lose sight of estimable work that has been on the shelves for more than a few years, let alone many decades. Plentiful rewarding reading exists among largely forgotten writers and their work, some of it better than much of the literature resplendent in shiny new dust jackets on bookstore shelves or in public library rental displays.

This bibliography will help illuminate the ways librarians have been treated in fiction. I hope that it also will bring together readers and books whose paths might otherwise have never crossed. There is some very fine fiction in which librarians prosper, suffer, triumph, and fail. It deserves wider reading.

— Grant Burns
Fall 1997

I. Novels

1. Abbe, George. *Voices in the Square.* New York: Coward-McCann, 1938. 333p.

Town librarian Miss Bunce breaks the surface for no more than a few pages in this tale of small-town youth, but her appearance is a notable example of stereotyping run amok. The local uppity adolescents who repair to the library to meet their friends and maybe land dates face a formidable adversary indeed in the personage of Miss Bunce:

"She was a huge, imposing woman with a heavy, red, disagreeable face, hairs on chin and upper lip. Her eyes, fierce and always penetrating, lifted from whatever she was doing and knifed the person entering.... Her melon-like breasts standing out vengefully; she stood there scowling, the rubber stamp lifted, like a judge ready to strike the death sentence...."

Abbe writes tolerably when he is not finding the devil in Miss Bunce, but somewhere deep in his own youth he must have been bitten in the stacks, or in some sensitive spot, by a librarian.

2. Ackroyd, Peter. *Chatterton.* New York: Grove, 1987. 234p. London: Hamilton, 1987. (Other editions.)

Philip Slack, he of the "lean and sombre" face, is a public librarian in London and a major character in this ambitious and inventive literary mystery. He visits his otherwise-unemployed poet friend Charles Wychwood on weekends, bringing with him, always, two bottles of wine. Philip is awkward in company and a bit caught up in his work but is a decent sort. Charles has acquired an old painting of the fabricating medievalist Thomas Chatterton, who committed suicide at the age of 18 in 1770. Details about the painting seem to suggest that Chatterton faked his suicide as well as he faked medieval literature. In the gloomy basement of the library, Philip pursues revelations about Chatterton among forgotten stored volumes. It is true that "he might seem slow or hesitant in his dealings with the world, but he always read swiftly and anxiously. He knew that his real comfort was to be found in books." Nevertheless, Philip shows a sympathetic attitude toward the poor and unwashed who often frequent the library.

Like several of the characters, Philip is a writer whose efforts have been frustrated. Charles cannot sell the poems he writes; Philip stumbled through 40 pages of a novel but could not find his own voice and gave up on the project. Yet, in the end, he believes that he will be able to take Charles's place as a writer, among other roles.

Characters here include not only Slack (the surname is not without significance) and other present-day types, but George Meredith, nineteenth-century painter Henry Wallis, and Chatterton himself. A readable and extraordinarily clever novel, *Chatterton* is, unfortunately, almost all head and very little soul.

3. Alington, C. A. *Gold and Gaiters.* London: Faber & Faber, 1950. 207p.

The aging archdeacon Castleton is in charge of a small library in an old English abbey. The library, a haphazard collection, contains one very special feature: a half-dozen Roman gold coins of great rarity. Castleton is very proud of his library but humble about his own role in it. He fears that he is too old for the job, although assured otherwise by his colleagues, and is keenly aware of the fact that he is an amateur bibliotechnician: "He was continually harassed by the fear that he was an inadequate librarian." When the Roman coins disappear one day, the archdeacon has new reason to doubt his library management ability. A gentle, good-humored mystery, with an attractive character in Castleton.

4. Amis, Kingsley. *That Uncertain Feeling.* New York: Harcourt, Brace, 1956. 247p. London: Gollancz, 1955. (Other editions.)

Main character John Lewis is a 26-year-old assistant librarian with the Aberdarcy Public Library. When passing out romance novels at random to patrons at the lending desk, he has a pet answer to his favorite question, "Is it a good book?" The answer: "You'll like it." The blend of savoir faire and contempt residing in this response catches Lewis's point of view quite well. He is, he says, "a sworn foe of the bourgeoisie," and he has little kind regard for anyone who either reveals ignorance or assumes importance. At a party populated by upper-middle-class types, he gets into a row with a local author who criticizes the library and its staff. He eagerly anticipates the next issue of *Astounding Science Fiction* magazine, while speaking of the books on his shelves at home with less than enthusiasm: "One book would tell me what I knew already, another what I couldn't understand, a third what I knew to be untrue, a fourth what I didn't want to be told about." A sense of being off his literary feed extends to life in general; Lewis neither particularly wants to do anything, nor does he particularly not want to do anything.

In spite of his diffidence, he believes that he is interested in an opening in the library's administrative area. This interest dovetails with his affair with the wife of one of the committee members responsible for making a decision on the administrative opening. There are some delightfully absurd passages in the novel, including Lewis's fleeing a would-be trysting place disguised in women's clothing, and his fantasy about the perfect job interview: "Are you interested in films, drinking, American novels, women's breasts, jazz, science fiction?" The imaginary interview is scarcely less ludicrous than the ensuing chapter-long real interview, in which Lewis faces the hiring committee.

How and why Lewis and his wife resolve the uncertain feelings of marital stress and the conflicts between careerism and true personal needs are the book's main issues. As is the usual case with Amis, the results are both entertaining and thought provoking.

5. Anderson, Sherwood. *Beyond Desire.* New York: Liveright, 1932. 359p. (Other editions.)

Vintage Anderson, this novel focuses by turns on the tangled relations between men and women, the dark recesses of individual souls, and the struggles of the working class, in this case Southern mill workers (with inspiration drawn from a 1929 strike in North Carolina).

A good two-thirds of the book concerns Ethel Long, the 29-year-old town librarian of Langdon, Georgia. Educated at the University of Chicago more to satisfy her father than herself, Ethel obtains a job in a branch of the Chicago Public Library, "far out on the West Side ... handing out dirty soiled books to dirty soiled people day after day ... having to be cheerful about it and act as though you liked it.... Such tired weary faces most of the working people had."

That passage suggests something of Ethel's scant pleasure in her work. Her real ambition is to satisfy her materialistic, acquisitive nature, as well as her animal lust (that old Anderson standby). While in Chicago, she uses a number of men for her own purposes, for better or worse. The worse includes a beating by a sadistic book collector. Ethel's suffering parallels her own cold objectives: "I could hurt a lot of men before I die," she thinks — and probably does.

One of them is young Red Oliver, the book's most important character. Fate waits for Red in the strike, but before it claims him, Ethel has her way with him. It is a dark and stormy night in Langdon when young Red walks into the library to find Ethel waiting for him. The seduction scene, with Ethel calling all the shots, takes place as rain pours in the open library windows. "It had all happened on a table in the library, the table at which he was accustomed to sit, reading his books."

Anderson can be a wonderfully awkward writer, but it is a mistake to become distracted by his lack of literary grace. He works ferociously to get into his characters' heads and hearts and is determined to address the most fundamental questions of human conduct at as unadorned and raw a level as possible. He succeeds in stripping bare Ethel's motives and inner life. The resulting picture isn't pretty, but it is very persuasive. There is not much of libraries here, but there is a lot of human nature.

Anonymous. *See* Klein, Joe.

6. Astley, Thea. *Reaching Tin River.* Port Melbourne, Victoria: Heinemann Australia, 1990. 223p. New York: Putnam, 1990. (Other editions.)

A superbly imagined, mysterious, and not a little eerie story of a woman looking for the center of her life, this novel makes no compromises with reader expectations, remaining true to itself and to its main character's lonely search.

The narrator, Belle, is the daughter of an American jazz trumpeter and his
drummer wife, Bonnie. Bonnie lurched back home to Australia by herself before
Belle's birth. Belle grows up with some advantages, including private school attendance paid for by her grandmother, but Bonnie slides by, just barely, playing
nostalgic music few want to hear and working on the side as a supermarket check-
out clerk. Belle puts in some years as a schoolteacher, until she applies for a
librarian traineeship in a Brisbane municipal library. She and Bonnie move into
an old house, where Bonnie tries to simplify her life by giving away her bed
and washing machine and knitting household items from the hair of her dog.
Driven from the house by her mother's eccentricity, Belle rents a flat of her own,
where she lives while contending with the head librarian. He summons his staff
with whistles and snapped fingers, "knows the Dewey system by heart — every
category — and refuses to listen to any proposed changes. A natural Luddite,
computers are killing him." He collects pigeon droppings for mulch. "It is like
being back with mother," notes Belle.

Belle passes her exams, receives a modest promotion, and makes friends with
the other librarians, all of whom "have a hair-shirt quality of endurance and a
gentleness the public service has never been able to damp out." She goes into
archival work and marries Seb, her section head, who soon makes the jump to
deputy librarian. The marriage is a mess from the beginning. "When your mother
is a lot more entertaining than your husband is," observes Belle, "it gets you
down to analyzing the pith of matrimony."

Seb is cold and self-absorbed. In the course of the marriage, he works his
way through several affairs. Belle finds escape and a certain purpose in her archival
research into the life of a nineteenth-century farmer, Gaden Lockyer. Her pursuit of Lockyer becomes intense to the point of obsession; one expects at any
point that her research and her fancy will merge past and present and place her
literally in the presence of the long-dead man. Indeed, as she reads his journal
entries, she sees herself described in them. By the time Belle reaches Tin River,
where she stays in a boarding house where Lockyer once lived, their meeting in
the flesh seems certain.

It is not as certain as it seems, however, and the novel is the stronger for it.
Belle is an adroitly drawn character, alert and self-critical, with a rueful humor.
Several other characters also stand out, among them Belle's father, with whom
she has a brief and painful (for the reader) reunion in New York City. It's a relatively short novel, but dense with numerous varieties of human experience.

7. Barbour, Ralph Henry. *A Maid in Arcady.* Philadelphia: Lippincott, 1906. 213p.

Mencken was right: The effects of Puritanism on American literature were pernicious. Barbour helps demonstrate the fact in this painfully stilted, ridiculously chaste romance, couched in prose so flowery the aroma of gardenias wafts upward from the pages. Hero Ethan Parmley is a Harvard Law grad who one day out canoeing spies a classical goddess come to life. She proves to be public librarian Miss Hoyt, although Ethan does not learn her true identity until late in the book, when we finally obtain a glimpse of her at work. Miss Hoyt, whether capering coyly in Grecian garb or leading Ethan to believe she is someone else, floats through the story like a bit of dandelion fluff. "'Do you realize,' she asked, 'that you have made me late for church?'" Goodness! It's a truly silly piece of work that may have dissuaded at least a few young women from pursuing library careers. It has pleasantly quaint illustrations, though, by Frederic J. von Rapp.

8. Barrangon, Eloise. *How to Travel with Parents.* New York: Dial, 1956. 242p.

This entertaining novel features 13-year-old Liz's narrative of her vacation travels with her family. Liz's librarian Aunt Maureen appears on a few pages. Maureen is "nice-looking in a wholesome sort of way." She attends foreign films and reads *Vogue* but wears the same perfume and same shade of lipstick year after year, to go with her dumpy clothes. She also habitually drops her dinner plates onto the floor. (She doesn't mind picking up the broken pieces.) Says Liz of her aunt: "Men seldom make passes at girls who talk about the Dewey decimal system even if they don't wear glasses."

9. Bassett, Sara Ware. *Within the Harbor.* Garden City, N.Y.: Doubleday, 1948. 252p. New York: Popular Library, 1948.

Libbie Lane, librarian of the New England burg of Belleport, caters to the ill, obtains speakers for the Women's Club, plays organ in church, and generally makes herself more than useful in her little town. Libbie is "respected and beloved" by the townsfolk, albeit a mere 21 years old. One day she breaks her leg (probably hurrying from the library to the church), and retired college professor Floyd Robertson agrees to fill in at her post on an interim basis. The job, "of course ... doesn't pay much," but Robertson declines to accept even the pittance Miss Lane received. He finds the library surprisingly well organized, though small, with a good collection. On finally meeting the convalescent Libbie a third of the way through the novel, he judges her not pretty, but beautiful in her own unique way: "He understood now why she drew people to her, why the village sang her praises, why she had a train of worshipers, and why even rough, untutored boys ... became courteous in her presence and leaped to do her bidding." Miss Lane is headed for hard times, but no one could believe that they would last long, not even with the theft of the library's most precious volume, an edition of Shelley's *Defense of*

Queen Charlotte. It's a middling entertainment in which mild people involved in mild romance and mild intrigue produce mild amusement.

10. Bates, Sylvia C. *The Long Way Home.* New York: Harcourt, Brace, 1937. 537p.

An interminable family saga spanning generations, this story eventually devolves to its focus on Ellen Swain, a hard-working, earnest young woman. Her mother assures her, two-thirds of the way through the novel, "You're going to accomplish something. You're going to show what women can do." Late in the novel, shortly after World War II, Ellen receives an offer to assume the head librarian's position in the public library of a rather rural county. The offer comes from the woman financing the library's construction. To her credit, Ellen Swain protests: "But I'm not a librarian. I didn't even go to college."

Not to worry. Undeterred, the benefactress notes that education and professional preparation are trifles: "You can read, can't you? Don't talk to me about librarians. I always fight with them. You won't look down your nose" (which point of view trained librarians apparently adopt). Ellen takes the job and is assigned the task of building the collection in modern novels, poetry, and drama. She can't be trusted with serious stuff like history and economics, but her slim education doesn't seem to be a handicap in the assessment of creative literature. There is relatively little action in the book that actually involves the library; considering the level of ignorance at play in the story about what makes a qualified librarian, it is probably just as well.

11. Berckman, Evelyn. *The Fourth Man on the Rope.* Garden City, N.Y.: Doubleday, 1972. 234p. London: Hamilton, 1972. (Other editions.)

A good mystery with strong characters, with a primary focus on two English librarians, archivist Alison Pendrell and Myra MacKinnon. Old school friends, they reunite some years later as staff members of the private Champernowne Library, an old (1703) establishment in the quiet village of Beechen Hayes. Alison, a divorcée with an adolescent son, has come to Beechen Hayes on a temporary assignment, to organize a large collection of papers donated by one of the county's old residents. Alison lives in a boarding house with a number of other major characters, including Myra and Mrs. Lees-Milburn, an ancient boarder who professes to possess a quantity of intimate letters sent her mother by Robert Browning and other noted authors.

Myra, eager to get a look at the letters, challenges the old woman with derisive comments about their value. She attempts to enlist Alison in her effort; when Alison refuses, their old friendship rapidly crumbles. Alison has her own concerns, including the welfare of her son, off on a European tour, and her troubling feelings for the library director, Tom Durant. Tom's wife, a faithless, strident woman, wants to divorce him and grab the loot she anticipates Tom's dying father will leave him. She throws tantrums in his office, her ravings audible to the library staff, who uniformly pretend they hear nothing in order to spare Tom embarrassment.

Alison finds herself attracted to Tom, an attraction that she sees as "a threat to her whole way of life, sexless, industrious and thrifty." She has been giving everything to her son as atonement for inflicting on him a wretched father. She has almost completely effaced her own needs; their unexpected resurfacing does not square with her established self-perceptions.

The main characters here are particularly well drawn. Alison and Myra have grown apart since university and represent opposite extremes. Where Myra, a reading room assistant, is mercurial, judgmental, vituperative, and scheming, Alison is discreet, gentle, and a peacemaker. She shows kindness to others, regardless of their positions; she is as considerate and generous to a young library aide as she is to her aging landlady. Library director Tom Durant is the sort of superior that all librarians might desire: patient, unflappable, sensitive to his staff, and genuinely serious about his work. Among the supporting characters, the impecunious and tart-tongued grand dame Mrs. Lees-Milburn is a standout.

Suspicious goings-on, murder, plot twists, and other effects keep the novel moving along, but Berckman's way with characters is what makes it a real reading pleasure. Berckman dedicates the novel, by the way, to "All Archivists, Keepers and Librarians on both sides of the water who place at the public disposal their untiring patience and courtesy."

12. Betts, Doris. *Heading West.* New York: Knopf, 1981. 359p. New York: Scribner Paperback Fiction, 1995.

Nancy Finch, 34-year-old public librarian, is kidnapped in the Appalachians by a psychopathic bank robber who calls himself Dwight Anderson. Dwight takes Nancy with him across country, in the company of a disgraced former judge they pick up along the way. To her family, Nancy is "Big Sister, Elder Daughter, Virgin Spinster." She summarizes her life thus: "Unsatisfactory Conditions, from which she was being abducted by an Unsatisfactory Kidnapper." Unsatisfactory or otherwise, Dwight's pointless abduction jolts Nancy from her routine in a manner that she welcomes. She neglects opportunities to summon help, apparently preferring to ride out the adventure with Dwight to whatever end it brings her. No end could be less appealing, it seems, than her stale routine in the branch library or her stale family life.

Nancy's travail with Dwight reaches a harrowing and unexpected climax in the Grand Canyon, where Nancy displays courage both mental and physical. Although much of the dramatic tension evaporates long before the end of the novel, the lengthy post–Dwight Anderson coda is a penetrating look into Nancy's character. The kidnapping is instrumental in enabling her to wrench herself free from the blinders of her previous existence. In spite of the threat posed by Dwight, Nancy feels a certain admiration for him: "Dwight did exactly what he wanted," she says late in the novel, "and if he was never satisfied, he was never guilty either. It was fascinating.... Part of me is like him."

And it is this part, perhaps, that allows Nancy to absorb "what the Cherokee knew" as noted near the story's beginning: "not that they moved while the world was fixed in existence, but that the world moved with a roar and that in it they thinly, barely existed, perhaps as much as a snowflake standing in a fire."

13. Bishop, Morris. *The Widening Stain.* (Pub. under pseud. W. Bolingbroke Johnson.) New York: Knopf, 1942. 242p. London: John Lane, the Bodley Head, 1943. Ithaca, N.Y.: Cornell Univ. Library Associates, 1976.

The Widening Stain is a mystery well above average in which the central character is a bright and resourceful librarian, and in which a great deal of the action takes place in a library. Gilda Gorham, in her early thirties, is second-in-charge at an old university library. The building is such a hodgepodge of additions that the locals call it "our architectural emetic." A summa cum laude graduate of the school, Gilda is all business on the job. She does not hesitate to let her new director, Dr. Sandys, know that she intends to uphold the library's rules in spite of faculty's pleading for special privileges. She is as no-nonsense with her staff as she is with her boss: When a young assistant affects a provocative wiggle in her walk, she instructs her, "Don't undulate around here.... Maybe you expect to be sent to Atlantic City as Miss University Library?"

On the night of the university president's address to the faculty at the start of the fall term, Gilda finds Professor Lucie Coindreau dead of a broken neck in the occult sciences wing of the library, "an ever-widening stain" of blood spreading about her head. The authorities deem the death an accident, but Gilda is not convinced, and her subsequent investigation leads to a not-inconsiderable list of suspects, including drama prof "Frolicsome" Francis Parry, with whom Gilda is building a little affair. The novel's title alludes not only to the blood on the floor around the dead professor, but to the idea that crime begets crime in an ever-widening stain. And indeed, after the first death, there is another.

The novel is engaging for its plot and its characters, particularly Gilda Gorham, and also for Bishop's witty and knowing perspective on academic jealousies, pettiness, and trivial pursuits. The book is not widely owned but is well worth pursuing through interlibrary loan.

14. Blackburn, John. *Packed for Murder.* New York: Mill, 1964. 191p. Also published as *Colonel Bogus.* London: Cape, 1964.

Packed for Murder is a spy tale in which Dr. Vasya Drozd appears for a few pages as the librarian of the Soviet Embassy in London. Dr. Drozd is a "knowledgeable" man who is nearly "bubbling with excitement" over the prospect of acquiring some letters of interest to the Marx-Engels Institute in Moscow.

Blackstock, Charity. *See* Torday, Ursula.

Bleeck, Oliver. *See* Thomas, Ross.

15. Bosse, Malcolm. *The Man Who Loved Zoos.* New York: Putnam, 1974. 214p. London: Gollancz, 1975. Also published as *Stricken.* New York: Dell, 1977.

The man who loved zoos is Warren Shore, nephew and ward of San Francisco librarian Victoria Welch. Warren is a traumatized Vietnam veteran who stumbles across a bus full of dead tourists in the city and loots them. Someone later makes it look as though the bus passengers died when the vehicle went over a cliff. Then Warren himself dies. Victoria, a widow, is convinced that Warren has been murdered because of what he knew about the bus, but police believe he was involved in a drug deal that went bad. Victoria decides to fight to clear her nephew's name. She is a small, apparently meek woman, but given a crisis to manage, she displays a striking toughness of mind.

Victoria lives in an apartment house down by the waterfront, among stevedores and drifters. "In her red pillbox hat and thick glasses, her figure stereotypically dumpy, she looked the part of someone who lived with books and believed in astrology [which she does, alas, but what connection does that have with living with books?], and at the same time she had the sharp eyes of a trained investigator, the resoluteness of a marine." Victoria's faith in astrology is annoying: She evaluates everyone she meets in accord with this pseudoscience. It is not a charming attribute for an educated person, much less for a serious investigator of factual matters. Nevertheless, Victoria is resolute in her pursuit of the truth about her nephew and the fatal bus. The case proves to concern a sinister federal operation involving an agricultural research station, murder, and cover-up. Alexander Boyle, an agent who admires Victoria's integrity and resolve even while she drives him to what might be a case of terminal despair, is her chief nemesis in the matter.

Balancing the positive portrayal of Victoria Welch is the characterization of her supervisor, Miss Sackman. Miss Sackman brags that she hasn't read a novel in five years "because they lacked educational value." Chief librarian Sackman thoroughly inventories her apartment every Saturday morning, down to the contents of the refrigerator. She is "possessive and devious with a cruel streak running behind her fixed smile." A pair of glasses hangs from her neck by a leather cord; she is painfully loquacious, obese, self-important, and suspicious. It is interesting that while Victoria Welch is treated with such approbation, her boss is little short of repulsive.

16. Bowes, Barry. *Between the Stacks.* London: Landesman, 1979. 192p.

If the Monty Python troupe were to run a branch library, the results would very likely resemble the action in this funny, episodic novel. The narrator is the senior assistant librarian at the Pike Lane branch, where the staff of ten ("the Magnificent Ten") carry on with their work in spite of themselves and in spite of their public. The story line, such as it is, concerns the narrator's upcoming interview for a job as branch librarian. He isn't sure whether he really wants the job; that he's mugged on the way to the interview by a disgruntled patron might suggest he look to a new line of work, and the interview itself, a bizarre disaster, sets the stage for a most unexpected change of employment venue.

But all those events come at the end, and on the way there, author Bowes provides a steady diet of laughter as well as a knowing look at life in a none too intellectually stimulating library. Eccentric (and worse) patrons are daily fare. Among them is the man who has borrowed and renewed *Welding for Beginners* for two years without a break; the man who comes into the library with a flower pot, complete with purple creeper, balanced on his head; the woman in the Mickey Mouse mask; and the Surveyor, who sits at a table all day and ogles the voluptuous new staffer in the children's department.

The narrator and his wife are having domestic difficulties, and he and Marianne, a library assistant, are on the verge of an affair. The narrator's struggle to recognize his real wants and needs kicks around below the surface of the novel. He has always "gone for the easy options" and has always hated making choices. It's too bad, perhaps, that he has to leave the library field to come to grips with his habit of sliding into the easiest groove available. Do not fear, however, that the novel is earnest in its depiction of the narrator's psychological stresses. No novel whose high point is an hilarious rescue on the library roof could be fairly accused of earnestness.

17. Bracken, Catherine. *Roman Ring.* London: Cassell, 1968. 170p.

Roman Ring is a passable mystery set in Italy, where a ring of book thieves is launching an assault on the rare-book market. The ring's operatives pilfer rare editions from both public and private libraries, concealing their nefarious work by switching relatively inexpensive editions for the libraries' valuable versions. The "financial brain" behind the scheme is Franco Camerino. After World War II, Camerino eked out a living as a librarian while doing bookkeeping on the side. Apparently his bibliographic knowledge and his ledger balancing produced a good combination, for the former librarian is a meticulous organizer. That he has no scruples whatever about gutting libraries of their prize volumes makes him all the more efficient. One of Camerino's functionaries is Santoni, sole employee of a front business the ring uses. Santoni catalogs and evaluates books for the ring — and steals them, when he finds good ones.

18. Braine, John. *The Jealous God.* Boston: Houghton Mifflin, 1965. 286p. London: Eyre and Spottiswoode, 1964.

Jealous God is a relentlessly somber novel of guilt and repression. Main character Vincent Dungarvan, a Catholic high school teacher, picks up 27-year-old librarian Laura Heycliff one day in the library. She agrees to meet him at an espresso bar. "It was too good to be true; it wasn't possible that he should be about to take out a girl who not only spoke well but who was pretty in an acceptable way, not tartish, not twitchily refined, not dowdy and quiet...." Laura smokes: "Perhaps it keeps me from worse things," she offers. "I'm wild and hard," she says. "I don't go to church any more." Vincent's initial estimation about truth and goodness seems on the mark when he learns that Laura is divorced. His rigid Catholic traditionalism throws a major obstacle in the path of their affair and leads to endless anguished soul-searching by both parties. Vincent's mother, who longed for him to become a priest, refers to Laura as "that dirty little whore." Laura is convinced that Vincent merely dallies with her, that he will leave her for "a nice Catholic girl." She feels guilty about using birth control. Vincent feels free to let her know when she has committed a "sin," such as feeling hopeless about their situation.

It hardly seems possible that the attitudes exhibited by Vincent can approach those of mainstream Catholicism. He is absolutely humorless, obsessed with death, and driven by guilt and self-righteousness. Laura, a not-unattractive character who deserves far better than a fate entwined with a grim religious fanatic, allows herself to be sucked into Vincent's dreary visions. That the novel's "happy" ending depends on an important and relatively innocent character's suicide should be reason enough to leave this work as it is, an emblem of a view of a world well on its way to perdition.

19. Braun, Lilian J. *The Cat Who Knew Shakespeare.* New York: Jove, 1988. 201p. Boston: G.K. Hall, 1988. (Large print.)

Polly Duncan, a "charming though enigmatic woman," is town librarian of little Pickax City (population 3,000), county seat of remote Moose County. She helps hero and cat fancier Jim Qwilleran with his historical research and has dinner with him from time to time. She always insists on going home early, although Qwilleran wouldn't mind testing his idea that she looks like "a comfortable armful." Fashionable dress is not her forte, but Polly has a lovely voice and knows Shakespeare backward and forward. She serves as the romantic interest for amateur detective Qwilleran in this light snack of a mystery. Oh, and one snowy night, she doesn't leave early.

20. Brautigan, Richard. *The Abortion: An Historical Romance, 1966.* New York: Simon & Schuster, 1971. 226p. London: Cape, 1973. (Other editions.)

The 31-year-old narrator is the perpetual librarian, 24 hours a day, seven days a week, at a curious San Francisco library where people deposit books they have written. After "registering" them with the librarian, they are free to place them anywhere they like in the stacks. "It doesn't make any difference where a book is placed," says the narrator, "because nobody ever checks them out and nobody ever comes here to read them. This is not that kind of library. This is another kind of library." The narrator is quiet, a little shy, and possesses a gentle good humor. The main business of the story concerns his girlfriend, Vida, whom he accompanies to Tijuana to obtain an abortion. Vida's body bothers her, generally; the narrator assures her that her statuesque beauty is not the burden she has come to regard it. On his return from Mexico, the narrator finds himself ousted from his position as librarian. He does not particularly mind, although he claimed earlier that he loved his library work. The novel is light and slight but is redeemed by the librarian's gentle nature and by Brautigan's gift for the occasional nice phrase.

21. Brean, Herbert. *A Matter of Fact.* New York: Morrow, 1956. 245p. London: MacDonald, 1958.

Rosemary Derby was the librarian at an exclusive private club in New York City until her brother Harry's murder conviction. The club sacked her at that point. We first meet her in a little pizzeria. "She had dark-blond hair and a slender face with a wide, patient mouth and dark, observant eyes that seemed not to want to see as much as they did." Her other brother, intoxicated, attempts to beat up Officer Ryan, whose objective is to consume an anchovy pizza in a nearby booth. Ryan helped send Harry to the pen. After Ryan dispatches her drunken brother, she herself assaults Ryan, ineffectively, in a fit of grief and rage. Feeling guilty, Ryan later offers to arrange for Rosemary a job in an ad agency. She demurs: "'Perhaps you don't understand the difference ... between library work and stenography.'" Rosemary, "a very decent sort of girl," is the catalyst for Ryan's decision to revisit the murder case, in hopes of getting her brother off the hook. Aside from that role, her presence in the novel is limited.

22. Breslin, Howard. *Let Go of Yesterday.* New York: Whittlesey House, 1950. 271p.

There's only a bit of cheap stereotyping here, in a passage about a main character's job doing research for hire. Speaking of the library he frequents, "It's a wonderful library...." he says. "But it's also the biggest mausoleum in this town.... And the librarians are a tribe all their own. They're nice enough, efficient, ready and willing to help you find things, but none of them ever smile. I don't think they go home nights. I think they file each other away on the shelves."

23. Brinig, Myron. *The Sun Sets in the West.* New York: Farrar & Rinehart, 1935. 360p. London: Cobden-Sanderson, 1935.

The Sun Sets in the West is a frequently interesting and readable novel of the Great Depression's effects on a Montana mining town. Packed with characters, the story features a subplot concerning young David Sandor, son of a local storekeeper, and town librarian Gertrude Field. David is an omnivorous reader who catches Miss Field's attention at an early age. As she watches him grow up, she finds herself attracted to him in a way that threatens to bloom into romantic involvement in spite of the two-decade difference in their ages. Miss Field "was a slender, virginal spinster of forty with flower-like blue eyes and the soft pale complexion of a Madonna. She was frail and alone and mysterious.... When Miss Field entered the library, the world without was obliterated, and she, herself, became a character in a book."

Miss Field feeds David's reading habit; when he is older, she invites him to her house, where they discuss books and read to one another, sometimes throughout the night. Their friendship becomes strong enough that when David faces a crisis in his family life, he comes to Miss Field for (literally) tea and sympathy. Throughout their relationship, the reader recognizes a powerful erotic undercurrent that Miss Field holds in check, although not without difficulty. In spite of their blameless conduct, word of the late-night meetings between David and Miss Field filters from suspicious neighbors back to city officers, who use the appearance of wrongdoing as an excuse to terminate Miss Field and close down the library, thereby saving some city funds. Miss Field is devastated: "She was trapped in a town that, without rows of bookshelves, had become the ugliest, most God-forsaken in the world." The description of her gathering her belongings and leaving the library where she has worked hard and honestly for so long is pathetic: "Her body and mind had no life to them, as weightless and insignificant as feathers."

A sad and angry novel with overtones of socialist sympathies, published in what for large numbers of Americans was a sad and angry year. (The title alludes to what for many Depression-battered citizens seemed the last place of hope, California.)

24. Bristow, Gwen, and Bruce Manning. *The Gutenberg Murders.* New York: Mystery League, 1931. 275p.

In this early library mystery, the real star is a newspaper reporter, Wade, who also works as a special assistant to the New Orleans district attorney. Quentin Ulman is an assistant librarian at the Sheldon Memorial Library. According to Wade, "His racket is wine, women, and books." Ulman is under suspicion of stealing rare books from the library, including the library's prize acquisition, nine leaves from a Gutenberg Bible. Ulman's involvement becomes a little more problematic when he turns up murdered, and incinerated, at the end of the first chapter.

The "old duck," head librarian Dr. Prentiss, appears convinced that Ulman was culpable. Dr. Prentiss himself is quiet, reserved, interested in nothing but rare books, and content to work in solitude. He cares a great deal about his reputation as a capable collector. He is "the scholar of pictures and legends, tall and slender, with a droop to his shoulders that suggested much bending over a desk and long delicate hands that seemed made for caressing the crumbly pages of old books." Dr. Prentiss proves once again, however, that you can't judge a book by its cover, literally or metaphorically.

A talky affair, the novel is nevertheless occasionally amusing. For one stranded on a remote island or trapped in an elevator, there would be worse ways to pass time than reading it.

25. Brookner, Anita. *Lewis Percy.* New York: Pantheon, 1989. 261p. London: Cape, 1989. (Other editions.)

Literary scholar Lewis Percy takes a job in a British public library, apparently without benefit of anything resembling actual library education. His duties are vague, he "catalogs" articles that he finds "in publications," and compiles some sort of index. An acquaintance informs him, "You could do this job with both hands tied behind your back." The chief librarian, Percy's boss, is Arnold Goldsborough, "florid, large, shapeless, with rosy curls blossoming above his collar," and with a cautious eye "like that of a halibut." Goldsborough himself is a literary critic in the fashionable deconstructionist mode. He is "a marauder, a manhandler, busy taking the text away from the author and turning it into something else." He looks forward to automating the library, including Lewis's precious index, with some glee. He is not, however, an interesting character, and he occupies not overmuch space in the novel.

26. _____. Look at Me. Pantheon, 1983. 192p. London: Cape, 1983. (Other editions.)

British librarian Frances Hinton describes herself as "an observer." She idealizes handsome men and beautiful women and longs to attract their attention. "Look at me," she wants to say to them, "Look at me!" She claims to "love" the lives of these glossy folk but is proud of the fact that she is not "in love with anyone."

When the novel opens, Frances seems in the grip of repression. She is severely self-controlled, apparently (because she is so rigid) unfeeling, afraid of excitement, and seeking refuge in a job and a life that she acknowledges are dull.

She works as an assistant in the reference library of a medical research institute. There she is in charge of acquiring and organizing pictorial material, artwork depicting depression, madness, and other variations on human emotional wreckage. The melodrama of her specialty is in ironic contrast to the tightly wound life she herself leads.

Yet Frances is young and physically attractive. She also writes fiction, because she must. "When I feel swamped in my solitude and hidden by it ... writing is my way of piping up."

Frances's development as a character hinges on her falling in love, which she does, with vigor.

Few could complain about Brookner's style, but the characters in *Look at Me*, including Frances, achieve at best an appeal rooted in their psychological impairments. At worst, their neurotic disabilities, including those of Frances, are more annoying than interesting and leave an aftertaste of the clinic.

27. Browne, Douglas G. Death in Seven Volumes: A Mr. Tuke Mystery. London: Macdonald, 1958. 192p.

Strange goings-on, eventually involving murder and missing persons, in the private London Library prompt its young head librarian, Roger Gournay, to solicit a visit from the authorities. The curiosity at first seems limited to hanky-panky with presentation sets of a seven-volume philosophical treatise. Gournay is businesslike and capable in the ten or so pages he occupies, but he serves no real function other than to explain the matter to the inspector (and to the reader). That work done, he disappears from the novel. There is, however, an energetic chase scene consuming some eight pages later in the book, in which Mr. Harvey Tuke, of the Department of Public Prosecution, pursues a suspect through the stacks of the London Library.

28. Burks, Allison L. *Tight Rope.* New York: Duell, Sloan and Pearce, 1945. 215p.

Stella Moore walks a tightrope of well-intentioned duplicity in her masquerade as Dorinda LaCroix in this mystery set before World War II. Anne Delahay, town librarian in a little community a few hours' drive from Los Angeles, is one of Stella's favorite locals. Attractive, friendly, and discreet, Anne has the makings of a good confidante and companion. Her association with Stella proves unrewarding for her, however, for the tale's culprit inadvertently murders Anne in a most heinous manner upon mistaking her for Stella. Although Anne receives enough positive ink from the author to arouse some disappointment on the reader's part at her killing, she is a significant character only to the extent that she serves as a tool to advance the plot.

29. Burr, Anna Robeson. *The Jessop Bequest.* Boston and New York: Houghton, Mifflin, 1907. 402p.

A chapter in which the heroine visits the Chillingworth Library gives some insight into popular notions of both libraries and librarians. The old library has "successfully resisted all attempts at modernization." Nevertheless, unlike many libraries that maintain closed stacks, one may (if "of ripe age and established morals") browse the shelves in person. The library's catalog is a slovenly thing, but few really care, for "the society in its walls is the only leisure class in the world," an aimless bunch who "have all time at their backs." The library is "dusty, dusky, and dingy." As for the librarian who presides over this quasimausoleum, he warrants not even a name. He is an "exhausted" old fellow, yet pitifully eager to please the heroine, and receives the author's patronizing sympathy as "the poor librarian" when a visitor rails at him over the misplacement of a book.

30. Cameron, Eleanor. *The Unheard Music.* Little, Brown, 1950. 278p.

This densely written novel features Jane, a 30-year-old reference librarian in the town of St. Albans. Jane has missed out on her first real love, an artist, thanks to the selfish manipulations of her late aunt. Jane is a cool-demeanored sort, but takes a very solicitous attitude toward the aging genius composer Matthew Hinden.

The book concentrates on a set of characters whose closely interwoven lives allow Cameron to emphasize the importance of art and music. Jane is a complex character who "loved to pitch herself at a problem, at a challenge, an idea." But she is also "a woman of reflection," not of achievement, with "an inordinate love of learning, of quiet brooding and meditation." In spite of those latter qualities, Jane is not a stereotypical bookworm recluse, but neither is she content with her life. While her acquaintances do more romantic things, Jane suffers "a most desolating sense of fixity, of being sunk irretrievably into this rut which she had worn for herself day after day." An inner voice suggests that the best choice might be to cast her routine existence aside, foreswear "this sitting behind reference desks and answering intolerably dull questions." Yet Jane loves life or at any rate "certain secret fragments of it" chiefly obtained from books and music.

Unheard Music suffers at times from a density of style, too much explaining and not enough showing, and some occasionally suffocating excursions through Jane's most personal thoughts. One wishes from time to time that Jane would stop ruminating and start acting. Still, she is not an uninteresting character.

The novel's grasp of librarianship is sound. Cameron offers some telling insights on the difficulty of running a public library with an unsupportive governing board. Mrs. Topping, the sympathetically portrayed longtime director of the library, relies on Jane to help her endure "the constant cutting of the book fund, the shabbiness of the library, the dirt, the smell of the rest rooms … the lack of room, the bad lighting, the need for higher wages." At one point, when Mrs. Topping tells the board that what her staff earns is "shameful," a board member of inherited wealth responds with a banal and patronizing argument the likes of which far too many librarians have heard: "But Mrs. Topping you are all priestesses in the temple of learning, and that, surely, is something, is it not?"

The title refers to Matthew Hinden's final symphony, growing from the working world of men and women, from "the sounds their lives sent up, an unheard music," the "resonance of their existence." It also alludes to the unheard quality of the symphony itself, and perhaps to the unheard melodies of Jane's own life, melodies yet to be played.

31. Card, Orson Scott. *Wyrms.* New York: Arbor House, 1987. 263p.

In the chapter "Heffiji's House," we meet a strange female creature, Heffiji, who lives in a shabby hilltop house along a riverbank. She has "all the answers. Every one of them." She solicits these answers from all comers and provides them to others, free, on request. "I don't know anything, but I can find everything," she says. Her entire house, in fact, is a library, although at first examination a disorderly one. Papers are scattered throughout in apparent chaos, but Heffiji, an otherworldly archetype of the reference librarian, has committed to memory the location of every answer-bearing scrap of paper.

32. Carey, Elisabeth and Marian W. Magoon. *I Smell the Devil.* (Pub. under pseud. Carey Magoon.) New York and London: Farrar & Rinehart, 1943. 247p.

Two graduate students, one of whom claims to be able to "smell the Devil" when trouble brews, help solve a murder mystery on the campus of Cowabet College. The chief victim is rare-books librarian Miss Christopherson, whose corpse is removed from the scene (reputedly modeled after the Hatcher Graduate Library at the University of Michigan) before the reader has a chance to get acquainted with her. Given the library setting, it is curious that there is so little emphasis on librarians as characters. The director, Dr. Wines, is in some evidence but mainly as a prop to assist police investigators. He shows little in the way of personality other than a somewhat annoyed air of authority. Miss Christopherson's assistant, Miss Allen, initially seems more upset about the safety of the rare book collection than about the death of her supervisor, but as narrator Adelaide Stone explains to the police, "It's clear you don't know much about librarians. It's 'books first' every time...." A bit of stereotyping, then, in a fairly humdrum mystery.

33. Carr, John Dickson. *He Who Whispers: A Dr. Fell Mystery Story.* New York: Harper, 1946. 250p. London: Hamilton, 1946. (Other editions.)

In this mystery set in 1945, historian Miles Hammond hires young librarian Fay Seton to catalog a large private library that Miles has inherited from his uncle. Fay was involved in "unnamed bad conduct" a half-dozen years earlier in France. The bad conduct proves to have been the death of her employer, a death ruled suicide. Miles, quite taken with Fay's gentle grace, refuses to believe that she could be a killer. Yet Fay seems more than simply a wrongly suspected librarian. Some detect qualities not just suspect but dark and sinister about her, perhaps even supernatural. Even so, Miles seems to be falling in love with this "odd girl with the red hair." Before we leap to conclusions, another character refers to Fay as "one of the most completely wronged, bedeviled and — and *hurt* persons I've ever heard of." As it turns out, Fay is suffering from a most peculiar, and scarcely credible, mental illness. She seems if not guilty, nevertheless doomed. As critical as Fay is to the novel's events, she is less a character developed through her own observable actions than she is one elaborated through others' conversations about her. The book is not altogether satisfying, with a long-winded denouement concerning who did what to whom and why.

34. Chesterton, G. K. *The Return of Don Quixote.* New York: Dodd, Mead, 1927. 302p. London: Chatto & Windus, 1927. (Other editions.)

Michael Herne is the librarian hero in this sociopolitical satire. Chesterton spends considerable time establishing Herne as "eccentric" and "dreamy." Herne delights in earning his living by caring for the Seawood Abbey library; he is "certainly of the sort that is remote from the daylight, and suited to be a shade among the shades of a great library." His lack of sociability comes "not from positive dislike of society but from an equally positive love of solitude." Herne is so caught up in his favorite historical period (that of the Hittites) that he at first resists taking the role of medieval king in an amateur theatrical production. He eventually yields and engages so thoroughly in the role that he refuses to relinquish it. His obstinacy leads to a chivalric restoration in England. Herne's faith in a mythic past does not persuade the workers of his world, who refuse to join his Medieval solutions. Ultimately, Herne abandons his grander scheme for social change for more modest chivalric aims. If Herne were not so deliberately cast as an oddball, completely out of touch with contemporary times, his role as the catalyst for change might be more persuasive. But possibly not, too. The novel's main characters, including Herne, are little but two-dimensional stick figures that Chesterton uses to score ideological points in this "parable for social reformers."

35. Churchill, Winston. *Coniston.* New York: Macmillan, 1906. 543p.

A long, creaking moral romance, *Coniston* features a secondary but important character, Miss Lucretia Penniman, who is founder and librarian of the Brampton Social Library, in the shadow, more or less, of Coniston Mountain. "Miss Lucretia" was "one of the first to sound the clarion note for the intellectual independence of American woman." She served as a social and literary beacon for the community, advancing its tastes and politics, even visiting the sick to read to them. She moved on to Boston, where she became the "editress" of a literary journal, the *Woman's Hour.* In Boston, she takes under her wing Cynthia Ware, a Coniston County girl. Miss Lucretia comes and goes in the novel, displaying a crusty integrity and forthright interest in others. Late in the book the 70-year-old Miss Lucretia returns to Brampton to give a fiery speech at a mass meeting in defense of Cynthia, who has been dismissed wrongly from her schoolteacher's position. It is hard to imagine any contemporary reader diving into this novel for pleasure, but no one can dispute Miss Lucretia's noble nature.

36. Converse, Florence. *Sphinx.* New York: Dutton, 1931. 311p. London: Dent, 1931.

A resolutely dull mystery cum travelog, *Sphinx* follows a group of tourists through Italy. One of them, Miss Longstreet, is "a Carnegie librarian from Ohio" who loosens up enough to fall in love. Loosening is something Miss Watson sorely needs. Reserved and prim, "never been kissed," she is an irritating fussbudget. When she visits a museum, she complains about the catalog and nitpicks over the guidebook. She worries that a traveling companion may become too familiar with her. She corrects other people's pronunciation. She knows Greek mythology well enough to treat her audience to an "encyclopaedic monologue" on the topic. A hint of Miss Watson's stiff sense of rectitude (and perhaps the author's belief that only romantic love can liberate her) is that we do not learn her first name (Amy) until page 137 and then only as a result of an exchange with her boyfriend inchoate, Mr. Peterson. Late in the story Miss Watson asks Nils Peterson if he actually thinks of her as a "highbrow." She characterizes herself as "just a little middle class assistant librarian from a small town in the Middle West." Nils objects: "Middle West, maybe ... but middle class, never!" Oh, the pulses are pounding! A forgettable novel, but useful as a catalog of librarian stereotypes.

37. Corle, Edwin. *Burro Alley.* New York: Random, 1938. 279p. New York: Bantam, 1953. (Other editions.)

Roberta Grace, a 38-year-old library cataloger from Denver, has come on vacation to a resort town in New Mexico. She is feeling very frustrated, for this is the last night of her vacation, and nothing has really happened. Her physician urged her on this solo trip, telling her to do things she had never done, to "be a different person." Her life, like J. Alfred Prufrock's, is measured out by the spoon.

Corle introduces Roberta on page 74. The story of her weary, lonesome, and awkward life weaves in and out through the rest of the novel, which Corle packs with a wide variety of characters seen in a single twelve hours of afternoon and evening.

In spite of herself, Roberta picks up Amador in a bar and invites him to her room. He proves to be a con artist and persuades Roberta to empty her pocket-book for him.

Roberta's story is a nicely executed portrait of a pathetic, rigid woman's search for a life that seems to lie hopelessly out of her reach. One could argue that Roberta represents a stereotype, but Corle draws her with too much depth for that. Roberta Grace is a real person, and a sad and affecting one.

38. Crider, Bill. *Dying Voices.* New York: St. Martin's, 1989. 196p.

Elaine Tanner is the new head librarian at the Texas academic backwater, Hartley Gorman College. She plays an important early part in the mystery of the murder of a famous poet and former English department faculty member who returns to the campus for a seminar. Miss Tanner has succeeded the elderly Miss Watson, whose devoted but inept administration left the library something less than the crown jewel in the campus plan. Crider is an amusing writer with an insider's grasp of academic nonsense, and the grasp extends to the library. A good share of the holdings now in Tanner's domain "had come from such sources as former professors who, looking for a tax dodge or some such thing, donated all their books to the library upon their retirement. Thus there were many old and useless volumes which, despite the fact that they helped inflate the book count ... did no one any good at all." Tanner does some good for the image of librarians. She is eccentric; her office contains a shelf of trophies that she has amassed as emotional pick-me-ups in secondhand stores, and she calms herself by blowing soap bubbles in her office. She is also smart and delightful and provides worthy assistance to English prof and amateur sleuth Carl Burns.

Cunningham, E. V. *See* Fast, Howard.

39. Daly, Elizabeth. *Night Walk.* New York: Berkley, 1963. 157p. New York: Rinehart, 1947.

The Rigby Library in the town of Frazer's Mills is the domain of Miss Hattie Bluett. Miss Bluett has been the librarian there her entire career, and she has no ambition to go elsewhere. "She thought Frazer's Mills the most desirable place in the world, and she ran the Library as she chose." She has no objections to working late and doesn't mind forcing others to do the same. "She's in a class by herself," says one local, in a not completely complimentary manner. "Our library is an anachronism," continues the observer. "It'll die with Hattie Bluett. She'll be found disintegrating among the ruins." "She takes it so seriously," says another. "She does love it so when she can collect a fine."

One evening, as Miss Bluett works overtime in the library, she hears suspicious noises but finds no one when she investigates. It turns out that she narrowly escaped victimization by a killer that late evening. Her reprieve proves temporary: Some two-thirds of the way through the book, the killer bludgeons Miss Bluett to death while she's on the job, a pencil clutched in her hand. *Night Walk* is a pleasant enough mystery starring the author's urbane sleuth, Henry Gamadge.

40. Dannay, Frederic and Manfred Lee. *The Four Johns.* (Pub. under pseud. Ellery Queen.) New York: Pocket Books, 1964. 164p. Also published as: *Four Men Called John.* London: Gollancz, 1976. (Other editions.)

The Four Johns is set on and around the campus of the University of California-Berkeley. Mary Hazelwood, "one of the busiest bodies on the campus," disappears one day. The main suspects in the disappearance are all named John, from John Pilgrim, a "beatnik of distinction," to librarian and UC stacks supervisor John Thompson. Thompson is "persuasive, hedonistic, and enterprising, a librarian who likes his assistants well stacked." He is a "compact, sunburned man of thirty-five," with a mild disposition. He does, however, lead a mysterious existence: Each Friday after work, he disappears from campus, not to be seen again until Monday morning. When an investigator follows Thompson as the latter blasts off in his MG late one Friday, he discovers an astonishing truth: John Thompson is living a double life. During the workweek, he's a stack superintendent–roué and lives in a bachelor apartment in the city; from Friday evening to Monday morning, he's a devoted family man who lives in the suburbs with his wife and children. Is he guilty of more than duplicity? This is a competent Ellery Queen potboiler.

41. Davis, Clyde Brion. *The Anointed.* New York and Toronto: Farrar & Rinehart, 1937. 277p.

Harry Patterson is a rough-hewn sailor with spiritual yearnings and a desire to learn "to navigate" his mind. On a stop in San Francisco, he meets Marie Snyder, a young librarian with the San Francisco Public Library.

"I fell in love with her the first time I saw her in the library," Harry admits late in his first-person narrative. It is in the book's last 50 pages where Harry relates the impact Marie has had on him. In spite of his unlettered and awkward nature, she quickly recognized his intelligence and potential and helped him set course on a self-directed reading program, with a little Dickens and George Eliot (!) for starters. Marie's understanding and helpful approach lead Harry away from his dead-end job as a deckhand.

"I've never seen a woman that could compare with Marie for goodness, and smartness, too. And when you get to know her, she seems beautiful also," gushes Harry.

Harry is a little too wide-eyed to be altogether persuasive, but Marie Snyder, whom Harry decides to marry, could hardly stand in a better light from the point of view of sheer wonderfulness.

There is a naïveté in the story that is both touching and a little comical. When Harry first asks Marie out, she responds, "'I really don't go out with strangers. And the library frowns on the girls making dates with patrons.'" Fortunately for his self-improvement program, Harry is persistent.

42. Davis, Dorothy S. *A Town of Masks.* New York: Dell, 1952. 190p. New York: Scribner, 1952.

A Town of Masks is a murder mystery with some fairly serious efforts to portray the inner life of a small town and its residents. Elizabeth Merritt, the young town librarian of Campbell's Cove, is the heroine and the real force behind the solution of a homicide committed by one of the town's leading citizens. Although Merritt takes a backseat insofar as her space in the story is concerned — the killer receives far closer attention — Davis presents her as intelligent, courageous, and attractive.

43. Davis, Lavinia. *Reference to Death.* Garden City, N.Y.: Doubleday, 1950. 221p.

So many librarians in fiction are cranky, peculiar, befuddled, or otherwise wanting that when one comes across an example of the profession who happens to be an agreeable person, one wants to savor the experience. The savoring is brief in this mystery, for even before we meet Miss Miriam Purvis, she has expired from a fall from her office window. A suicide note lies on her desk beneath a paperweight.

Early in the book, Miss Purvis, town librarian in the little community of Stillbridge, Connecticut, summons her old acquaintance, the aging scholar Alden Bancroft, to her aid. Dropping his research at the New York Public Library, Bancroft rushes to the call. Too late to save Purvis, he investigates some curious circumstances about her death. Was it really suicide, or did she know too much about the wrong subject? We learn a good bit about the late Miss Purvis through Bancroft's digging. She was a natural listener and "loved helping people." She lived modestly but enjoyed the outdoors and read extensively in good literature. One young man she helped describes her as "'one of the kindest people who ever lived.'" Bibliomaniac's note: A 1928 edition of the *Beilstein Handbuch* plays an important part in revealing the truth in *Reference to Death.*

44. De Bruyn, Gunter. *Buridan's Ass.* Berlin: Seven Seas, 1973. 254p. Translation of *Buridans Esel.* Halle, Germany: Mitteldeutscher, 1968.

The author, a former Berlin librarian, turns in a witty, literate novel, or, as he calls it, tongue-in-cheek, a "report on love, women, morals, librarians, manners, contemporary life, society and Berlin." The story, set chiefly in East Berlin, concerns 40-year-old library director Karl Erp's affair with librarian trainee Fraulein Broder, 22. Erp, a former horticulturalist, soldier, and POW, is a success in his profession; everything that he has dreamed of obtaining he now has. That is, he has everything but satisfaction, in spite of his position, his car, his comfortable home, his wife and children. When Broder, fresh from library school, begins work in the library, Erp is fodder for her. She is beautiful and smart but has "an eye for the weaknesses of people and things," with "more intelligence than feelings and flesh."

When Erp at last visits Broder with "a lighthearted act of adultery" in mind, the two talk for hours, she ultimately vexing him with her question about why he belongs to the Communist Party. It is an inauspicious and chaste overture to their affair. In a snit over her question, Erp writes her a tart, stupid letter of self-defense, defense against charges that she did not utter. As for Broder, she has come to an understanding of the gap between ideals and reality, art and life, but still expects more from others, including Erp, than they can give. She discovers that Erp's "greatest weakness was that he had so many small weaknesses." Nevertheless, her thoughts hum with the theme of illicit love, "love by the hour," involving Erp.

Erp moves out of his house over Christmas, leaving almost everything behind, including his family, to move in with Broder. He resigns as library director, acknowledging that the two of them cannot work in the same facility.

The author's ironic, dry humor is a delight; he frequently steps aside from the narrative to discuss what might or should happen next and nudges the reader with wry observations. He permits Erp himself to be witty enough to make amusing allusions to Marx ("A spectre is haunting our profession," notes Erp, paraphrasing the opening of the *Communist Manifesto*). The title itself alludes to the medieval fable of the ass who, when faced with two bundles of hay, dies of starvation because it cannot choose between the two. Parallels between Erp and the unfortunate ass are clear; driving the point home, one of Erp's colleagues mentions the fable one day when Erp cannot decide whether to join Broder for lunch or sit at a nearby table with some other staff members.

If the novel's setting in the German Democratic Republic renders it at all passé, it is only to a slight degree. In spite of the demise of East Germany, *Buridan's Ass* transcends political issues to remain a novel rich in human insight, clever humor, and well-wrought prose.

45. Dee, Sylvia. *Dear Guest and Ghost.* New York: Macmillan, 1950. 259p.

Twenty-five-year-old Thelma Helmakobbler is a librarian at a branch library in New York City. She accompanies her family on a move from the city to a house on Staten Island. The house is occupied by a somewhat mischievous ghost. Following an ill-developed romance with the principal of her brother's school, Thelma marries the man. "The maid of honor and the bridesmaids looked exactly like what they were — librarians dressed in organdy. They wore tortoise-shelled or steel-rimmed glasses and they seemed about to warn you that no talking was allowed in the library." We do not see Thelma at work, although she dotes over her collection of first editions and displays a tediously proper attitude toward books in general. This is a featherweight novel, with characters who appear to have escaped from a 1950s television sitcom, featuring Mom, Dad, Bud, and Sis (Thelma). All that's missing is a laugh track.

46. Deeping, Warwick. *Exile.* New York: Knopf, 1930. 330p. Also published as *Exiles*. London: Cassell, 1930.

Deeping presents a rather nice reversal of expectations in the character of Julia Lord, who operates an English lending library and teashop in Tindaro, Italy. Deeping initially sets off the warning signals of conventional librarian stereotyping. Miss Lord "allowed herself no sense of humor ... she had chosen to be cold marble." To her new assistant, Miss Billy Brown, Miss Lord's face looks as though it "had been kept in ice." She takes a cold bath every morning. If she has redeeming qualities, they seem to lie in her self-possession and her efficiency: she is "dignified, deliberate and complete." She knows her public; she has operated her library for many years and has found that the chief problem in the job, as it is everywhere, is human nature: "The greedy and the selfish and the inconsiderate had to be dealt with in a library as everywhere else." Miss Lord takes satisfaction in her labors, regardless of the nattering annoyances posed by human nature. "She was never dull or bored when she was working." She fears none of her sometimes imperious, frequently monied patrons and is businesslike and nononsense, "always direct."

Yet Miss Lord is considerably more than a crisp, hardheaded librarian. When she arranges flowers, she touches them "gently and tenderly." She is sensitive to young people, treats Billy with restrained kindness, and takes a keen interest in the young woman's welfare when she drifts into questionable company. She struggles with conflicting desires to intercede in Billy's personal life or to let her work out her own problems. She chooses the second course and then blames herself when Billy becomes engaged to a local blackguard. "'O, damn sex!'" exclaims Miss Lord, "'It spoils everything.'" As Billy reaps the consequences of her bad, albeit sincere, judgment, Miss Lord displays strength of character by refusing to truckle to library patrons who feign offense at Billy's conduct. When Billy comes under fire from the local bluenoses, Miss Lord stands firmly at her side.

Exile is more Billy Brown's story than Julia Lord's, but Miss Lord receives extensive attention and is critical in Billy's development as an adult. It becomes clear, eventually, that Miss Lord's wise and compassionate treatment of Billy depends to a great extent on her own youthful experiences and mistaken choices. She is a likeable character in a surprisingly candid work of popular fiction.

47. De Leeuw, Adele. *With a High Heart.* Toronto: Macmillan, 1945. 207p. New York: Macmillan, 1946.

Considering its predictability and that it escapes reasonable classification as juvenile fiction only by a slim margin, *With a High Heart* is a surprisingly readable novel of a young woman's coming of age, both in her profession and as a person. To her total dismay, top-flight "vibrant" library science student Anne McLane is assigned a summer-long practicum at an unappealing county library that gets by on a minimal budget. "It probably has a staff of four or five spinsters and it'll be dull as ditchwater, and I'll die of ennui," laments Anne. Miss Nichols, the librarian, proves to be "shrewd but kindly"—and also accident prone, for early in the summer she breaks her leg in a fall down stairs. The job of driving the bookmobile lands in Anne's lap, for no one else on the staff (no spinsters among them, by the way) knows how to drive. Thrown into the breach left by Miss Nichols, Anne proves herself an energetic and resourceful librarian, or almost-librarian. She works well with the people that she had expected to be little but yokels and sees it through in spite of difficult patrons and assorted crises. The novel is very much in the spirit of its wartime composition. The effects of war are felt on the library, including a shortage of gasoline for the bookmobile, but the staff do what must be done to make things work and provide the best service they can. The title comes from Anne's realization that she can savor her life more fully if she takes it as it comes, "with a high heart," rather than insisting that it meet her preconceived requirements. It may take a jaded reader at the millennium's cusp a bit of effort to slip into the book's sensibility, but the effort will not go unrewarded.

48. Dell, Floyd. *Moon-Calf.* New York: Knopf, 1920. 394p. New York: Sagamore, 1957.

This is Dell's largely autobiographical novel about a small-town boy in America's heartland growing up to be a writer. Felix Fay develops a love of reading very early in his life and as a boy dreams of being a writer so admired that people will one day point out in reverence the house where he lived as a child. He discovers the public library in his second year of school. The librarian, "a strict but kindly old lady," feeds Felix's reading habit, although not always with the sort of books he would have chosen himself had he been courageous enough to do so. The well-intentioned librarian is providing him with popular boys' tales when the lad's taste runs more to Victor Hugo.

It is Helen Raymond, chief librarian in the town of Port Royal, who becomes one of the great influences in Felix's life. Miss Raymond, not much older than Felix, serves as the major stimulus toward Felix's maturing as a writer.

"He had seen her afar — that is to say, as she came and went about the library with a light step, disappearing all too quickly into that secluded and sacred region, her private office. He knew her name, and her official position. But to him she was not so much the librarian as the spirit, half familiar and half divine, which haunted this place of books.... Something in her light step, her serene glance, personified for him the spirit of literature; she *was* its spirit, made visible in radiant cool flesh."

Clearly young Felix sees Miss Raymond as a goddess. He cannot imagine having a human relationship with her. Miss Raymond, though, has other ideas. She has read one of Felix's poems in her literary club and conceives a quick interest in the young man. He is a talented writer, though with many rough edges.

"It was part of her duty, as she conceived it, to encourage people who showed any enthusiasm for books — not merely by official helpfulness, but by revealing herself to them as a fellow-enthusiast." Miss Raymond corners Felix in the stacks one day and compliments him on his poem. He goes away "intoxicated." Soon they are meeting regularly in her office, talking literature and life, if with a certain formality. Miss Raymond does not feel quite comfortable about becoming too casually familiar with the young man too soon.

Helen Raymond had been "dreamish" as a college student; she found it necessary to learn how to hide this quality from her professors. When she reads more of Felix's poems, his dreamy poignancy seems to awaken memories of her own excursions in the rare air of fantasy. She reads his poems carefully, critically and decides "I want to *help* him."

Over a period of several months, Felix writes many poems, "each as an excuse which would permit him to see Helen Raymond.... It was as if she had forbidden him to come, save as a poet."

There lies between the lines of the passages of Felix and Helen Raymond a frustrated sexuality. It's frustrating because of Helen's sense of playing the benefactress, the tutor, the more lettered of the two and most likely because of her status as chief librarian while Felix's career has not yet amounted to anything. It's frustrated because Felix, in spite of the rapidly growing maturity that Helen notes in him, cannot set aside his original vision of her as something both more and less than human, the "half divine" spirit of the library. One wishes that on one of Felix's visits to Helen's private office they might dispense with the poetry and proceed to a more physical expression of things beautiful and joyful. They do not.

Helen Raymond eventually disappears from the novel, moving away to become the librarian in another town. But she is the catalyst for Felix's growth as a writer, for his entry "to a wonderful world of friendship with poets and novelists and beautiful women."

49. Denniston, Elinore. *Girl on a High Wire.* (Pub. under pseud. Rae Foley.) New York: Dodd, Mead, 1969. 218p. London: Hale, 1971.

Twenty-three-year-old Cathy Briggs finds her public library work "about as varied and exciting as a treadmill." Her small-town library is such a dull place that she can close it down for an hour in the middle of the day to run a personal errand without bothering would-be patrons. Fortunately for Cathy, her filthy-rich aunt dies suddenly and leaves her an estate worth millions. Cathy does not make a large bequest to the town library, but she does face a tangled skein of greed, murder, and romance (the last of which she hungers for considerably). Her status as a librarian seems devised only to show what a humdrum life she led before her aunt's death opened the door to adventure in this run-of-the-mill mystery.

50. Derleth, August. *The Shield of the Valiant.* New York: Scribner, 1945. 511p.

An entry in the author's *Sac Prairie Saga*, this novel of life in the small Wisconsin town of Sac Prairie features detailed portraits of several characters. One of the major figures in the town and in the novel is the librarian, Miss Mergan. The book opens with an account of her receiving a diagnosis of lung cancer. What troubles her most is not the prospect of death but that of leaving Sac Prairie forever, where she has worked long and hard. "She had fought for Sac Prairie so long that she was frightened now at the thought of what the village would become without her." For years she has been a liberal force on the board of education and has kept the library open to books of all kinds, "regardless of those who were against this or that on various trumped-up grounds of bigotry and ignorance." She fears that no one will take up her work. She worries about her patrons, especially adolescents and children. She is gentle with the young and helps them with their books and reading in a caring, personal way. Not one to let her own mortality keep her from constructive action, she trains a new librarian and persuades one of her young proteges, Steve Grendon, to run for her seat on the school board. He is anxious over his ability to do a job that will stand up to hers. Could he match her fair play, her honesty and courage? "Whose challenging wit would take the place of hers? Whose valiance and quiet determination would encompass hers?"

A passage (pp. 182–185) written with restraint and control details Miss Mergan's final day in the library. It is a simply stated, unsentimental, and moving few pages. When Miss Mergan leaves the library for the last time, snow is falling. She turns to look back, but the old red-brick building is lost to her sight. She sees "only a void of swirling flakes"—a nice symbolic touch in this story-within-the-story.

DeWeese, Jean. *See* DeWeese, Thomas Eugene.

51. DeWeese, Thomas Eugene. *The Doll with Opal Eyes.* (Pub. under pseud. Jean DeWeese.) Garden City, N.Y.: Doubleday, 1976. 182p. London: Hale, 1977. New York: Popular Library, 1978.

Soon after her graduation from library school at the University of Wisconsin, Roslyn Stratton obtains a job as a librarian in the midwestern town of Fowler.

Roslyn was born in Fowler but has not seen it in two decades since she and her parents moved away when she was an infant. Although Roslyn is dedicated to her work and happy to have an opportunity to begin her career in Fowler, there is something unsettling about the town and some of its inhabitants. Her initial strange sense of familiarity with the place and its people evolves into a disturbing sense of dissociation, and the recurring nightmare ("forms, huge and indistinct, hovering over her") that has haunted Roslyn throughout her life begins to reassert itself. As the mystery unravels, Roslyn discovers a shocking case of confused identity, in part through noting that the eyes of a doll in a photograph inexplicably match the opal ring she has owned since her infancy.

The mystery component of the novel is reasonably effective, although, as is the case with so many mysteries, once answers begin to surface, the story's tension sags. From a librarian's point of view, the most interesting aspect of the novel is author DeWeese's occasional and none-too-subtle proselytizing for the profession. DeWeese clearly conceives of Roslyn as an enlightened librarian, not a prim fuddy-duddy afraid of comic books or even television. Indeed, Roslyn enjoys watching old horror movies on the tube. She has a revealing discussion with the local sheriff, who asks her why she became a librarian. She "saw so many bad librarians" as a child, she says, that she "decided to get into the system and try to convert it from the inside." Roslyn acknowledges the "grandiose" nature of this ambition but doesn't dismiss its sincerity.

Nonlibrarians who serve important functions in libraries will welcome DeWeese's positive remarks on those individuals. Library aide Jenny Wellons, for example, is a cheerful older woman who does much to keep the Fowler P.L. running smoothly. She also shares Roslyn's opinion about the tediousness of the authoritarianism both see heaped too often on innocent would-be readers by librarians and teachers narrowly devoted to "good" literature, sometimes driving people away from reading anything at all. (Anyone who endured *Silas Marner* as a high school sophomore will be glad to second their opinion.)

The usual effect of baldly preaching a point of view in a work of fiction is to put bumps in the story, and the effect of DeWeese's occasional dalliance with such preaching achieves the usual. The preaching is infrequent, however, and does not gravely mar a fairly entertaining mystery, nor does it turn a nicely realized character, Roslyn Stratton, into a puppet.

52. _____. *Hour of the Cat.* Garden City, N.Y.: Doubleday, 1980. 179p. London: Hale, 1980.

Hour of the Cat is a fairly entertaining mystery, somewhat overseasoned with proreading, prolibrary propaganda. Valerie Hamilton is the new librarian in Hazleton, Indiana. She's quite a package, albeit a small one, at five feet tall. She plays a mean game of table tennis, is a competent amateur guitarist, and stands up to the forces of censorship with equanimity and a level voice. Someone has planted a false story in the local paper announcing her engagement to her acquaintance, attorney Martin Forster. The same day the story appears, her cat,

Muldoon, comes home with a message attached to his collar. It proves to be a death threat against Valerie. She soon learns that Martin's first wife, Sandra, was murdered shortly after their marriage, and it seems that someone is seeing in her whatever it was that prompted Sandra's killing. The mystery alternates with scenes of Valerie's work. She compiles bibliographies for high school teachers, attends a library fund-raiser, reads *Publishers Weekly* and *Library Journal* reviews, orders books, and confronts a group of the local guardians of the public's reading morals at a library board meeting. She also equips herself with a water pistol filled with concentrated ammonia to defend herself should the anonymous threatening notes and telephone calls give way to more direct action.

53. Dickens, Charles. *The Life and Adventures of Martin Chuzzlewit.* London: Oxford University Press, 1975. 841p. London: Chapman and Hall, 1844. (2 vols.) (Many editions.)

In this populous novel with a complex plot, librarian Tom Pinch displays the unpretentiousness of a babe and the heart of a saint. We meet Tom as a draftsman in the architectural firm of Mr. Pecksniff. He is "an ungainly, awkward-looking man, extremely shortsighted, and prematurely bald." Tom is more than ready to believe the worst of himself, however ill-founded the criticism may be, even when it issues from the loathsome hypocrite, Pecksniff. "Tom Pinch's heart was very tender, and he could not bear to see the most indifferent person in distress." He plays organ in the church without compensation.

Tom eventually sees the true character of Pecksniff; after his vile boss sacks him on a pretense, Tom accepts a position as a private librarian at £100 pounds a year. It is a mysterious assignment, for Tom does not know the identity of the individual who has hired him by proxy. Tom's new job site is in an out-of-the-way house. "On all the floors were piles of books, to the amount, perhaps, of some thousands of volumes." Those not stacked on the floor are "scattered singly or in heaps; not one upon the shelves which lined the walls." It is Tom's task and one that he gladly accepts to organize and catalog this jumble of books. He proceeds, under his own supervision, to put the mess in fine order and produces "a very marvel of a catalogue." We learn late in the novel that Tom's anonymous employer is none other than the elder Martin Chuzzlewit, whose beneficence toward Tom is but one act in his redemption from selfishness.

54. Doderer, Heimito von. *The Demons.* New York: Knopf, 1961. 2 vols. (1,334p.) Translation of *Die Dämonen.* Munich: Biederstein, 1956. London: Quartet Encounters, 1989. (Other editions.)

Austrian von Doderer labored nearly three decades on this massive novel featuring well over 100 characters. The setting is chiefly 1926–1927 Vienna. One of the multitude of characters is Leonhard Kakabsa, who rises from ordinary workman to the post of librarian on the estate of a prince. Although Kakabsa is absent from the story for hundreds of pages at a time, he is a major character and one warmly regarded by the author. When we first meet Kakabsa, he is a young, lukewarm Social Democrat working in Vienna. He likes an uncluttered life and is surrounded by people suspicious of intelligence. An irresistible change begins when one day, on his way home from work, he steps into a bookshop and buys a Latin grammar. The bookseller sees in Leonhard a man whose potential wants encouragement, and he provides it. Leonhard embarks on a program of self-instruction in the classics, which eventually leads him to regular visits to a university library. He rarely misses an evening in the reading room.

Prince Alfons Croix has inherited a palace containing a large, ill-organized private library. Prince Croix becomes acquainted with Kakabsa and offers him a post as his librarian. "'I don't want a middle-class academician reeking of general education,'" he tells Leonhard. He offers to pay for Leonhard's complete education, including a doctorate. And, indeed, the earnest, uncomplicated but hardworking and gifted Kakabsa later earns a Ph.D. and what is apparently a lifetime sinecure as Prince Croix's estate librarian and curator. We never actually see Leonhard working as a librarian but are assured that he went on to a fine career in the prince's employment. One of the author's central themes concerns the necessity of accepting life as it is, in its complexity and lack of tidiness. This acceptance is facilitated in Leonhard's case by the unlikely (one is tempted to say fantastic) intervention of Prince Croix.

55. Dolson, Hildegarde. *Please Omit Funeral.* Philadelphia: Lippincott, 1975. 237p.

A curious and rather awkward blend of murder mystery and free-speech sermonizing. Marcy Coving is the 24-year-old librarian of the Wingate, Connecticut, high school. She is a wholesomely lubricious sort who favors halter tops and miniskirts and inspires secret thoughts among the male students who observe her at work (where she dresses more demurely). She is a devoted advocate of the freedom to read. A local right-wing activist complicates Marcy's life by sending a student to borrow a number of "offensive" books, which she then destroys. The books include *Grapes of Wrath*, Eldridge Cleaver's *Soul on Ice*, and local author Laurence Dilman's *Wayward the World*. Laurence intervenes in the smut crusade, and seems to persuade its prime mover to back off, but on the very evening when a truce appears in the offing, Laurence dies suddenly. Is it a heart attack? Is it murder? It is a question that will not likely rivet many readers to their chairs, for the novel simply does not evoke reality, either as a mystery or as an argument for free speech.

56. Downes, Anne M. *So Stands the Rock.* New York: Stokes, 1939. 341p. New York: Grosset & Dunlap, 1939.

Set in small-town New England near the turn of the 19th century, *So Stands the Rock* is a sentimental, overlong soap opera. Matilda (Tilly) Lawrence, "so intelligent, but she is shy, awfully shy," is the youngest woman ever to attend

Wells College. She comes back to the town of Winston to teach school and after school works without pay as the librarian. Though shy, she is candid and bright. She's also "a genius at giving people the books they need." Tilly nurtures the literary talent of young Angus Shawn with books and sympathy. With money from the sale of her family house, she offers to buy him a printing press to start a newspaper. There is a strong romantic link between Tilly and Angus, but this is the sort of fiction in which upstanding people nobly overcome the temptations posed by powerful feelings. Tilly is not sufficiently self-effacing to forego asking the school board for a stipend for her library work, but they vote against it on the grounds that they're already paying her for teaching. In spite of her flirtation with economic self-interest, Tilly is such a good, generous, and selfless person — "born with love in her heart" — that her characterization defies belief.

57. Dumas, Alexandre. *The Chevalier D'Harmental.* New York: Collier, 1910. 431p. Translation of *Le Chevalier d'Harmental.* Paris: Dumont, 1842. (Many editions.)

The Chevalier D'Harmental is a historical romance set in the early part of the 18th century. Jean Buvat, "Le Bonhomme Buvat," is a not terribly bright fellow whose chief talent is a fine manuscript hand. As a result of his kindness toward a child, he is rewarded with a position in the royal library. The position does not pay handsomely, but Buvat cherishes it. Some years later he again shows his large-heartedness through his earnest care of Bathilde, the daughter of his deceased neighbor. He secures a nanny for the child and lives with the two of them in a small apartment. Buvat works tirelessly for the child, teaching writing in his spare time to earn money for her dowry. During a stretch of hard financial times, Buvat continues his work at the royal library without pay — for a good six years!— because he cares so much for his job and the library itself. At the far end of this travail, Buvat stumbles across a secret document that leads to his invaluable service to the state, and, ironically, to endangering his beloved Bathilde's husband-to-be. It will surprise no one that all ends well. As for Buvat, he is no genius; that is true. He is, however, loyal, honest, brave, loving, and generous.

58. Dunn, Nell. *Tear His Head Off His Shoulders.* London: Cape, 1974. 176p. Garden City, N.Y.: Doubleday, 1975.

Sometime-narrator (the voice shifts between third- and first-person) and main character Jeanette Rawling is a librarian in her early 50s. She has recently moved from Exeter to work in a London library. The book opens with her impressionistic reflections on her affair of a few years before with Jack, a married man. "All I wanted was the luxury of his presence," she claims, and it is clear that she has not gotten over his loss. In her London apartment building, she makes close friends with Queenie, a working-class woman her own age. She and Queenie become soul mates, sharing their most personal accounts of their romantic trials.

Jeanette agonizes over Jack: "I am bleeding from missing him.... I am torn apart.... Every morning for the last ten years I have woken up thinking of him." As the reader learns more of her time with Jack, questions develop about the health of their relationship. Not only does the extramarital tang sour the flavor of their affair, but a current of violence lay close to the surface. Jeanette and Jack abused each other physically.

As Jeanette reveals to Queenie further details of her strange life with Jack, she and Queenie draw ever closer. Their relationship threatens to become something more than supportive friendship; at one point, Queenie invites Jeanette to move into her flat with her. Jeanette does not take advantage of the offer, but she does follow up on Queenie's assistance in trying to drive the devil of Jack from her existence. The novel's title derives from a bizarre episode in which Queenie helps Jeanette manufacture an effigy of Jack on which Jeanette can vent the rage she feels over his alleged betrayal.

There is little library action in the novel, but when Jeanette speaks of "the sanctuary of the warm mahogany library" where she works and of the quiet intimacy of reference work, the library seems an island of reasoned calm in the tempest of her emotional life. "It's very hard to show your love ... very hard," is Jeanette's concluding line in a novel of white-hot intensity.

59. Dutourd, Jean. *The Horrors of Love.* Garden City, N.Y.: Doubleday, 1967. 665p. Translation of *Les Horreurs de l'Amour.* Paris: Gallimard, 1963.

The *Horrors of Love* is the story of the Don Juanesque figure Edouard Roberti. One of the women who captures his obsession during a "rather bitter little affair" of some two months is a librarian, Odile. Odile receives a few pages of attention before the pages run to triple digits. An "Amazon type" in her late 20s or early 30s, Odile was "a striking, well-built girl with beautiful pale blue eyes." Odile was a "semi-intellectual" who ordinarily took up with talentless painters, journalists, and university students. She proved demanding and baffling to Edouard. She shared none of his radical political ideas and didn't like the writers, poets or artists he admired. She despised Mozart and Renoir, admired Bartok and abstract painting; whatever Edouard was or liked, Odile was not, and loathed. Yet when she dropped him to marry someone else, Edouard was desolate, enraged, and in a way delighted with his romantic distress.

60. Dutton, Charles J. *Murder in a Library.* New York: Dodd, Mead, 1931. 302p.

Stereotyping is rampant in this mystery set in one of the "best known" public libraries in the country. Ruby Merton, the reference librarian in charge of the reading room at this estimable facility, is a "thin, angular and rather ill-tempered old lady." Everyone in the city knows her: "Her sharp tongue had made her a public character." She is eccentric in all respects, "like many of her type." She is a "repressed neurotic, whom life had soured," and has few friends. One rainy morning a visitor finds her dead — strangled — at her office desk, slumped down near a pile of *Publishers Weekly* copies. The murder case involves a number of stolen rare pamphlets. Did someone on the library staff steal them? Not likely, for, as Dutton writes, "As a rule librarians were not bookish people, so one could bar out almost three-fourths of the staff." A purported suicide note from chief librarian Henry Spicer admits his theft of the pamphlets and murder of Merton. Yet everyone knows that Spicer was genial and happy and "one of the best informed men in his field in the country." Subsequent investigation reveals that Spicer, too, was murdered.

Although Spicer escapes the stereotyping hook, Ruby Merton is typical of the librarian breed advertised here. One character describes librarians in general as "a bit unnatural." Libraries, furthermore, are "filled with narrow, repressed neurotic women." They are places "filled with books, with nice young girls and cranky old maids." One wonders how delighted the staff of the Des Moines Public Library was to see the book dedicated to them!

Two points in the novel seem ironically up-to-date: Dutton describes the library's reading room as a haven for the homeless looking for refuge from bad weather, and the culprit in the case has a nasty cocaine habit.

61. Eco, Umberto. *The Name of the Rose*. New York: Harcourt Brace Jovanovich, 1983. 502p. London: Secker & Warburg, 1983. Translation of *Il Nome della Rosa*. Milan: Bompiani, 1980. (Many editions.)

A remarkable combination of murder mystery, history, and philosophical discourse, *The Name of the Rose* purports to be a 14th-century manuscript by a monk, Adso of Melk. Adso's first-person narrative is set in a German monastery where for generations authoritarian librarians have overseen the building and preservation of a great library, perhaps the greatest in Christendom. They have done more than build and preserve, however, they have ruled access to the library's collection with a closefisted parsimony. No one may obtain any volume from the library without the librarian's permission. Adso plays second banana to the brilliant investigator William of Baskerville (echoes of Conan Doyle!), an English Franciscan who has been dispatched to look into matters of heresy in the monastery. Heresy takes a back seat to murder as seven killings in seven days shake the monastery's occupants and compel William to exercise his formidable detective powers.

The present librarian, Malachi of Hildesheim, is the only resident of the monastery empowered to visit the library. Malachi, whom the reader almost immediately distrusts, is a chilling presence. "He was tall and extremely thin," writes Adso, "with large and awkward limbs. As he took his great strides, cloaked in the black habit of the order, there was something upsetting about his appearance.... In his physiognomy there were what seemed traces of many passions which his will had disciplined but which seemed to have frozen those features they had now ceased to animate. Sadness and severity predominated in the lines

of his face, and his eyes were so intense that with one glance they could pene-
trate the heart of the person speaking to him, and read the secret thoughts, so it
was difficult to tolerate their inquiry and one was not tempted to meet them a
second time."

The crux of the intrigue is the library's possession of the only copy of an
otherwise lost work, the second volume of Aristotle's *Poetics*, allegedly dealing
with comedy. Eco uses the "lost" book to illustrate conflicting points of view about
nature, truth, and freedom of intellectual inquiry. Librarian Malachi, one regrets
to admit, fulfills the dark promise of Adso's impression quoted above. Although
Malachi himself is not the master hand behind the homicides, he is far from
guiltless. It's a challenging but rewarding novel, rich in historical detail and
insight.

62. Engstrand, Sophia B. *Wilma Rogers.* New York: Dial, 1941. 352p.

One of those rare books that combines a good, readable story with advo-
cacy of a profession, *Wilma Rogers* is an almost completely forgotten novel
that deserves a better fate. The title character, a 26-year-old librarian, has
left New York City and Columbia University for Milo, Illinois. Milo, a town
of 5,000, finds its chief distinction in the presence just outside of town (far
enough so that it avoids having to pay city taxes) of an immense corn process-
ing plant.

Rogers finds the Milo library a "mean, bare, little hopeless place." Rather
than succumbing to dismay, she vows to do her professional best to see that Milo
gets the library and the library service that it deserves.

It's a tall order. Milo is a town of airless provincialism. For the past quarter-century, the library has been in the inept hands of Miss Templeton, an
untrained and grossly prejudiced woman now on open-ended leave to tend to
family business out of town. The library board is a mixed bag, with a few progressive types contending with some not so progressive.

Through an injudicious (and steadfastly, infuriatingly chaste) affair with
Walsh, the president of the library board, who also presides over the corn pro-
cessing plant, Rogers obtains the political and financial clout required to build
a new library in Milo. Through her hard work and devotion to the job, she
changes the town's ideas about what libraries and librarians should be.

Author Engstand seldom steps into mere didacticism, even though she finds
many opportunities to show a librarian at work and to proselytize for professional librarianship. She neatly weaves into the story numerous scenes of the
librarian's life, from meeting with the board to developing a friends-of-the-library
group to defending inclusion in the collection of materials that do not automatically assume every American value is beyond question.

The affair with Walsh reveals Rogers as anything but a creature foreign to
normal human appetites and conflict. It shows her, rather, as a complex, deeply
human individual of mixed virtues but with good intentions and professional
devotion paramount.

Published on the heels of the Great Depression, the novel features a pronounced, although not shrill, proletarian sensibility. The struggle between classes, represented by that of the hard-working poor whites and blacks of Milo and the affluent quasisuburbanites from a nearby subdivision, is seldom far from front-and-center. Rogers herself lives in a working-class boardinghouse. The novel includes a rousing climax in which the righteous will of the people of Milo triumphs over the nefarious schemes of a handful of would-be patricians.

Wilma Rogers is not great art. Its assumptions are too certain for that. But the book holds up surprisingly well today and offers insights on the library profession as pointed and true as they were in 1941. It is also fun to read, and Wilma Rogers stands out in the ranks of fictitious librarians.

63. Erdman, Loula G. *Three at the Wedding.* New York: Dodd, Mead, 1953. 275p. London: Hodder & Stoughton, 1954. *Redbook*, May 1953.

Frances was the minister's daughter in Kelso, Illinois, where she had been working as a librarian for several years when the stranger, Tom, visited the library one afternoon. He proved to be a published poet. Frances and Tom fell in love; he was, unfortunately, married to another. Frances cried. Tom obtained a divorce. She and Tom married. They lived, if not happily ever after, then in a reasonable facsimile thereof.

In spite of its sentimentality, *Three at the Wedding* is a sincere argument for small-town life at its best: honest, uncomplicated, unspectacular, but characterized by hard-working, quietly productive people. (As one sign of its middle-American solidity, little Kelso's downtown coffee shop is nothing other than the Busy Bee Café. What else?) The novel uses as a jumping-off point the wedding of Tom's daughter from his first marriage to examine the lives of a number of interconnected people. Far from great or even good literature — it is too much a part of the world it describes to pretend to anything but popular entertainment and reinforcement of the values that Frances, or the author, has received from previous generations — the book is nevertheless a fairly readable and useful aid for understanding an important strain of American ideas. As for librarian Frances, she is undistinguished by very much but a simple desire to lead a decent life. If that means submerging her own ambitions in favor of her husband's, that does not appear to distress her. "Frances often thought that a woman's greatest work would be to make it possible for a man to keep his pride and self-respect. If need be, she must hold herself back in order to do this — perhaps even conceal her own capabilities, her keenness of mind, her rightness of judgment." Self-effacement is the order of Frances's day, indeed, of her world, for women. The idea that she would pursue any career other than as a domestic pillar of reliability is unthinkable. She even abandons her career: "Tom did not want her to work, so she gave up her job at the library.... Her home was her work, and she wanted no other."

Many readers will shake their heads in wonder at Frances's willingness to set aside career aspirations, even her own judgment, and will condemn out-of-hand a society that would encourage her to follow the route she takes. But Frances is not without dignity or passion, and it might be advisable, even while dismissing the culture she represents, to acknowledge the ironic strength of her character. It is fitting that the book's final chapter belongs to Frances and Tom.

64. Fairbank, Janet A. *Rich Man, Poor Man.* New York: Houghton Mifflin, 1936. 626p.

Rich Man, Poor Man is a still reasonably readable historical novel that attempts the grand sweeping treatment as it follows its characters from the 1912 contest for the U.S. presidential nomination through World War I, to a few months before the stock market crash of 1929. Barbara Jackson, a young librarian in Elida, Kansas, is one of the two most important characters in the story. Her husband, Hendricks, is the other. Barbara is notable as an early example of a librarian whose interests go far beyond the walls of the library. She was already involved in Progressive politics well before meeting Hendricks, the son of a rich Chicago banker, and their marriage (encouraged by the "portly" Elida head librarian, Miss Jessup) does nothing to quell her commitment to the cause. A suffragist, a pacifist during the war, a campaigner for the "rights of the people" in the 1920s, Barbara eventually drifts so far from her husband's place in the world that they divorce. Actual library scenes are minimal in the story; once Barbara leaves Kansas for Chicago, her library days are over. Even so, it's nice to see a librarian taking on the big political issues of the time.

65. Fante, John. *The Road to Los Angeles.* Santa Barbara: Black Sparrow, 1985. 164p.

Fante wrote this gritty novel of an aspiring author's struggles with rotten day jobs and difficult women in the early 1930s under contract to Knopf. The book did not see publication until after Fante's 1983 death. Readers familiar with another Black Sparrow author, Charles Bukowski, will see some parallels between the two. Here, Fante's alter ego Arturo Bandini reads compulsively when he is not working on the docks or in a cannery. He borrows his books from the Los Angeles Public Library, where he becomes overwhelmed by the beautiful librarian, Miss Hopkins. He finds her legs particularly appealing. One day, she catches him staring at her: "Our eyes met and she smiled, with a smile that said: Go ahead and look if you like; there's nothing I can do about it, although I'd like to slap your face." Bandini visits the library every afternoon to borrow books and ogle Miss Hopkins. He finds her at work "floating on white legs in the folds of her loose dresses in an atmosphere of books and cool thoughts."

In one striking passage, Arturo covets a book that Miss Hopkins actually carried in her own hands. "Who knows? Perhaps she perspires through her fingers as she reads it. Wonderful!" He obtains the book, on Catherine of Aragon, and uses it in a ritual featuring an improvised shrine to Miss Hopkins. "Oh fair white Miss Hopkins.... Oh queen of all the heavens and the earth." Miss Hopkins appears on only a few pages in this novel but is surely the only librarian in fiction honored by pagan sacrifice involving a cricket.

66. Fargo, Lucile E. *Marian-Martha.* New York: Dodd, Mead, 1936. 257p.

A real curiosity, this novel relates the adventures of two close friends, Marian and Martha (so close that their own friends often refer to them as Marian-Martha), as they work their way from high school through college and library school to professional library positions. The book was an entry in the publisher's Career Books series. Rather than attempting a straightforward discussion of library work, *Marian-Martha* tries to draw interested readers into library work through their identification with the main characters. The book aims clearly at adolescent girls, although there are male librarians (directors, to be sure) present in its pages. The author, a former school librarian, avoids anything along the lines of serious conflict in the story, a tactic that keeps the book from approaching the status of serious fiction. Her message is that a knack for organization, an ability to work well with others, and — of course — a confirmed pleasure in reading combine to give a young woman a firm footing for a career in librarianship. A certain touching innocence prevails: it is almost impossible to imagine such a novel being written today, much less published. Nevertheless, Fargo's vision of librarianship is still quite sound, and her fictional exposition of its mid–1930s details is not without interest. Times do change: In the public library where Martha first works, a cook prepares a daily hot lunch for staff members. On the other hand, some things never change: The shorthanded staff must sometimes gobble their lunches quickly to be sure that their stations are covered throughout the day. The story is enhanced by many cheerful illustrations by Dorothea Warren.

67. Fast, Howard. *Sylvia.* (Pub. under pseud. E. V. Cunningham.) New York: Carol Communications, 1992. 332p. New York: Doubleday, 1960.

Irma Olanski is a Pittsburgh librarian, 36, "a tall, dry woman approaching a loveless and lonely middle age," in the view of narrator and private investigator Alan Macklin. Over drinks in a bar with Alan, Irma refers to herself as "an unimaginative spinster." Alan sees Irma as "a stiff, sexless, and desiccated librarian"— not that sexless, apparently. Before the night is out, he and Irma are in bed together, in "a few hours of rare and true intimacy." Irma has proved to be more in tune with the human touch than her early negative description would suggest; it is her seldom-fulfilled but deep desire for human contact that placed her in an important role in the novel. As a young librarian, she took in Sylvia, a hungry, abused child Alan now searches for as a young woman, and served as a surrogate parent for several months. "I just loved that damned kid," says Irma. Irma's part spans two chapters and 50-plus pages. In the space allotted her, a tension develops between her and Alan that leads the reader to believe both could see further into themselves with each other's help than without. Alan's obsession, alas, is Sylvia. He would have been better off if he had stayed in Pittsburgh.

Historical note: Doubleday originally published *Sylvia* under the Cunningham pseudonym as a result of Fast's groundless blacklisting achieved through the efforts of J. Edgar Hoover's FBI and the U.S. House Committee on Un-American Activities. Fast and his publishers generally found the assumed name a better dustjacket bet in the political air of the time.

68. Fergusson, Harvey. *Hot Saturday.* New York: Knopf, 1926. 261p.

Set during a single sweltering Saturday in and around a small New Mexico town, *Hot Saturday* is a nicely conceived and well-executed story of its type, that of the liberated postwar woman looking for sexual satisfaction or something close to that. Marriage is the ostensible objective of the main character, 20-year-old Ruth, but that may be a concession to the public (and publishing) mores of the era. It is obvious that Ruth's hormones are running as hot as the weather, and she means to heed their call.

Her best friend is town librarian Alma Budlong. At 33, Alma was unable to overcome her father's quashing of her own love affair with Rupert Elwood. Ruth pities Alma, who seems to be "drying up" on the job: "Alma began to look old just about the time she went to work at the library." Considering Ruth's preoccupation with her own body, it is not surprising that she evaluates Alma's physical attributes in not-very-flattering terms: "Her figure was still good and she had pretty ankles, but her neck was beginning to wrinkle and she had a few gray hairs — and then her glasses.... That was another trouble with working. You wore glasses and looked tired."

Yes, it's all downhill for Alma from this point. But in spite of her incipient decrepitude, Alma is not quite ready for the scrap pile. She has a flair for social relations and makes easy acquaintance with the distinguished and influential. She was one of the first respectable women in town to take up cigarettes and laughs off the jibes of the local prim-lipped crowd. She has been an effective librarian: "She made the city council double the appropriation for books and she made the board of governors buy whatever books she told them to buy." She has dumped the tired old "proper" fiction and brought in H. G. Wells and Arnold Bennett "and even Dreiser and Mencken." Too bad, Ruth thinks, that Alma is at her worst with men, laboring to seem younger than she is. "Men seldom saw the real Alma who was genuine and funny." There is reason to believe that author Fergusson does not share Ruth's pity for Alma; he does, at any rate, make it clear that she is a capable librarian and a woman of complex and not altogether unadventurous character.

69. Fisher, David E. *Katie's Terror.* New York: Morrow, 1982. 263p. London: Hale, 1983.

Katherine Townsend, 38, achieved modest success as an actress (that is, she worked enough to qualify for unemployment compensation every six months) but spent her free time in the New York Public Library. On the day of her "great awakening," she realized that she wanted to be a librarian. Her hobby is studying local newspaper stories of homicides around the country; she has successfully aided the authorities through her research on some cases. Katie's lover, Peter, is a struggling actor. He is also a homicidal maniac, although he has successfully kept this other self from Katie's awareness. When Katie begins receiving a series of obscene and threatening phone calls, including at her desk in the library reading room, she fears that the caller will try to kill her.

From its clanking, pedestrian title (reminiscent of something intended for 13-year-old girls) to its awkward characterization of the villain, the novel barely manages to boil the pot. Katie Townsend receives due respect as an intelligent, talented, attractive, and focused woman, and there is plenty of action in the New York Public Library, including some of the life-or-death afterhours sort, but the whole is so marginally ept that it's hard to care how the librarian in question fares.

70. Flint, Margaret. *Deacon's Road.* New York: Dodd, Mead, 1938. 310p.

Deacon's Road is a story of rural Maine told at a measured pace. Attractive and intelligent Shirley Wells is a fresh college graduate with a degree in library science (or its equivalent). Her parents insist that she take a summer off as a constitutional before taking up duties in a library. She goes to Parkston, Maine, where her cousin lives. Shirley enjoys Parkston and has no trouble fitting in with the local young crowd, but she cannot fathom how people of her own generation can choose to remain their whole lives in the area's bucolic changelessness.

Shirley becomes romantically involved with young Ephraim Squire, who dreams of resuscitating the old family farm on Deacon's Road. Shirley leaves Eph mopey when she moves to Foxboro to work in the public library. He cannot understand why she will not renounce her own career to embark on a farm life with him. He develops notions about "catching and taming" the "exotic" Shirley, who at last, against her better judgment, agrees to marry him.

The major focus in the novel is not on Shirley, but on Eph's perceptions of her. Shirley is, nevertheless, an impressive character: she is adaptable, yet not a chameleon willing to change her colors to suit a background prepared for her by a potential husband. She shows considerable development in the course of the book, from an 18-year-old eager to marry to a young woman in no haste to take a step her judgment tells her is a mistake. In the end, she provides Eph something he needed: "That's what Shirley was — Eph's adventure," concludes the novel; in the process, she grows significantly.

Foley, Rae. *See* Denniston, Elinore.

71. Fontaine, Don. *Sugar on the Slate.* New York: Farrar, Straus and Young, 1951. 278p.

Amy Beasley ("That's *Mrs.* Beasley," she reminds students) is the librarian in this novel of life in a junior high school. She appears approximately midnovel for a span of some 15 pages; the author portrays her as testy, narrow, and fundamentally ridiculous. She has a degree in library science, but can't decide whether she is "basically a teacher or factually a clerk." She is "short, chunky." She believes "that a library should inspire beautiful thoughts." To further that end, she has made window draperies for the library and has decorated the window sills with overgrown ferns and potted palms donated from local matrons' conservatories. She has plastered the library walls with "inspirational" quotations from Shakespeare, Virgil, the Bible, and Edgar Guest ("It takes a heap o' readin' to make a room a library," perhaps?). She regrets that the Dewey system prevents her from arranging the library's books as she would like, in a pleasing color scheme — red here, green there, and so on. Her big moment in the tale concerns her apprehension of a student who mutilates books in a novel manner: He tears off margin strips from the pages and eats them (bibliophagism?). He's working his way through the *World Book*, but savors single-volume works, too: "Bartlett tastes like boiled artichokes," an observation that probably fairly captures the level of both seriousness and humor that the novel achieves.

72. Fowler, Helen and Bernard Harris. *The Careless People*. New York: Morrow, 1955. 255p. Sydney: Angus & Robertson, 1954.

Esther Southy is the head librarian of an Australian publishing house, as well as a budding book illustrator. The library is "a gracious and pleasant place," where Esther "sat enthroned throughout the days." The "inmost core of her unhappiness" is her desperate need to believe that Martin, her married lover and a junior partner with the publisher, longs to be with her as much as she wants to be with him. She passes Martin off as her brother among the locals in the rural village where the two rendezvous. Her barrister husband, Graham, is a solicitous and protective sort and resents Esther's showing an interest in anyone but himself. Martin encourages Esther's artistic ambitions; Esther is preoccupied with the need to keep a cover on the affair. As the book opens, Esther is waiting for Martin to return to the cottage where she is working on illustrations for a book of poems. Martin suffers a serious accident on the way to the cottage. Will Martin be found in time to save his life? Will his wife and Esther's husband discover their secret? Will Esther find true happiness? It's romantic melodrama worthy of daytime television.

73. Fox, Paul. *Four Men*. New York: Scribner, 1946. 537p. London: Cresset, 1947.

Four Men tracks the lives of four World War I submarine crew members. One of them, Will Giles, who becomes a physician, also becomes involved romantically with youngish branch librarian Emma Bass. She is, in fact, his first patient. She appears at his door with her "dead, straw-colored hair," and her "frightened-looking, unprepossessing head." She quickly recites a list of symptoms ranging from headaches to insomnia; Dr. Giles decides without examining her that nothing ails her but "hysteria." He does not like Miss Bass, "with her beautiful figure and her plain, feverish-eyed head." In a subsequent visit, she pours out to him a tale of her "enforced spinsterhood, of a monotonous and friendless existence," and an "intolerable loneliness." All she has achieved through her seven years in the library is a "painful realization of emptiness." Dr. Giles tells her that her problem is her lack of character, a diagnosis for which she expresses her solemn appreciation.

Emma Bass comes and goes at intervals in the course of the novel. Her appearances almost always incur description of a hostile sort, of which the following is typical: "She looked at once repellent and touching ... in her toneless, drearily neat clothes, with her eyes shining as with sickness in her bloodless face." Even when she wonders how she might better appeal to Dr. Giles, Fox cannot let her thoughts emerge without describing them as "at once feeble and unscrupulous." Yet Bass is not without redeeming value: When Dr. Giles is in financial trouble, she props him up emotionally, as well as giving him and his mother groceries, and she willingly types his manuscripts when he submits articles to a magazine.

One of the most curious aspects of Bass's characterization is that, however closely tied she is to Dr. Giles, she remains always in his view, Miss Bass, not Emma. It is a strangely distant take on someone who stands by her man as readily as does Bass. Poor Emma, so beaten down by Fox's disparaging description, finally drinks herself to delirium over Dr. Giles's refusal to marry her. A sad and pathetic case, our Miss Bass.

74. France, Anatole. *The Revolt of the Angels.* New York: Dodd, Mead, 1914. 348p. London: Lane, 1914. Translation of *La Révolte des Anges.* Paris: Calmann-Levy, 1914. (Many editions.)

This satiric fantasy of war in heaven dwells at length on the trials of a hapless librarian. Former teacher Julien Sariette is the curator of the d'Esparvieu family's quite fabulous private library, which runs to well over 350,000 volumes. The collection includes a great many rare books and manuscripts, to whose well-being Sariette is wholly devoted. M. Sariette is, perhaps, the ultimate example of the librarian who wants to know that every book is safe in its assigned place. One morning he comes into the library to find someone has heaped and scattered books in disarray, an act of slovenliness repeated daily for weeks to come. As the anarchic treatment of the priceless collection continues, Sariette slides into a state of high anxiety. "He has become a complete idiot," confides one character. As the novel proceeds with its theme of celestial confrontation and the triumph of humanity and science over religious superstition, Sariette continues his pathetic decline. In the end, driven altogether mad, the unfortunate librarian turns in a frenzy on his own beloved library.

75. ____. *The Shirt.* In *The Seven Wives of Bluebeard;* bound with *The White Stone* as Vol. 14 of his *Works.* New York: Gabriell Wells, 1924, pp. 125–231. Translation of *La Chemise*, in *Les Sept Femmes de la Barb-Bleue, et Autres Contes Merveilleux.* Paris: Calmann-Levy, 1909.

Chapter 5 of *The Shirt* is "The Royal Library." Monsieur Chaudesaigues presides over the library; he enjoys a reputation as "the wisest man in the kingdom" on the subject of happiness, a topic of central importance in this short novel. Chaudesaigues receives a group of visitors who are much vexed by the question of happiness with a discourse on how the multitude of books in the royal library is making an "uproar" with their conflicting views: "They argue about everything … God, Nature, Man, Time, Space…." He assures his callers that as a result of listening to this cacophony, "I shall go mad." The librarian defines happiness for his visitors and tells them how to find a happy man. The key to the search? "The examination of chickens." Failing investigation of "sacred chickens," one looks for a happy man among those on their death beds, according to Chaudesaigues. His visitors heed him and continue their search.

76. Frank, Pat. *Alas, Babylon.* New York: Bantam, 1976. 312p. Philadelphia: Lippincott, 1959. London: Pan, 1959. (Other editions.)

"It was strange, she thought … that it should require a holocaust to make her own life worth living." Alice Cooksey, librarian of a small Florida town spared the direct effects of nuclear war, finds that the townsfolk are reawakened to the importance of the library, post–Big One. Early in the novel Alice asserts her independence, in an anecdote about how she refused to remove from the library material sympathetic to the civil rights movement. One passage describes her three-decade tenure as librarian as a losing struggle for adequate funding. In the aftermath of nuclear war, with no electricity to power modern amusements and self-help a matter of prime concern, books and reading achieve a central status, and Alice wins a new importance through her expertise. She appears only a few times in the story, but her appearances are in a consistently positive light. *Alas, Babylon* is a better-than-average early work of atomic apocalypse fiction.

77. Frost, Frances M. *Innocent Summer.* New York: Farrar & Rinehart, 1936. 365p.

Miss Louella Barton, public librarian in this novel of small-town life, receives little attention, but what print she gets is cold stuff. She is "nervous as seven cats and cranky." She resents being asked where a book is in the stacks. One character, young Sam Evans, "always felt guilty about escaping her sharp-tongued wrath" when he slipped into the stacks on his own while she was busy chasing other youngsters out of the library for giggling and whispering. She snaps at a girl who asks where she can buy a copy of the *Oxford Book of English Verse.* Her eyeglasses tremble "on her huge red nose." After date-stamping a book, she shoves it back at a young patron saying, "Well, don't stand there all day!" Like some other authors, Frances Frost seems to have had some unpleasant library experiences in her formative years.

78. Garrett, George. *The King of Babylon Shall Not Come Against You.* New York: Harcourt, Brace, 1996. 336p.

A quarter-century after Martin Luther King Jr.'s assassination, reporter Bill Tone visits the central Florida town of Paradise Springs to work on an assignment involving violent events in the town at the time of King's murder. He meets young librarian Eleanor Lealand in the library. The chain-smoking Lealand seems "thin, nervous, intense, vaguely unhealthy and oddly dangerous." Later Tone writes to a friend that of all the people he has met in Paradise Springs, Lealand is "the nicest of the bunch ... a young (and very pretty) librarian who, for some reason (God knows) has been kind and friendly and is trying to help on the project, too." Tone falls more-or-less in love with Lealand and moves in with her. "She hates to cook after a hard day in the library," he confides in another letter, "but I can't exactly ignore the fact that she is wonderful in bed. Just what the doctor ordered." The two have intelligent, playful "conversations by moonlight." At one point, Lealand writes Tone a long letter in which she tries to enlighten him on some aspects of popular culture. Tone, poor fellow, does not understand an allusion to Sonny and Cher's "I Got You, Babe."

Things don't quite pan out for Tone and Eleanor, but their relationship is a highlight in a thoughtful novel, even if the story is sometimes reminiscent of a set of depositions given by the locals. Lealand almost completely disappears from the novel's last third, but she does have a valedictory page in which she remarks, "It was a good thing to be in love again. While it lasted."

79. Garve, Andrew. *The Galloway Case.* New York: Lancer, 1964. 144p. New York: Harper, 1958.

The librarian at the center of this effective, tightly written mystery never graces its pages alive. Robert Shaw, a public librarian in Streatham, is found floating in the River Thames on an Easter Sunday. The 35-year-old mystery aficionado has been bludgeoned and drowned. Title character Galloway has been found guilty of Shaw's murder. According to Galloway, an accomplished mystery novelist, Shaw was attempting to blackmail him over an allegedly plagiarized story, but Galloway denies dispatching Shaw into the Thames. An investigation among Shaw's colleagues reveals the departed to have been "a quiet, mild-mannered little man — a bit humorless, but entirely inoffensive." Shaw was conscientious, was considerate of his staff, and had contributed articles on the mystery genre to library journals. Who did what to whom? Who wrote what, and when? The story wears well and will be a treat for devotees of snappy mysteries.

80. Gifford, Thomas. *The Wind Chill Factor.* New York: Putnam, 1975. 369p. London: Hamilton, 1975.

Paula Smithies is the town librarian in Cooper's Falls, in northern Minnesota. She is widowed, her journalist husband having died in Vietnam. One day, as she seeks to bring order to the long-neglected library, she finds some curious documents in German and a locked metal box among some archival material. Paula is romantically involved with a man she knew as an adolescent, the book's narrator, John Cooper. She drives a yellow Mustang convertible — "her freedom symbol" — and turns up dead at her desk in the library rather early in the book — so sad. She was a lively, pleasant type; one hoped that she would share in the discovery of truth in this tale of intrigue. On the other hand, even though Paula had some attractive qualities, our sadness at her loss is tempered with the knowledge that death freed her from further involvement in the novel's neo–Nazi nonsense.

81. Giguere, Diane. ***Wings in the Wind.*** Toronto: McClelland and Stewart, 1979. 108p. Translation of *Dans les Ailes du Vent.* Montreal: Tisseyre, 1976.

Amedee is a librarian in her early thirties, recently released from a hospital where she apparently received treatment for depression. She is trying to get on with her life. "I drag myself to work. I always look as if I were recovering from a drinking bout.... I have the impression that I'm not even there." She lives alone but for her Yorkshire terrier puppy, Rosalie. "I can pass whole days in a fog of shapeless meditation, a state of acute autism, staring down into the abyss, my life riddled with holes...." She collects paintings, books, and antique furniture and once in a while attends a film. She has no friends following the death of her beloved Rosalie. "Rosalie follows me like a dark angel." She likens the world to "a vast impersonal library" in which her life "is just a card in one of the many drawers where our imperfections, weaknesses, and failures are compiled." Amedee's tale takes up the first half of this work; she is effectively absent from the second half.

82. Gill, Bartholomew. ***The Death of an Ardent Bibliophile: A Peter McGarr Mystery.*** New York: William Morrow, 1995. 275p. London: Macmillan, 1995.

In this clever and sometimes gruesomely graphic whodunit set in Dublin, Ireland, Brian Herrick, keeper of Marsh's Library, lies dead on a table in the library of his own house as the tale opens. Charlotte Bing, Herrick's deputy at Marsh's, ushers investigator Peter McGarr to the body. Herrick is naked, and, having been dead in a warm room for most of a week, is not in mint condition. Bing believes that Herrick's personality was split between the proper bibliothecal scholar and the fiery, Swiftian wit of Herrick's newspaper column. Herrick, in fact, modeled himself on Swift. McGarr learns that Herrick also videotaped in his house hours of "Frollick" in which the librarian orchestrated elaborate sexual charades. Bing is convinced that Herrick was stealing rare books from Marsh's and substituting forgeries. As for Bing, the 45ish administrator delights in her work in the Marsh Library, "perhaps the finest example of a seventeenth-century scholar's library anywhere." She works with enthusiasm even at such plodding tasks as inventory. With her ashen hair, hazel eyes, and fair features, Bing "might even appear rather beautiful," were it not for her severity. The investigation of Herrick's murder is involved and entertaining, even though Herrick himself arouses scant sympathy: "Herrick had become such a wreck of a human being that he was virtually friendless and would be missed neither at work nor in society." Gill works in detailed references to Swift in a way that enhances, rather than burdens, the flow of the narrative — and creates a killer whose heartless calculation makes the skin crawl. It's good, if somewhat disgusting, fun!

83. Goodrum, Charles. *The Best Cellar.* New York: St. Martin's, 1987. 160p.

Goodrum, a librarian, presents credible characters and a convincing setting, but he studiously avoids mere narrative in favor of advancing the story through dialog. Betty Crighton Jones, 29, is a public relations officer at the Werner-Bok Library in Washington, D.C. Durance Steele, a chic young historian just about to get off the Ph.D. boat, comes into the library one day to do some studying. She comes with an enigmatic attitude blending hostility toward academia and warmth toward Betty. Betty invites Durance to stay in her spare room for a period while pursuing her research. When Betty receives a bizarre and threatening obscene phone call — from a woman — she suspects that Durance was the intended recipient. The story involves academic hanky-panky and major questions about what happened to several thousand books from the Library of Congress that may have been saved when the British sacked Washington in the War of 1812. Goodrum's favorite librarian-cum-sleuth, Dr. Edward George, is on hand to investigate. George, now 70, is "working harder than ever" and enjoying life to the fullest. George and Director Brooks of the Werner-Bok engage in some interesting discussions (or Goodrum editorialisms) on changing fashions in research and library use and reading. Unfortunately, interesting discussions do not by themselves make interesting novels, and *Best Cellar* is swamped in page after page of dialogue, interesting and otherwise.

84. ____. *Carnage of the Realm.* New York: Crown, 1979. 152p. Also published as *Dead for a Penny.* London: Gollancz, 1980.

Retired Yale librarian Edward George is visiting friends in Washington, D.C., and is also busy fretting that library automation is a real menace, that it is not only inaccurate but losing to oblivion pieces of the scholarly record. The murder of historian Karl Vandermann provides him other fodder for his active mind. It draws George into a web of mystery involving rare coins, their collectors, and a dental assistant with a knack for forgery. The sleuthing includes some searching of automated databases; just as pay dirt seems in the offing, the computer system crashes, perhaps confirming George's fears. Or are they Goodrum's? At any rate, the everprescient George once again demonstrates his detective mettle. Although Goodrum relies excessively on dialog, the novel is fairly readable.

Whether the implicit target audience — librarians with an interest in numismatics — will keep it in circulation as long as a penny struck by Henry III remains to be seen.

85. ____. *Dewey Decimated.* New York: Crown, 1977. 190p.

Although generally well regarded by reviewers, this murder mystery involving rare books, set in a large Washington research library is, like Goodrum's others, excessively talky. Talk is usually not a terribly exciting form of action, and Goodrum's characters don't help, with conversation that, in this outing, is seldom arresting or witty. The story does feature Goodrum's charming hero, however, the retired librarian Dr. Edward George. Dr. George conducts himself in the same admirable manner here as in Goodrum's other novels.

86. Gosling, Paula. *Hoodwink.* Garden City, N.Y.: Doubleday, 1988. 185p. London: Pan/Macmillan, 1993.

Molly Pemberton is the librarian — "such a suitable occupation for a widow of a certain age" — in the town of Grantham. She conducts herself "with exemplary professionalism and kindness." She lives alone with her cat, Mr. Braithwaite, with whom she discusses current crime stories. Molly's late husband, a policeman, left her with a lasting interest in the seamy side of life. As she offers some useful assistance in a murder case to her husband's old colleagues, she herself becomes endangered as a result of a furniture mix-up. Molly comes and goes throughout; we do not see her at work, but she is a capable, positive character in this serviceable mystery.

87. Gray, James. *The Penciled Frown.* New York: Scribner, 1925. 297p.

A frequently amusing satire that follows young writer Timothy Wynkoop's modestly budding career, *The Penciled Frown* features librarian Birdie Yost as Wynkoop's almost-bride-to-be. Mrs. Yost is separated and on the verge of divorce when she decides that the up-and-coming newspaper drama critic Timothy is the true love of her life. We meet Birdie in the book's opening section. She has a habit of "chirping and hopping about," hence her nickname. Her avian characteristics don't stop at her locomotive traits: "Her eyes like a bird's were bright without being intelligent."

Book II of the novel belongs to Birdie and her pursuit of Timothy. She pushes him into poetry, convinced that he has written a good deal of the stuff. He hasn't, but she has and requires little prodding to embark on a reading of her own "perfect" poems. She is a dreadful poet, her "perception dulled by her own enthusiasm."

"It takes so much out of one emotionally," laments Birdie, "reading the poems which one has lived and written. I think I have a little headache."

Birdie's romance with Timothy blossoms into a sharing of his work–that is, Timothy Wynkoop works, and Birdie shares her opinions and suggestions. She pouts freely when he rejects them. No master of his own fate, Timothy lets Birdie manipulate him into marriage plans, plans that include Birdie's mother, a woman Timothy errantly inspires to write bad fiction. The three will live in a "ducky little apartment," according to Birdie.

Luckily for Timothy, the engagement founders in an argument over a piece of atrocious artwork that Birdie plans to hang in their forthcoming ducky domain. It is the beginning of a sudden end for the lovers, and Birdie demands to have her letters back.

"I'm afraid I didn't keep them," admits Timothy.

Birdie is little more than a simpering, scheming idiot, although a fairly satisfying one in the sense of comical parody of the self-absorbed and talentless. Librarians may not enjoy seeing one of their own made to look foolish (although we barely see Birdie at work), but if anyone deserves to look foolish, it's Birdie. Besides, Timothy fares almost as badly as his would-be bride under author Gray's satiric hand.

88. Guilloux, Louis. *Bitter Victory.* New York: McBride, 1936. 574p. Translation of *Le Sang Noir*. Paris: Gallimard, 1935.

Schoolteacher and part-time public librarian Louis Babinot is a secondary character in this fine novel set in a French town during World War I. Babinot possesses "an ungainly nose," through which he talks. He is a bloviator to rival Warren G. Harding. He fancies himself a poet and recites his poems aloud to himself as he strolls the streets, reveling in his literary craftsmanship. He is an avid collector of firearms and considers himself quite the patriot. In an appalling passage, Babinot attempts to press on two passing French soldiers his patriotic doggerel. When they refuse it, he pursues them and secures a belt whipping for his fatuous efforts. Later he lies about the origin of the whipping injury to boost his listeners' opinion of him.

Babinot is a vain, hypocritical, blustering xenophobe: "All that was reasonable and tender in Babinot had deserted his face, which was henceforth incapable of expressing anything other than the inhuman passions of patriotism and war...." His obscene enthusiasm for the war conceals from all but the most perceptive his crumbling character, the doom in his heart as he anticipates the death of his son in battle. This trace of genuine humanity is one of Babinot's few redeeming traits; otherwise, his is a biting portrait of mindless nationalism and obtuse, envious enthusiasm for things military.

89. Harris, Charlaine. *Dead Over Heels: An Aurora Teagarden Mystery.* New York: Scribner, 1996. 205p.

Slick but amusing, *Dead Over Heels* is the sort of book that passes time nicely when one is waiting for one's car in an auto repair shop (the site of this bibliographer's reading of the novel). Thirty-two-year-old librarian Aurora Teagarden is an admirable heroine. The tale opens with Aurora, better known as Roe, out in her yard with Angel, her friend and bodyguard. A corpse falls from an airplane and hits the ground a few feet away. The victim, a police detective, had been involved in a long antagonistic relationship with Roe. The body's airmail delivery begins a series of unsettling events. The worst of them is the beating death of Beverly Rillington, Roe's librarian colleague at the Lawrenceton, Georgia, public library. Roe solves the mystery fairly handily after a satisfying period of perplexity.

Roe is a spunky sort with a notable lusty streak (which she satisfies with her Vietnam veteran husband). "I've got libraries in my blood," she says and clearly enjoys her work with books and patrons, including story hour with her youngest patrons. *Dead Over Heels* lacks the depth of vision (of life, death, meaning, or absurdity) that it would require to amount to more than a popular entertainment snack, but in that category it is quite tasty.

90. _____. *Real Murders.* New York: Walker, 1990. 175p. Bath, England: Chivers, 1991. South Yarmouth, Mass.: Curley, 1991. (Large print.)

Real Murders is a rousing, enjoyable mystery. Aurora Teagarden belongs to the Real Murders club, whose members study famous crimes. A member of the club turns up savagely murdered before one of the meetings; the details of the crime parallel those of the historical homicide that Aurora planned to present at that evening's gathering. Aurora finds herself pulled ever deeper into the mystery, matching wits with a serial killer who delights in imitating crimes of long ago. The story benefits from Harris's lively style as well as from Aurora's character.

Roe has fulfilled her childhood dream by becoming a librarian. She is energetic and has a nice sense of humor. In addition to demonstrating true grit in criminal matters, she reveals a keen eye for details of library work and boneheaded administrative moves. The new library director, Mr. Clerrick, decides without consulting anyone to keep the library open late three nights a week, with no additional staff. Aurora notes that "Mr. Clerrick, with his usual efficiency and lack of knowledge of the human race" handed out everyone's new schedule without discussion. "Mr. Clerrick was going to put an advertisement in the newspaper telling our patrons the exciting news. (He actually said that.)" Aurora herself has "a neat and tidy life in a messy world, and if sometimes I suspected I was trying to fulfill the stereotype of a small-town librarian, well, I had yearnings to play other roles, too." Play them she does in this fast-paced, well-plotted novel.

91. Harriss, Will. *The Bay Psalm Book Murder.* New York: Walker, 1983. 190p. London: Hale, 1983.

Add another murdered librarian to the pile. When the distinguished, if somewhat crotchety, Los Angeles University librarian Link Schofield is found stabbed to death in his parking garage, it looks like a simple case of stupid low-level theft: The thugs netted $14 from Schofield's pockets, while leaving clutched in his hand the library's copy of the *Bay Psalm Book*, valued at $300,000. His well-known contempt for the book—"'It's ugly, and it's absolutely unreadable!'"—make his possession of the copy out on the streets very curious. Schofield's daughter enlists his best friend, English professor Cliff Dunbar, in an independent investigation to learn the truth behind Schofield's murder. What we learn about Schofield is entirely secondhand, but it is clear that he was a highly competent and much-respected librarian, with 40 years' service to his credit. Among his accomplishments was building the library's superior medieval collection from scratch. The catalyst for the entire plot is Schofield's alert discovery of some discomforting details about the library's copy of the *Bay Psalm Book*. A readable and clever mystery, this one will be especially enjoyable for anyone with a background in rare books, printing, and bookbinding.

92. Havighurst, Marion B. *Murder in the Stacks.* Boston: Lothrup, Lee and Shepard, 1934. 249p. Oxford, Ohio: Miami University, 1989.

It doesn't take long for English professor Tom Allen to turn amateur sleuth after his good friend, librarian Don Crawford, is found dead in the Kingsley University library stacks. There are plenty of possible culprits from which to choose, including two other librarians. One, Bertha Chase, apparently has been involved in a secret marriage with Crawford. "I had never liked Bertha Chase," says Allen, "with her baby blue eyes, her mincing steps and provocative manner; but there was a helpless quality about the girl that made me loath to call her, even to my own mind, a murderer." Library head Mark Denman also comes under suspicion. He's an unpleasant, even nasty sort who likes to surround himself with attractive female assistants. That Crawford could have been secretly wed to Chase while at the same time pursuing an affair with a student assistant astounds Allen. How "that quiet hermit" who routinely went about with his pockets bulging with random correspondence could have the energy or the gall for such an enterprise defies reason.

Much of the action in this readable mystery, in which a rare essay by Charles Lamb plays a vital part, takes place in the library itself. Boyd achieves a nicely created sleepy little college town setting throughout, but one must question the rather amazing fact that college authorities do not call in the police when two serious library "accidents," one of them fatal, occur within 24 hours. Nevertheless, it's an agreeable book, with one of the great academic understatements of all time: "Idealistic as a college community seems to outsiders, gossip is not unknown within the sacred precincts."

93. Hawkes, Judith. *Julian's House.* New York: Ticknor & Fields, 1989. 354p. New York: Penguin, 1991.

One of the major characters in this complex haunted house tale is 79-year-old Colin Robinson. Colin, public librarian in a little western Massachusetts town, is a charming fellow fully in command of his domain. He has even persuaded the town council to buy a new microfilm machine for the library. Deeply interested in local history, Colin teams up with young Sally Curtiss and her husband, David, to investigate the mysterious goings-on at the old house they have just bought. The book's three parts ("David," "Colin," and "Sally") focus by turn on the three characters. Colin receives very nice treatment in Hawkes's hands: "He had a dog, cooked for himself, looked after the yard ... but his real existence was the library: mending a dogeared book, explaining the card catalog to a class of youngsters ... or pursuing his own researches — prying some obscure fact from its niche in the past, emerging from the dusty files like a miner, clutching his nugget of truth." Colin is alone a good deal but seldom feels lonely, so thoroughly interwoven is his own life with that of the town. Hawkes shows that Colin is, in effect, surprised at his age, for he is in many ways very close to the shy, book-loving boy he was 60 years earlier. He's shy, yes, but with many ambitions. The relationship between Colin and Sally and David is especially right: Far from being merely an old coot to be tolerated, they find in Colin a knowledgeable and valuable ally in their pursuit of the paranormal.

94. Hayes, Marjorie. *Homer's Hill.* Philadephia: Lippincott, 1944. 224p.

Presented in the form of a diary by Boston school librarian Hester Hamlin ("Hester Hamlin: her book,/Shame on him who takes a look!" says the warning facing the title page), this novel takes the reader deep into the World War II home front. Hamlin, who describes herself as an old maid, arranges to take care of businessman Mr. Lovell's house, daughter, and temporary ward in New Hampshire the summer of 1943. The story is set in a rural area known as Homer's Hill. The book provides a very interesting portrait of how the war affected so many aspects of life. Such war-related matters as gasoline rationing, victory gardens, volunteer hospital work, and continuing news of the war from its various fronts turn up in almost every entry. Hayes handles very nicely the contrasts between great events of the war and little domestic scenes, such as air raids on Berlin and bunnies missing from the family's hutch. Hamlin meets many of the well-drawn local characters and fits in well in the community. She has a nice touch with Mr. Lovell's daughter, Susy, and his ward, Pat. Pat is another reminder of the war: She has come from England to visit for the duration after a German bombing attack destroyed her school and killed her roommate.

Hamlin is an alert woman of multiple interests. She follows the war closely, of course; she also pays thoughtful attention to domestic political events, from labor strikes to the Detroit race riot of 1943: "Twenty-three dead, two hundred injured and the Army has taken over. Democracy not showing up very well this week." She reads poetry and quotes it frequently and writes some poetry herself. We learn how she became an "old maid" when she has a nightmare of her sweetheart's death in World War I. She awakens in tears from her dream: "Sun was just rising and I lay and watched the gay colors streak across the sky. It seemed incredible that in such a world of beauty men could choose to wage war. Wish it were only a bad dream, from which we could all waken to the sunrise."

It's a novel certainly very much of its time but one whose intimate portrayal of a strong character making do is touching, historically informative, and a pleasure to read. Hamlin sees it through and does a nice job of it. So does Marjorie Hayes.

95. Heidish, Marcy. *The Torching.* New York: Simon & Schuster, 1992. 236p. New York: Avon, 1993.

The Torching is a complex mystery in which bookstore owner and author Alice Grey finds aspects of a long-ago case of alleged witchcraft she is researching coming to replicate themselves in her own life. Mr. Archer and Mrs. Lind are librarians in the historical research library where Alice does her investigations. Mr. Archer, an elderly man with a reedy voice, "was a wisp of a man, thin as a stream of his own pipe smoke." He maintains a pet white rabbit who has the run of the library. Alice finds in Mr. Archer a ready ear: "Mr. Archer, I always felt, understood me." Alas for Mr. Archer, he meets an unpleasant demise early in the book, and Mrs. Lind, "a large, middle-aged British woman" who "always seemed somehow slightly damp," comes under suspicion as the mystery unfolds. Neither of the librarians, unfortunately, is at great evidence in the story.

96. Hersey, John. *The Child Buyer: A Novel in the Form of Hearings Before the Standing Committee on Education, Welfare & Public Morality of a Certain State Senate, Investigating the Conspiracy of Mr. Wissey Jones, with Others, to Purchase a Male Child.* New York: Knopf, 1960. 257p. London: Hamilton, 1962. (Other editions.)

Library books come up for scrutiny in a section of this novel, which takes the form of hearings before the state senate committee noted in the novel's subtitle. Pequot town librarian Elizabeth Cloud's spirited testimony before the committee occupies several pages in midbook. Cloud acquits herself handily as she describes to a hostile group of state legislators her practice of assisting bright, curious children in satisfying their reading interests. When one of the lawmakers starts raving about public libraries "dealing out sex and sadism," Cloud speaks plainly: "If you come down to the Town Free Library in Pequot with the intent of pulling out books and making a bonfire of them, sir, I'll be there to welcome you — with a fourteen-gauge shotgun."

97. Hill, Donna. *Catch a Brass Canary.* Philadelphia: Lippincott, 1965. 224p. Also in *Best-in-Books.* Garden City, N.Y.: Doubleday, 1965.

Nell Kettridge is the new acting head librarian of the Amsterdam Branch public library on Manhattan's West Side. The library is a decrepit facility with a small staff. Nell dislikes the library and has no interest in ingratiating herself with her subordinates. She thinks that she is not really interested in "any piddling career in the Public Library" but in enjoying the cultural advantages of New York City. "Books were the reason she had chosen this profession," and dealing with human beings not even a distant second. Notions of "Wrangles with the public, confusion at the desks, racket in the children's room, damages, losses, and fines; envy dissension and strife, all of it hated involvement with people's problems" form the background of Nell's ideas about library service. She would rather work with figures and reports and prefers her tiny basement "office" to the hurly-burly of public and staff interaction.

It sounds as though Nell is one more case for the librarian-as-recluse files, but not so. In this sentimental, idealistic, and old-fashioned liberal novel, Nell learns that she is good at the very things that she believes she most dislikes. The vehicle for her self-discovery is Puerto Rican youth Miguel Campos, who applies for a job as a page in the library. In spite of her initial aversion, Nell hires him and soon comes to his defense when other staff members treat him with cruel prejudice. The novel belongs more to Miguel than it does to Nell, but next to him, she is the most important character present.

98. Hilton, James. *Random Harvest.* Boston: Little, Brown, 1941. 327p. London: Macmillan, 1941. (Many editions.)

Woburn, a former public librarian, is a minor character in this novel of English upper-middle-class life immediately preceding World War II. He is "an elegant young man," and "a very adaptable young man" who catalogs private libraries. His work takes him from England to the Continent; he hopes that he can do his next job, scheduled for Nice, before war begins. He dabbles in fiction and has written a number of stories, but admits that his writing shows no real originality, "only a technique." As England's participation in the war becomes inevitable, Woburn resolves to join the air force.

99. ____. *So Well Remembered.* London: Macmillan, 1947. 300p. Boston: Little, Brown, 1945. (Many editions.)

A few pages approximately one-third of the way through this novel dwell on Dick Jordan, librarian of the Browdley Public Library. Jordan, a close friend and political supporter of main character George Boswell, agrees to hire as a junior assistant Olivia Channing, a young woman whose local history, through no fault of her own, is badly tarnished. Jordan is portrayed as a man who, due in part to his "weak heart" and his "nagging wife," seeks to avoid any conflict on the job. He tells Boswell that he "nearly had a heart attack" when a patron became abusive toward Channing, calling her names with no provocation on her part.

100. Hinkle, Vernon. *Music to Murder By.* Bath, England: Chivers. South Yarmouth, Mass.: John Curley, 1987. 294p. (Large print.) (Other editions.)

H. Martin Webb, Harvard music librarian, comes home one day to find his good friend Jerome and Jerome's estranged wife messily murdered in his bedroom. Subsequently he discovers another body, that of a male porn star. Webb puts his sleuthing skills into play as yet another in the roster of librarians who probably should have had offices down the hall from Sam Spade. Aside from his intensely emotional responses to music, Webb is a handball fanatic with a certain wry humor. He is also a member of the Irish Republican Army (albeit a peaceful one). Other than these considerations, there is little to distinguish this mystery from a host of its fellows, except, perhaps, that the occasional "offensive" word is represented with prissy blanks in the text. This may mean that Webb, as the narrator, is prissy. There could be another explanation for the mysterious omissions.

101. Hitchens, Dolores. *Enrollment Cancelled.* (Pub. under pseud. D. B. Olsen.) Garden City, N.Y.: Doubleday, 1952. 190p. Also published as *Dead Babes in the Wood.* New York: Dell, 1952.

    A series of murders turns the quiet campus of southern California's Clarendon College upside down. College librarian Miss Pettit is particularly distressed, for she is acquainted with all the victims and discovers one of them immediately after her slaying. Pettit, 30ish, lives with two other single female college staffers. She is not unattractive but has "the sort of shy, stiff manner that rebuffed men." She appears frequently during the novel, for there is an important link between the library (or, more precisely, between some of the library's books) and the killings. Pettit, "the little librarian," is not an attractive character. Several consider her excessively straitlaced, a professional virgin, and "hysterical." In the end, the bloom of love is on Pettit, ironically over her involvement with a police investigator who earlier intimidated her.

102. Hodges, Hollis. *Norman Rockwell's Greatest Painting.* Middlebury, Vt.: Erickson, 1988. 261p. (Other editions.)

    Mary Ostrowski, retired and widowed Massachusetts public librarian, is attractive "in her own way." She has "an alert, almost birdlike look." She lives alone in a too-large old house and frets about her age. She posed long ago for a painting by Norman Rockwell, one some think his greatest. She gives piano lessons to neighborhood children, reads the *New York Times*, and keeps up on current literature. She falls under the influence of an obscure self-help book on aging. The book has a lot to say on the romantic possibilities of those past 60. Following the book's counsel, she has an affair with a nice retired plumber whom she picks up in a hotel. One might think that their match was made somewhere other than heaven: she likes Berlioz; he doesn't know that Beethoven is dead. Their affair falters when they part at the end of their initial accidental rendezvous, since they neglect to ascertain certain vital data — like one another's names. Love triumphs in the end. Or maybe it overcomes through attrition, an effect that any reader dogged enough to persevere to the end of this shallow, if not preposterous, novel will also likely undergo.

103. Hodson, James L. *Harvest in the North.* London: Gollancz, 1934. 447p. New York: Knopf, 1934. (Other editions.)

Harvest in the North is set in England's Lancashire mill region in the 1920s. Henry Brierley is one of several characters who appear and reappear for the story's duration. Brierley, an aspiring playwright with, evidently, some real talent, works as a librarian. He has a weak spot for pub singer Trix Bishop. Bishop is an uncultured young woman who helps support a hard up family. She and Brierley are close, but she realizes that as a modestly paid librarian (four pounds a week), he offers no real solution to her financial problems. Yet he takes "pride and delight in having to love her with her faults of speech, crudities of manner." At her urging, he embezzles 200 pounds from the library's acquisitions funds to invest in the stock market. He makes a killing on the market and quits his loathed library job to concentrate on writing. Brierly learns at length that writing is an even less reliable way of making money than being a librarian, so he takes the balance of his market earnings and buys a mill. He and Bishop do not follow through on his early visions of love, sweet love. This is an awkward, if well-intentioned, novel concerned with the effect of money, or its lack, on its major characters.

104. Hood, Margaret P. *The Scarlet Thread.* New York: Coward-McCann, 1956. 186p.

It's the oldest story in the book: woman wants man; man is keen on another woman; woman kills her rival. The motive: jealousy; the method: a stout bit of thread; the place: the top of the stairs. Myra Hopkins is the librarian and the deadly killer-by-sewing-supplies in this mystery of loquacious local color set in Fox Island, Maine. Myra, often promised marriage, continually held at bay, longs to be the mistress of the Moors, an old house on the island. Poet Phillip Waite, owner of the Moors, keeps Myra at arm's length even while engaged to her. According to her doctor, Myra is "'a fine person. A bit on the serious side, strait-laced. Although you can never tell about these prim women. Too much repression sometimes weakens their control in one wild burst of passion.'" Myra's passion is more orderly than that, however, and one imagines that a first-degree verdict is probably in the future for this "tortured spinster" whose cheeks flush when she has a secret to conceal.

105. Horner, Joyce. *The Greyhound in the Leash.* Garden City, N.Y.: Doubleday, 1949. 313p.

The idea behind this novel set in 1938 is provocative, although not unique: What would happen if an individual were able to live more than one life? Evalina Grant gets that opportunity here as we see her following several different lives whose natures depend, perhaps, on the men she chooses to marry — or not marry; or, perhaps, on the qualities within her that lead her to choose more or less the same sort of man each time. In one of her lives Evalina is a librarian. In spite of the book's generally laudatory reviews, this bibliographer found the book staggeringly dull. The premise is fine, but Evalina proves in every version such a fundamentally tedious character that it is hard to imagine anyone caring what happens to her. Horner's prose is literate, certainly, but it also alternates between long, long passages of banal dialogue and even longer passages of pointlessly cluttered description. It's a challenge to any reader's sensibilities.

106. Hurley, Doran. *Says Mrs. Crowley, Says She!* New York and Toronto: Longmans, Green, 1941. 254p.

Says Mrs. Crowley, Says She! is a collection of sketches about life in a Catholic parish. Constance Carey, "tremendously educated, with a high college degree," is assigned parish librarian. Her task is to turn the old parochial school library into a facility that will serve the entire parish. "And trust Connie to take it into her head to supervise and regulate our reading and try to raise our literary standards," notes one observer. Constance appears from time to time throughout the book, frequently as an up-to-date irritant to the novel's title character, who prides herself in her old-fashioned religion. In the chapter "The Library," Constance makes the mistake of suggesting that a quantity of musty old tomes in the library be discarded to make way for newer, livelier acquisitions. The new priest intervenes to save the precious collection of Catholic histories. The abrupt reversal of her ambitions must be a bit difficult to bear for a young woman who "has insisted upon becoming the Old Parish authority on all things liturgical and ecclesiastical." Nevertheless, Constance "is a sweet, good girl" and "a good Catholic." This is not, however, a good book. It is pious pap.

107. Innes, Michael. *Operation Pax.* New York: Dodd, Mead, 1951. 304p. London: Gollancz, 1951. Also published as *Paper Thunderbolt.* New York: Berkley, 1966. (Other editions.)

Although this novel features the Bodleian Library, there is very little here of librarians. The depiction of the infrequently mentioned "Bodley's Librarian," however, is worth a note: He is an aged specimen, bald, who carries simultaneously several pairs of spectacles upon his high, domed forehead. Sometimes he actually uses as many as three pairs at the same time, depending on the visual difficulty of the text he must consult. Michael Innes is the real life J.I.M. Stewart.

108. Iverson, Andrina. *The Gifts of Love.* New York: Farrar, Strauss, 1946. 275p. Published in condensed form under the name Andrina Gilmartin. *Ladies Home Journal* 63 (April 1946): 17–19.

The Great Depression and World War II loom over this first novel, which won a Hopwood Prize in 1945. They loom, but rather than overpowering personal stories, they place them in perspective. Main character Jane Rankin began her work as a librarian in a small college somewhere between Detroit and Cleveland at the Depression's onset. Thanks to her regular paycheck, she found herself with more money than she had ever seen at a time when she read in the newspapers about bread lines and panhandlers in the big cities. She is the protégé of Miss Erwin, the university librarian. Miss Erwin, who has a small part in the book, is "funny, frustrated, sex-starved," and believes "that pretty women were created for men's pleasure." Miss Erwin reads Hemingway and Waugh and is not easily shocked.

Jane is a very bright (Phi Beta Kappa) young woman with a complex emotional makeup. The daughter of a chemistry professor, she confesses at the age of 19 her true love for a professor friend of the family, a colleague of her father's. When he gently deflects her passionate profession, she slinks away in shame and despair. Her reaction seems more than superficial; coupled with her grasp of her father's first unhappy marriage and her sister's not-so-happy marital situation, it colors her trust in her own feelings for years to come. When she becomes emotionally involved with Warren Gregory, a young engineer, she experiences considerable difficulty in accepting at face value not only her own feelings but Warren's. Jane has long guarded against losing control of her own life and identity: "Was there never to come the time when she'd be free to be herself? When people wouldn't feel at liberty to correct, admonish, reproach?"

Narrated from Jane's point of view in lengthy flashbacks, the novel is an adept examination of her emotional conflicts, self-doubt, fear, and desire. Iverson delves into Jane's psychology sympathetically and instructively. The Depression and the war — never overwhelming in their insistence, yet undeniably evident — form a background suggesting that Jane's personal struggles, however demanding, are far from global in their import. Jane's library work, never prominent in the story, more-or-less disappears from view following her marriage to Warren, although in 1941, nearly ten years later, she is still working part-time at the library.

109. Johnson, Stanley. *Professor.* New York: Harcourt, Brace, 1925. 312p.

Professor is an astringent satire of academic life featuring a surprisingly positive characterization of the college librarian. English professor Parkhurst is the focus of the novel, but Charlotte Lee Sears, librarian at Thurston College, performs limited but important occasional duty. She is a beautiful, white-haired, 31-year-old widow, "working for two reasons — because I have to make a living and because I like library work." Parkhurst seeks her out as a confidant, speaking at length with her, hoping to gain from her insights on his character and his romantic failures. She addresses him with perceptive candor: "All your values are wrong," she says, "outside of that you seem to be all right." In another important conversation between Sears and Parkhurst (and the author implies that there have been several others not recorded in the narrative), Sears forces the professor to acknowledge his hiding behind a mask of irony, his hypocrisy, his relentless "compromising between things as they ought to be and things as they have to be." Yet Sears cannot bring Parkhurst to grasp the understanding of what he lacks most seriously, a "soul," as she puts it, or, more verbosely, an ability to feel the inner lives of others and to make sympathetic allowances for them. In addition to her role as Parkhurst's confidant, Sears shows her involvement in the life of the college at large by organizing and managing a faculty picnic, in hopes that camaraderie in the outdoors will make this diverse, crabby bunch a more cohesive lot. Sears may be the only important character in the book treated with unreserved approbation and free of negative stereotyping.

Johnson, W. Bolingbroke. *See* Bishop, Morris.

110. Johnston, George H. *My Brother Jack.* New York: Morrow, 1965. 415p. Sydney and London: Collins, 1964. (Other editions.)

In Melbourne, Australia, young David Meredith is working as a fledgling newspaper reporter. There he becomes reacquainted with Helen Midgeley, four years his senior, whom he first met as a teenager when she was an art student. Now, he finds that she manages a subscription lending library. She startles him with her fashionable dress and her confident manner. In her small sitting room in the library, he notices that her reading includes such left-wing classics as *Das Kapital* and *Ten Days That Shook the World*. She wears a locket containing a photo of Sacco and Vanzetti. Helen seduces David efficiently and expediently in the library after closing. It is a venue that becomes their regular romantic rendezvous. Their relationship continues for several years, yet they have almost no contact outside the library. "Here I was with my own secret mistress," reflects David, "who was beautiful and clever and kind, and who asked for nothing, it seemed, except my occasional attention."

When Helen realizes the extent of David's potential as a journalist, she engineers their marriage. Her first visit with his family is an ominous disaster, from her general discomfort with the unpolished bunch to her repugnance at being dirtied by one of the family infants. She even picks an argument with David's revered brother, Jack, over the Spanish Civil War.

After their marriage, David and Helen move to a house in a nice subdivision (a "mental desert," in David's subsequent estimation). Helen's sympathies for the downtrodden mysteriously ebb; although she still refers to herself as having been a librarian, she now concentrates on life as a newly arrived socialite. The second half of the book records David's growing independence and success as a writer and Helen's slow fade from his existence and her failure to transcend her taste for superficial satisfactions. The author implies that Helen's newfound life as a seeker of shallow glamor and material pleasure owes to the very modest circumstances of her background. Whatever the rationale, her abrupt transition from advocate of the working class to Sybarite is not entirely convincing.

111. Keller, David H. *The Eternal Conflict.* Philadelphia: Prime Press, 1949. 191p.

A woman (or Woman, as she is called in the novel) with the powers of a goddess draws elderly librarian Henry Cecil back in time to live in her castle. She abducts Cecil, recently canned from his public library job in a cost-cutting move, because she wants to employ him as her personal librarian. Although the abrupt change of scene leaves Cecil rattled, he is clearly impressed by the Woman's powers and tantalized by his new opportunities. The Woman creates a library from nothing, according to Cecil's specifications, containing all the lost books of the world, including those from the Library of Alexandria. Cecil spends most of his time in the library, either playing checkers with a German mathematician the Woman has also abducted, reading the ancient texts, or writing novels. From time to time he draws information from arcane volumes that helps the Woman achieve her desires. Occasionally, he challenges her assumptions. "You have the very disgusting habit of forcing me to think," she tells him. Cecil also gives advice to a hunter the Woman has spirited to her domain on how to please her. When the Woman decides to abandon her castle, she leaves it to Cecil and the mathematician, knowing that all their needs will be satisfied merely through their wishing so. "Perhaps we are dead," observes Cecil, "and perhaps this is our Paradise." A symbol-laden (often densely laden) and quite nicely written fantasy whose focus is the "eternal conflict" between men and women, a conflict Henry Cecil helps the author explore.

112. Kelly, Mary. *March to the Gallows.* New York: Holt, Rinehart, Winston, 1965. 192p. London: M. Joseph, 1964.

Young Hester Callard is in charge of reference services at London's Colwell Central Public Library. Her friend Tony, a would-be writer, dismisses thrillers as "poison"— and Hester acknowledges that for every Mann or Camus she lends, a load of "bilge" also goes out. Yet she also admits that the "poison" is in her blood. Her former Irish lover (crushed by falling scaffolding on his way back from lunch, poor lad), used to castigate her for swallowing "dreams and lies" rather than living her own life. That life is less than she hoped for; she plods along at the library under her tedious boss, Mr. Hadstock. She hears the usual ignorant, well intended remarks directed at librarians: "I should think it would be terribly satisfying to work with books."

"Once I'd dreamt of college libraries [she's naive in her own way, it is clear], dusty parchments, discovering another Vercelli Codex. Well, I still had the dust"— and the bilge. Hester yearns for a little "adventure" in her existence. It comes to her one day when the theft of her handbag leads her into a web of mystery and personal danger. Unfortunately for the reader, the mystery is talky, slow, and dull. Too bad, for Hester, who is casually profane, rather brave, and sometimes actually amusing in spite of the fatiguing story, deserves a better setting for her character.

113. King, Stephen. *Insomnia.* New York: Signet, 1995. 663p. New York: Viking, 1994. London: Hodder & Stoughton, 1994.

In a novel that stands in limp contrast to King's earlier, better work, librarian

Helen Deepneau plays a bit part. She has the misfortune of being Ed Deepneau's wife. Ed is a vehicle for bad business of a supernatural sort; when the dark force moves in, Ed's pleasant personality checks out. He beats Helen savagely, driving her to leave him. She has an MLS and lands a job with the Derry Public Library, courtesy of Mike Hanlon (see Item 114). "I think they ought to make Mike Hanlon's birthday a national holiday," says Helen, who later narrowly escapes a burning building, turns to feminism, and wins a nice insurance settlement upon Ed's death. King continues to treat librarians positively, but the relentless readability of his earlier novels is almost wholly absent from this overlong, ill-focused exercise.

114. ____. *It.* New York: Viking, 1986. 1,138p. London: Hodder & Stoughton, 1986. (Other editions.)

This immense novel of good versus evil exhibits all the best and worst features of King's work: compulsive readability, verbosity run wild, believable characters portrayed with honest sympathy, gratuitous vulgarity, a fine eye for the details of ordinary life, and a fundamentally silly premise. *It* also features a librarian, Mike Hanlon, in a critical role. Hanlon is the town librarian of Derry, Maine; he calls his old, widely scattered childhood friends back together some 30 years after the events that first brought them into the grip of terror in their struggles with the monstrous alien entity know as It. Hanlon also contributes an "unauthorized town history" of Derry, which appears in a number of interludes scattered through the novel. The manuscript, purportedly found in the Derry library vault, contains Hanlon's observations recorded afterhours in his library office.

As a child, Hanlon was one of the local "losers," in his case because he was black. Now, he notes, "On one level of my mind I was and am living with the most grotesque, capering horrors; on another I have continued to live the mundane life of a small-city librarian." He is the only one who hears the rumblings of It's awakening, for among his friends only he has remained in Derry, in the home ground of the evil embodied by It. Hanlon initiates the reunion of the old circle in the renewed battle against It. Hanlon acquits himself well, both as town historian and as a participant in the battle. In the occasional scenes in which Hanlon performs library work, he also acts like an actual librarian.

115. ____. *The Library Policeman.* In his *Four Past Midnight*. Viking, 1990, pp. 401–604. London: Hodder & Stoughton, 1990. (Other editions.)

Insurance man Sam Peebles visits the old Junction City Public Library one day to root up a little material for a Rotary speech. The deserted library gives him an uneasy feeling, highlighted by some grim "public service" posters, including one referring to the "library police," who allegedly come after boys and girls who keep their books past due. When librarian Ardelia Lortz wheels a book truck into view, Sam's discomfort scarcely abates. Ardelia seems pleasant enough, but there is something cold about her. She provides Sam some speech aids, but the two come very close to a full-scale argument over the posters. In their exchange, Ardelia presents a clear impression of authoritarian self-certainty. Inevitably, Sam loses the books she retrieved for him, and a message on his answering machine from Ardelia threatens him with the library policeman over his tardiness. Sam returns to the library to pay for his lost books and finds the place wholly different. It is busy and cheerful, and no one on the staff has heard of Ardelia Lortz. The librarian in charge is the gentlemanly Mr. Price. Sam spends the rest of the novel investigating the truth about Ardelia Lortz and his own connection with the long-vanished library of his first visit. An effective and readable horror tale, told with King's usual aplomb.

116. Klein, Joe. *Primary Colors: A Novel of Politics.* (Pub. under Anonymous.) New York: Random, 1996. 366p. London: Chatto & Windus, 1996. (Other editions.)

Miss Baum, a middle-aged Harlem librarian, appears on a few pages in this *roman à clef* claptrap satirizing the presidential campaign process. Baum is "pushing fifty, hair dyed auburn to blot the gray." She is "condescending ... in the reflexive, unconsciously insulting manner of public servants everywhere." She is a "pretty typical library bureaucrat" who doesn't mind a roll in the hay with a prominent politico. Shortly after this book's publication, *Newsweek* columnist Klein made headlines with his fairly despicable dissembling about his authorship. His coyness in this regard is no more off-putting than his style, which relies on such advanced compositional devices as PUTTING EVERYTHING IN CAPITALS TO MAKE SURE WE GET THE POINT. As cheesy a piece of fiction as the novel is, it is altogether fitting and proper that a real-life New York City librarian filed suit against Klein, seeking the modest recompense of $100 million, for allegedly abusing her in his portrayal of the essentially characterless and transparent Baum. Cheesy book, dubious lawsuit, a waste of time all around. Read the ingredients list on a box of Velveeta; it will be a more nourishing and edifying experience.

117. Knight, Kathleen M. *The Trouble at Turkey Hill.* Garden City, N.Y.: Doubleday, 1946. 220p. Also in Holding, Elisabeth. *The Innocent Mrs. Duff* (bound with the title novel and with A. E. Martin's *Death in the Limelight.*) New York: W.E. Black, 1946.

Marcella Tracy, the town librarian in an island community near New Bedford, narrates a murder mystery. Although it portrays Tracy as perceptive and resourceful, the novel's concerns with libraries, or librarianship, are barely marginal. It's a decent bit of mystery-thriller work, however.

118. Kristof, Agota. *The Proof.* New York: Grove Weidenfeld, 1991. 154p. Translation of *La Preuve.* Paris: Editions du Seuil, 1988.

In a country wracked by war and revolution, young Lucas survives on vegetables he raises in the family garden. All the other members of his family have apparently been killed in the conflict. One day he learns that there is a public library in his devastated town, and he goes there hoping to find something interesting to read. Clara, the 35-year-old librarian, is a widow. Her husband was executed for "treason." Her hair turned white overnight in reaction to her husband's killing. She fears, at first, that Lucas is a spy, sent to trick her into giving him books proscribed by the authorities. Lucas gains her trust slowly; one evening he finds her drunk in a bar, helps her home, puts her to bed, and comforts her when she has a nightmare about her husband's death. Lucas tends her when she is sick. "I've treated you badly," she says. "You treated me like a dog," he answers. "It doesn't matter."

She allows him to read banned books that she has saved from the library and hidden in her cellar. Although Lucas lives with a woman and her child, refugees from the fighting, he and Clara become lovers. Clara and Lucas both disappear from the story, although Clara resurfaces in the end, having been released from prison. She is toothless, demented, incapable of caring for herself, demolished by the war and her memories of her husband. The proof alluded to in the title comes in a postscript, in which the authorities cast a final note of grim irony on this short, sad, well-written novel.

119. Lambert, Gavin. *In the Night All Cats Are Grey*. London: W.H. Allen, 1976. 155p.

A claustrophobic, intense novel of a man who does his best to remain socially isolated. Abandoned in a movie theater at three weeks of age, the narrator grew up in an orphanage. He is now a 30-year-old librarian in London, where he has lived in a basement flat for 12 years. "I've never thought of myself as having a story. I'm just someone who happened." He has one acquaintance outside of work, the 54-year-old Ruth, whom he met in a tea shop. They go long periods without seeing each other. Grace Garland, his 53-year-old neighbor, invades his isolation, and the two develop something resembling a friendship. The narrator finds in Grace a deliverance, of sorts, from his emotional solipsism: "For the first time in my life I was looking at myself through another person's eyes. I didn't want to disappoint Grace." The story evolves quite contrary to what one might expect, that is, a conventional "awakening" of the narrator to the realm of positive human feeling. He instead slides into a lethal madness. Aside from its melodramatic and not-altogether-credible conclusion, the novel is a chilling study of a man who stands apart from the world. The book's atmosphere is leaden, oppressive: "The sky looked heavy, with dirty clouds that didn't move and a drizzle that felt like cold sweat." Like Dickens, the narrator walks the streets of London for hours at night, unable to sleep. "I live alone in my empty past," he observes. He does spend a fair amount of his narrative in the library and makes at least one pointed comment on reference work: "Disturbing things…often came out when you work at a library. They make me feel that the more I learn the less I know."

120. Lane, Rose Wilder. *He Was a Man.* New York and London: Harper, 1925. 380p.

He Was a Man is a fairly readable novel of a man's rise from ignorant poverty to international fame as a writer — a fictionalized biography, of sorts, of Jack London. Mr. Stein, a librarian, appears on fewer than two dozen pages, but it is he who helps put young Gordon Blake's career in motion. Blake is an untutored fellow when he meets Stein, but he is a haunter of libraries and has tried some writing. Stein finds him a compelling storyteller, and encourages him to commit his experiences to paper in the form of articles for the Sunday paper. He is instrumental in helping Blake break into print; he provides vital editorial assistance, finetuning Blake's rough-and-tumble prose to suit the "family" audience. Stein impresses Blake with his urbanity: "Mr. Stein moved among the books, speaking with ease in smooth grammatical sentences, uttering words which he had met only in print." Before he disappears from the novel, Stein also introduces Blake to his future wife. In all, not a shabby performance for a librarian who has barely 20 pages to get his job done.

121. Langton, Jane. *The Transcendental Murder.* Harper & Row, 1964. 247p. New York: Penguin, 1989. Also published as *The Minuteman Murder.* New York: Dell, 1976.

Trouble is brewing in the local literary club in Concord, Massachusetts. Club member Mr. Goss alleges to have come upon some original correspondence revealing some of the Transcendentalists as not as immune to earthly delights as their reputations would have it. Goss himself soon turns up dead, murdered, and circulation librarian Mary Morgan finds herself pressed in as an assistant in the investigation. Morgan is an expert on the local scene and is writing a book on the Transcendentalist women. Her boss, the aging chief librarian Miss Herpitude, appears from time to time; she is "no ordinary librarian." She believes that books are to be used, not warehoused, and is even willing to cut pictures from books if a patron needs to make a tracing. (She does carefully replace the razored bits later.) She also has some important beans to spill regarding the investigation, but as she is about to speak, she becomes the victim of an encounter with a bust of Louisa May Alcott. Transcendentalist buffs (there probably are some, somewhere) will find the novel amusing, but for all the local color over which the author labors and in spite of her credible characters, the tale is slightly stupefying.

122. Larkin, Philip. *A Girl in Winter.* London: Faber and Faber, 1957. 248p. New York: St. Martin's, 1962. (Other editions.)

Set in England during World War II, this penetrating examination of a young woman's thoughts and feelings offers many arresting passages. A number occur in the public library where the heroine, Katherine Lind, works as a clerical assistant. The bane of her existence in the library is head librarian Mr. Anstey. Anstey is "a thin, wizened man," around forty, who "resembled a clerk at a railway station who had suffered from shellshock." He is a petty, condescending blowhard who is ready with no provocation to ream out a junior assistant at length over a trivial and readily corrected error. Lind finds Anstey insufferable, yet the chance discovery of a letter from him forces her to contend with the reality of his humanity, which is neither so shallow or mean as his daily behavior would suggest. Ironically, immediately on the heels of Lind's insight into Anstey, he treats her abysmally and stupidly for the way she helped a younger staff member through a dental emergency. Anstey's role in the novel is fairly minor, but Larkin makes him memorable in a handful of pages. Larkin describes Miss Feather, Anstey's second-in-command, as marked by "a withered, sly face, and a conspiratorial way of glancing on all sides as she spoke and rarely looking anyone in the face."

123. Le Carré, John. *The Spy Who Came In from the Cold.* New York: Coward-McCann, 1963. 256p. London: Gollancz, 1963. (Many editions.)

Whatever cold the spy came in from could hardly shiver one's timbers more thoroughly than Le Carré's librarian, Miss Crail. Main character Alec Leamas takes a job in the Bayswater Library for Psychic Research. There, in the chilly old churchlike building heated by black oil stoves, he reports to his boss, Crail. Miss Crail is officious, rule-bound, and rude. She spends a lot of work time arguing with her mother on the telephone. From time to time, she invokes an apparently imaginary superior, Mr. Ironside, when a subordinate tests her will. Crail obsesses about inane trivia — a coat hung on the wrong peg, for example — and when she is not arguing with her mother, calls her to report her underlings' sins. She rapidly develops an intense hatred for Leamas, without provocation, but "enemies were what Miss Crail liked." Crail earns only a few pages in the novel, but those are sufficient. Brrr!

124. LeClaire, Anne D. *Sideshow.* New York: Viking, 1994. 308p. London: Piatkus, 1995.

Soleil Browne is a 35-year-old librarian with Boston's Museum of Science. She has volunteered to be the "sleeper" in an exhibit designed to translate the brain waves of her dreams into a light and music projection. She learns that the physician who will monitor her "performance" is Andy McKey, with whom she had an intense affair several years earlier. As the exhibition progresses, Soleil finds herself pulled ever deeper into a long, disturbing dream that links her with people and events in 1932 Ohio, into a dangerous journey into her own past, and back into Andy's amorous regard. It's an effective psychological thriller with Soleil as a brave and resourceful librarian but one whose business as a librarian scarcely receives mention. At one point, the narrative notes, "She missed the library. The orderliness. The routine. The satisfaction of knowing she was good at her job." The book would be better without the occasional references to pop culture figures such as Sam Shepard and Jessica Lange, and the connection between past and present strains credibility, but it's still fun.

125. Lee, Austin. *Sheep's Clothing: A Detective Frolic.* London: Cape, 1955. 223p. London: White Lion, 1976.

Sheep's Clothing is an amusing British mystery with a light touch, starring Miss Hogg, a teacher turned private investigator. In her first case, she receives valuable help from her old college classmate Dr. Alfred Greenwood. Greenwood is head of the Burghley Library, Westminster, founded in 1583. The Burghley features the Harland Bequest, one of the world's finest collections of erotica ("outside the Vatican library, of course"). Greenwood is not present on more than a dozen pages, but author Lee provides a number of clues to his character. When Hogg meets him, he is busy perusing one of the library's books, apparently something from the Harland Bequest. He quickly closes the book on Hogg's entrance. He seems to be a man with time on his hands: His In and Out trays are both empty. Although he is almost completely bald and his skin has "the bleached appearance of one who rarely sees the daylight," with his engaging smile he still reminds Hogg of the young man she knew 20 years earlier. Greenwood's elderly assistant seems to admire him in a romantic vein, a point of which he may be oblivious. The mystery leads to a rare and wonderful addition to the Burghley: the "lost" ending of St. Mark's Gospel, something that would, quips Hogg, "sort of balance the Harland Bequest."

126. Le Guin, Ursula. *Always Coming Home.* New York: Harper & Row, 1985. 523p. London: Gollancz, 1986. (Other editions.)

In this remarkable novel cum anthropology of a life in a future California organized on tribal lines, libraries are important repositories for each tribe's experience and knowledge. There are numerous references to things being given to libraries not for purposes of an easy tax deduction but as a kind of sacred rite. Librarians, it follows, are significant figures in this future society, although their presence in the book is not frequently front-and-center. In "The Keeper" (pp. 60–62) Fletcher, a tribal librarian, tells a formal story about a woman who served a particular valuable function for her people but who strayed from her mission. In "Pandora Converses with the Archivist of the Library of the Madrone Lodge at Wakwaha-na" (pp. 314–317), Pandora — who seems a lot like Le Guin herself — and her niece, the archivist, discuss how materials are chosen for the Madrone Lodge library and how they are removed from the collection. The conversation moves to the archivist's challenging questions about how information can be developed and multiplied without "becoming yet another source of power to the powerful." In neither selection is there anything in the way of character development for the two librarians, but that they receive such attention in the book reveals much about Le Guin's ideas of the proper activity of librarians, as "information is passed on — the central act of human culture."

127. Lemarchand, Elizabeth. *Step in the Dark*. New York: Walker, 1977. 173p. London: Hart-Davis, MacGibbon, 1976. (Other editions.)

Alastair Habgood has been librarian of the Ramsden Literary and Scientific Society since shortly after World War II. Of medium height, he is "pale and scholarly in appearance. He wore spectacles, and his thinning hair was receding from his temples." Annabel Lucas, his disreputable assistant, is found dead in the library at the foot of a staircase, a nearby cupboard full of rare books ransacked. In the aftermath of Lucas's death, Habgood seems drawn and "mentally dislocated," although the return of the rare books perks him up a good bit. He provides some assistance to the authorities, who briefly entertain thoughts of his possible involvement in the dirty work. It's the sort of mystery one consumes with weak tea and crackers.

128. Levi, Primo. *The Periodic Table*. New York: Schocken, 1984. 233p. London: M. Joseph, 1985. Translation of *Il Sistema Periodico*. Turin, Italy: Einaudi, 1975. (Many editions.)

Levi's novel features librarian Signorina Paglietta on barely two pages, but her description is on an unforgettable par with that of Miss Bunce in Abbe's *Voices in the Square* (Item 1). She guards the factory library where the narrator does his research. She is "small, without breasts or hips, waxen, wilted, and monstrously myopic: she wore glasses so thick and concave that, looking at her head-on, her eyes light blue, almost white, seemed very far away, stuck at the back of her cranium." She is "like a watchdog," one that has been "deliberately made vicious by being chained up and given little to eat...."

129. Lewin, Elsa. *I, Anna*. New York: Mysterious Press, 1984. 301p. (Other editions.)

Main character Anna Welles, "a gentle soul" in the estimation of one acquaintance, is a public librarian and cataloger in New York City. Middle-aged, divorced, and lonely, she goes to singles clubs and lets herself be picked up. Early in the novel while under the influence of marijuana (!), she commits a ghastly murder, including mutilation. She does not remember the event and seems likely to escape detection. She and a police officer investigating the case become romantically entangled. Anna is, as she tells him, someone who feels sporadic "rage and fear and helplessness. Total despair. But mostly I feel nothing." Anna has worked 15 years in her Queens library with generally laudable efficiency, yet "when she walked out of the place, the job fell away from her consciousness, like a coat slipped off her shoulders and hung away in a closet."

What at first seems an outtake from the film *Reefer Madness* (gentle librarian driven to killer frenzy by the dreaded weed) eventually clarifies itself as a psychotic episode growing out of Anna's bottomless sense of worthlessness and loneliness. It's a none-too-pleasant but nicely plotted crime novel. Anna's ultimate fate is in keeping with her self-assessment.

130. Lewis, Roy. *A Cracking of Spines.* London: Robert Hale, 1980. 207p. New York: St. Martin's, 1981. (Other editions.)

Love drives men to rash actions, and here college librarian Edward Heyman succumbs. He succumbs in more ways than one, for before the loose ends of this mystery are tied up, Heyman tumbles to his death from a library skylight, having apparently slipped while attempting to abscond with a load of rare books. Rare books, in fact, are Heyman's true love. Before his tumble, he was the librarian of Radford College. He was a chain smoker, compulsively energetic, "a peculiar-looking man ... extremely emaciated, with a small intelligent face dominated by steel-framed spectacles so large they could have passed for a comedian's props." When antiquarian bookseller and the novel's narrator Matthew Coll investigates the theft of a number of valuable rare books from Radford College, he learns that Heyman's romance with the book had blossomed into something worse than shady. It's a nicely written story in which librarian Heyman's sins are mitigated by his positive qualities as a bibliophile.

131. _____. *The Manuscript Murders.* London: Robert Hale, 1981. 208p. New York: St. Martin's, 1982.

In this outing, narrator Matthew Coll is acting as an agent at a book auction for American university librarian Tom Duncan. His mission: to buy a rare 16th-century manuscript constituting the personal journal of Emilia Lanier, alleged Dark Lady of Shakespeare's *Sonnets*. Duncan is a former boxer who now fights to build a great library and a great career. He has given Coll the go-ahead to pull out the stops in his quest for the Lanier journal. Duncan is single-minded, ruthless, and given to abrupt rudeness. Coll becomes suspicious of the journal's authenticity when the Dutch professor who discovered it is murdered. Although Duncan expresses conviction that the document is genuine, he submits it to a variety of experts, including a graphologist and a psychologist, to obtain further verification. An engrossing mystery for rare-book aficionados in which an ambitious librarian concocts and carries out an elaborate, imaginative, and thoroughly illegal scheme.

132. _____. *Where Agents Fear to Tread.* New York: St. Martins, 1984. 192p. London: Robert Hale, 1984.

Henry Franklin is a 32-year-old county librarian. Although unprepossessing and apparently not moving up the career ladder fast enough to suit his ambitious girlfriend, he is one of England's top experts on Arabic manuscripts. When a number of valuable manuscripts stolen from the British Library reputedly turn up in Pakistan, the government sends Franklin off to ascertain the authenticity of the documents. Accompanied to Karachi by a secret service agent, Franklin promptly proves his mettle when attacked by a group of street thugs. Soon Franklin is involved in not only stolen manuscripts, but murder, as well as mistaken identity: Pakistani radicals take him for a free-lancer in the spy (if not soldier) of fortune trade. Franklin undergoes "a three-week spell of fantasy" involving Islamic fanatics, a sudden love affair, and heroic derring-do on his part. It's approximately as believable as a James Bond outing, and nearly as amusing. Franklin's character is little developed little beyond the basic premise of an extraordinary adventure befalling a reasonably ordinary man.

133. Lewis, Sinclair. *Main Street*. New York: Harcourt, Brace, 1920. 451p. London: Hodder & Stoughton, 1921. (Many editions.)

It might be easy to characterize *Main Street*, Sinclair Lewis's first major success, as little more than a window on a vanished world of small-town America. The town of Gopher Prairie, Minnesota, to which librarian Carol Kennicott moves with her physician husband, may indeed seem lost in time and space in its self-satisfied provincialism. For thoughtful residents of small or even mid-sized towns of the American Middle West, however, the suffocating grip Gopher Prairie exerts on its residents will not seem a sociological quirk of the past but representative of what often takes place today.

Lewis does not linger long on Carol's undergraduate career in an undistinguished Minnesota college nor on her year in a Chicago library school, where her study of cataloging, reference, and the like "was easy and not too somniferous." Carol is not gifted but is reasonably bright, with a genuine interest in high culture. She revels in Chicago's Art Institute and other attractions and leaves library school with aspirations to bring culture and beauty to some prairie town. Lewis glosses over her three years in a St. Paul, Minnesota, public library in a few paragraphs — where "never did she feel that she was living" — for his objective is to get her to Gopher Prairie as quickly as possible.

Carol's fantasies about bringing the light of the world to the midwestern outback die a hard death in Gopher Prairie. In spite of her best intentions and efforts, the community insists on transforming Carol to its own ways and views. Her well-meaning cultural initiatives are so much dust in the wind of the historical insularity of small-town life. Lewis is surprisingly sympathetic toward most of his characters in *Main Street*, much more so than in the scathing *Babbitt*, which appeared two years later. It is, perhaps, his gentleness with the denizens of Gopher Prairie that makes his depiction of its crushingly self-referential culture so effective. In addition to Carol Kennicott, who does bear out the desire of a good librarian to bring new truths and ideas to those around her, Lewis devotes a fair amount of space to Miss Villets, the Gopher Prairie librarian. The "spinsterish" Miss Villets is not an altogether objectionable soul, but she offers up some well-petrified views on librarianship. She reveals these in an early conversation with Carol, in which, among other things, she indicates disapproval of the way some large city libraries permit "tramps" and "dirty persons" in the reading rooms and they allow "nasty children" to ruin books.

"Well," says Carol, "I'm sure you will agree with me in one thing: The chief task of a librarian is to get people to read."

"You feel so?" answers Miss Villets. "My feeling, Mrs. Kennicott ... is that the first duty of the *conscientious* librarian is to preserve the books.... Some librarians may choose to be so wishy-washy and turn their libraries into nursing-homes and kindergartens, but as long as I'm in charge, the Gopher Prairie library is going to be quiet and decent, and the books well kept!"

So there! But however hard-nosed and ornery Miss Villets may seem, one cannot help pitying her when she later reveals her own real sense of powerlessness in the community. Speaking of her involvement in the local literary club (an utterly pathetic organization, by the way), Miss Villets acknowledges that the club relies for papers on members who lack her literary training, but "why should I complain? What am I but a city employee?" Later in the same passage, having mentioned some of the club's "important" members, she dismisses her own worth altogether: "No, you may regard me as entirely unimportant. I'm sure what I say doesn't matter a bit!" Carol briefly tries to counter this dismal assessment but to no effect.

In the end, Gopher Prairie's relentless abrasive action on the new, the different, and the upstart wears down Carol's idealistic ambitions and her anger at not being able to carry them out. It is hard to imagine any other end for her ideals, or for Carol — or for the countless young men and women who dream dreams, but whose dreams evaporate in the often arid cultural realm of provincial America.

134. Leyland, Eric. *Faint Shadow.* London: MacDonald, 1948. 224p.

One-time librarian Tony Webb is now an accomplished writer living with his wife in a cottage in rural England. The novel consists of his reminiscences about his life, especially the years before World War II, "a pleasant world to remember, even though the memory be but a faint shadow of that which was." Webb agreed with friendly advice received in prep school that it would be a good idea for him to "go in for librarianship." "I was already a librarian," he notes, "of the school library." He adopted the profession as a way to a "secure living" while working toward his future as a writer. He eventually spent nine years as a librarian before his "plunge into the uncharted waters of professional writing."

Webb offers some pointed opinions on public libraries: As potential "people's universities," they should not waste their money or their staff on the purchase and circulation of popular fiction. It annoys him immensely that libraries bow to public demand for cheap thrills and thus perpetuate their image as places of refuge for those seeking such thrills in the form of throwaway fiction.

By the age of 25, Webb had already published three books, all for adolescents. He climbed in the library profession to become head of the Moor Park library system but carried on a long debate with himself about the wisdom of leaving his post for the full-time writer's life. Somewhat past the novel's halfway point, he throws in the towel at Moor Park and moves to the country with his wife, there to be a book writer rather than a bookman. "I have a great deal to thank librarianship for," Webb states. "True I left the work, but only for the one other occupation which appealed to me — full-time writing."

Although competently written from a technical standpoint, the narrative is plodding and humorless.

135. Lincoln, Joseph C. and Freeman Lincoln. *Ownley Inn.* New York: Coward-McCann, 1939. 311p.

Dr. Samuel Payson, curator and librarian for 30 years of the Knowlton Library of American Literature at a Connecticut university, is certain that his job is on the line as a result of the theft of a rare and valuable copy of the *New England Primer*. *Ownley Inn* is a good natured, old-fashioned mystery. One of its enjoyable aspects is seeing Dickson Clarke, a member of the school football team, join Dr. Payson as a library assistant and through Dr. Payson's tutelage become happily immersed in the study of American literature and rare books.

136. Lively, Penelope. *Passing On.* London: A. Deutsch, 1989. 210p. New York: Grove, Weidenfeld, 1990. (Other editions.)

Passing On is a fine, perceptive character study, written with finesse and compassion. Helen Glover is a librarian in her early 50s. Her late mother, who died at 80, was overbearing and unsympathetic toward Helen, and even after her death looms over her daughter like a bad dream. Although plagued by her mother, Helen is no pushover. She is a competent, functional woman whose disappointments in life do not keep her from living constructively. Chief among these disappointments is her romantic history, which, as histories go, is rather brief. Her mother, who found sex despicable and communicated that finding to Helen, bears considerable responsibility for Helen's spotty love life.

As the novel opens, the issue of the moment concerns settling Helen's mother's estate. Much to her surprise, Helen feels a powerful attraction to Giles Carnaby, one of the lawyers involved in the business. "She had not felt thus for roughly fifteen years and had not expected to do so ever again." Yet she doubts her ability to attract men; as she examined herself in the mirror, her body "looked to her ... like an illustration in a medical journal."

Senior librarian Joyce Babcock, Helen's superior in the public library, is "a woman without vision or curiosity; her distaste for books was equalled only by her dislike of people." For Helen, however, "the library was a refuge.... There, Helen became someone else; she became brisk efficient well-liked Helen. Helen who had been there years and years, knew all the ropes, could be relied on to deal tactfully with difficult customers, with the intransigence of the county library system, with errant books and tiresome children." Joyce Babcock can fathom Helen's devotion to books no better than Helen's mother could.

Helen lives with her schoolteacher younger brother Edward in the old family house. She provides Edward, as she has throughout her life, a strong measure of emotional support. Late in the book, a crisis in Edward's life gives Helen an opportunity to stand firm for him, and she does.

The novel is full of subtle touches. When Helen meets at lunch with Giles to sort out their abortive affair, she notices, for example, that he sneaks a glance at his watch during a presumably heartfelt discussion. The gesture speaks volumes to Helen. Ultimately Helen finds herself able to escape the shadow and the voice of her mother through the strength she displays in dealing with Giles and the good judgment she shows in contending with her brother's crisis. It is no longer necessary for her to find refreshing—"invigorating, even"—the realization that she hates her mother. She transcends hatred and realizes that from all the disappointment "something can be retrieved."

137. Lockridge, Richard and Frances Lockridge. *The Distant Clue.* Philadelphia: Lippincott, 1963. 187p. London: Long, 1964.

Loudon Wingate, retired from his position as history professor at New York's Dyckman University, is now the town librarian in Van Brunt. One day he is found dead, a bullet hole between his eyes. Dead as well is a lawyer whom Wingate assisted in his historical research. Initially it looks as though Wingate mortally wounded the lawyer, who then seized the gun and shot Wingate. The action does not square with Wingate's reputation. Both current acquaintances and former colleagues found the old scholar easygoing, good-natured, and disinclined to quarrel. Unfortunately, Wingate's character is poorly developed beyond this point, a problem that makes it difficult to care very much whether he is (or was) guilty or innocent in the shootings. The book does, however, add another corpse to the growing pile of fictional librarians dead by violence.

138. Lodge, David. *Small World: An Academic Romance.* New York: Warner, 1991. 385p. London: Secker & Warburg, 1984. (Other editions.)

Having presumed her dead in a plane crash following a torrid one-night stand with her, Professor Philip Swallow finds Joy Simpson three years later very much alive and now working as the British Council librarian in Istanbul. "Alive! That warm, breathing flesh that he had clasped in the purple-lit bedroom in Genoa was still warm, still breathed." They take up where they left off, this time on a train. Joy tells Philip, during a break in the action, that her late husband lacked passion. She also tells him that her three-year-old child is his and describes herself as a well-trained, "good librarian." In this generally hilarious satire on academia, with the emphasis on globe-trotting scholars of literature, Joy Simpson plays a small but decidedly energetic part—joyful, one might say.

139. London, Jack. *The Valley of the Moon.* Middletown, Calif.: David Rejl, 1988. 182p. New York: Macmillan, 1913. London: Mills & Boon, 1914. (Other editions.) *Cosmopolitan* 54(5)–56(1) (April–Dec. 1913).

The widow Mrs. Mortimer, now a successful San Jose–area farmer, has effected a radical change from her former life as head librarian of the Doncaster

Library. She appears in Chapter 22, where she pleasantly receives on-the-road couple Billy and Saxon Roberts, who are fleeing labor strife in Oakland, California. She impresses the young couple with her business acumen and resourcefulness before they leave her behind. Mrs. Mortimer is of interest chiefly because she is probably based, at least in part, on Jack London's Oakland mentor, librarian Ina Coolbirth. (Those who seek out this novel of the working class may want to obtain the David Rejl edition; a reprint of the *Cosmopolitan* serial, it features the original typeface with the fine and plentiful illustrations by Howard C. Christy that graced the magazine.)

140. McCracken, Elizabeth. *The Giant's House.* New York: Dial, 1996. 259p. London: Cape, 1996.

Former librarian McCracken's novel received extensive critical attention in 1996 and for good reason. *The Giant's House* is a good study of love, death, and second chances. The narrator, reference librarian and public library director Peggy Cort, is a young woman adept at her profession, in which relationships with the public are superficial, stylized, and temporary but whose interaction with those in her personal life is cool, distant, and infrequent. "I was the perfect public servant," she says, "deferential, dogged, oblivious to insults. Friendly but not overly familiar." She is "a sad person ... a fundamentally unlovable person."

She meets James Sweatt in 1950, when he is on the verge of adolescence. James is a giant, already taller than most men, and growing rapidly. In spite of his physical problem, he is an intellectually curious and sociable boy; he and Peggy Cort quickly form a friendship that grows stronger with time. Particularly after his mother dies, Peggy takes a strong interest in the welfare of "the tallest man in the world." At one point she decides, in effect, that because of James, love is not beyond her experience: He can be "a love that would occupy all my time." And he very nearly does. Peggy knows that James's condition dooms him to a short life, and she tries her best to be for him as much as she can. "I loved him because I wanted to save him, and because I could not. I loved him because I wanted to be enough for him, and I was not." Their relationship spans the decade. Following James's death, Peggy finds that she has been given — by chance, by Providence, by fate — a second chance to keep him in her life.

The material for mawkishness is here in large helpings, but McCracken never indulges in cheap sentiment. Her characterizations of Peggy and James are sympathetic yet restrained, believable, and greatly touching. McCracken's background as a librarian comes to the fore in many astute passages on the work, particularly one about reference work: "A good librarian is not so different from a prospector, her whole brain a divining rod. She walks to books and stands and wonders: here? Is the answer here? The same blind faith in finding, even when hopeless. If someone caught me when I was in the throes of tracking something elusive, I would have told them: but it's out there. I can feel it. God *wants* me to find it." It's a fine book by an exceptionally capable young writer.

141. McCullough, Colleen. *The Ladies of Missalonghi.* New York: Harper & Row, 1987. 189p. London and Melbourne, Australia: Hutchinson, 1987. (Other editions.)

The Ladies of Missalonghi is set in the World War I era in frontier Australia. Lacking a public library, residents of the little town of Byron turn to Livilla Hurlingford's privately owned lending library. Her cousin Una is the assistant "librarian," and while she may not have formal training, she shows many good professional qualities. She endears herself to Missy, a young woman, with her "liveliness, understanding and kindness." Una is not only pleasant but strikingly pretty. She is also divorced. "My whole trouble, darling," she confides in Missy, "is that I have never loved anybody half so well as myself." In spite of her self reproach, Una has a ready sense of humor. She takes Missy under her wing, gives her emotional support and guidance, and helps her on her way to marriage. It's a romantic tale with some curious twists. McCullough, by the way, stepped into a nasty bit of speculation about possibly plagiaristic features of this novel, which bears some remarkable similarities in its details to Lucy M. Montgomery's 1926 novel, *The Blue Castle.*

142. MacDonald, George. *Alec Forbes of Howglen.* Leipzig, Germany: Bernhard Tauchnitz, 1865. 2 vols. 674p. London: Hurst & Blackett, 1865. 3 vols. New York: Harper, 1874. (Many editions.)

Alec Forbes is a young student at a Scottish college. He lives in a rooming house where he meets Mr. Cosmo Cupples, the acting librarian of the college. Mr. Cupples lives upstairs in a garret apartment. In addition to his effective management of the library, he gives lessons in Greek and Hebrew, deals in books, writes for lawyers, and composes the occasional poem. In spite of his gifts, Mr. Cupples has been kept from realizing his greatest professional possibilities by his addiction to drink. He is seldom without a large tumbler of whiskey at hand.

As Alec's college career progresses in fits and starts, he and Mr. Cupples draw ever closer. The little librarian helps Alec prepare for exams and counsels him wisely on his relationships with others. He enlists Alec as a student helper in the library, where he assigns him routine chores. Alec realizes that his mentor — for that is very much Mr. Cupples's role — dreads that the college will hire a regular librarian before he himself has a chance to effect his envisioned improvements in the facility.

At one point Mr. Cupples bravely protects Alec from angry thugs at the expense of receiving a beating that leaves him senseless in his own garret. His relationship with Alec is far from one of flawless harmony: In another passage, after Mr. Cupples has again valiantly saved Alec from a sticky situation, Alec strikes the librarian in a drunken rage, leaving his protector bleeding and unconscious in the gutter. This shocking episode leads to a remorseful rapprochement. When he awakens the next morning, Alec rushes to Mr. Cupples's garret, where he "knelt at Mr. Cupples's feet, laid his head on his knee, and burst into very unsaxon but most gracious tears. Mr. Cupples laid a small trembling hand on the boy's head, saying, 'Eh, bantam, bantam!' [his pet name for Alec] and could say no more."

Together, they swear off liquor. Mr. Cupples doubles his tobacco use and takes up tea. "Meeserable stuff," he calls it, "awfu' weyk tipple — a pagan invention a'thegither."

Leaving the scotch behind produces salutary effects. Mr. Cupples receives his cherished appointment as permanent college librarian, a position that he uses in the most conscientious and honorable fashion. The college's best students develop "a profound respect for the librarian. Not a few of them repaired to him with all their difficulties.... Indeed I doubt whether, within the course of a curriculum, Mr. Cupples had not become the real centre of intellectual and moral life in that college."

The novel's Dickensian sentimentality does not keep it from being genuinely affecting. Mr. Cupples is an immensely appealing character. He is charming, witty, courageous, and justly proud of his librarianship. The one obstacle that stands in the way of an enjoyable reading of the novel today is MacDonald's widespread use of dense, often nearly impenetrable, Scottish dialect in his dialogue. The reader who can adjust to such dialect — "I'm thinkin' that the buiks are beginnin' to ken by this time what they're aboot; for sic a throuither disjakit midden o' lere, I never saw. Ye micht hae taicklet it wi' a graip" — will have a good time with Alec Forbes and Cosmo Cupples.

143. _____. *Lilith.* Bound with *Phantastes* in *The Visionary Novels of George MacDonald.* New York: Noonday, 1954, pp. 1–260. London: Chatto & Windus, 1895. (Other editions.)

The narrator, Mr. Vane, inherits a great house with a library that occupies the major portion of the ground floor. Legend has it that Mr. Raven, the longtime librarian to the former masters of the house, encouraged them in the reading of "strange, forbidden, and evil books." *Lilith* is neither forbidden nor evil, but it is most certainly strange, a dense, dreamlike adventure that will tax the patience of any reader ordinarily attuned to realistic fiction. Even readers of fantasy will often find the novel rough going — rough, but not uninteresting. Although presumed long since dead, Mr. Raven has continued to manifest himself, from time to time, in the library. Mr. Vane sees Mr. Raven moving about the library, "a slight, stooping man, in a shabby dress-coat reaching almost to his heels." Vane follows Mr. Raven to unexplored regions of the house and finds himself in a wild country that he enters through a picture. There a raven (the sort with feathers) addresses him and shifts his form back and forth from bird to the old librarian. Bird or man, the raven/Raven becomes Vane's guide in the curious other world. When he is the librarian, Mr. Raven's face is alive; never has Vane seen "a look so keen or so friendly as that in his pale blue eyes, which yet had a haze about them as if they had done much weeping." Mr. Raven counsels Vane on how to conduct himself in the fantastic world and at times acts as his guide. His ultimate act of shape-shifting occurs when he is no longer bird or librarian but Adam, the first man. Life as dream, dream as life, *Lilith* requires more than a little suspension of disbelief, but it is a remarkable novel, if not a *sui generis*, then something very close to it.

144. McGovern, James. *No Ruined Castles.* New York: Putnam's, 1957. 287p.

Edward Downey is a young foreign service officer in West Germany in 1951. He directs the America Haus public relations center in the imaginary town of Crellenbach, where he does his best to recruit the German folk to "our side." His librarian, the young war widow Maria Bretzig, speaks good English and has "very nice legs." The two gradually grow close as Maria gives Edward German lessons and shows him the local sights. She is among those sights: Edward is transfixed by Maria in her bathing suit. "Downey realized that Maria was a very attractive woman. Her baggy, tweedy librarian's uniform neatly obscured this fact during working hours...." "She's a damned attractive woman," Edward tells an acquaintance. "I can't figure out what she's doing working as a librarian in a place like Crellenbach." What she is doing is surviving the best she can after seeing her life reduced to bare threads by the war. She has not only been widowed but left with a son, now five, by an American soldier. Maria shows her greatest strength near the end of the novel, when her "dead" husband appears among a group of POWs returned from Russia (an event that puts a temporary crimp in her romance with Edward). Maria is a pleasant character who receives a lot of space in the novel, but the book is uninteresting except as a literary artifact of the early years of the Cold War. A sidelight on that note: at one point, Edward's superior directs him to purge the library of "those pinko books," books of an alleged "subversive" nature. Edward complies, with little hesitation.

145. Mac Laverty, Bernard. *Cal.* London: Jonathan Cape, 1983. 170p. New York: George Braziller, 1983. (Other editions.)

Cal is a short novel of tremendous emotional power. Nineteen-year-old Cal McCrystal is a working-class Catholic youth who lives with his father in a town in Northern Ireland. Both have been threatened by local Protestant fanatics: Cal has been beaten up, and the thugs have threatened to burn them out of their house. In spite of the ominous atmosphere, Cal plugs on with his life. He plays guitar in his room, does his best to get along with his father, Shamie, and takes a job on a farm to get off the dole. A twist of the narrative's chronology reveals that the farm belongs to the Morton family, led by a Protestant man in whose murder Cal was an accomplice approximately a year earlier. The man's wife was public librarian Marcella Morton, 10 years Cal's senior, and still living on the farm with her husband's parents and her small daughter.

Cal becomes obsessed with Marcella. He visits the library to look in awe at her. When the thugs make good their promise and burn down his house, Cal hides out in a rough cottage on the Morton property. Marcella intervenes and arranges for him to live there, for the time being, and helps him make the place habitable. The tension between Marcella and Cal is evident from the first time he speaks to her in the library. The two are drawn together in a sudden and fiery affair, the first of Cal's experience. There is no chance of their knowing any long-term happiness. Cal is tormented by his need to confess his role in the murder (it is not mere accident that leads him to borrow *Crime and Punishment* from the library), and his old IRA cronies refuse to let him abandon his participation in their terrorist campaign.

Marcella and Cal are the innocent — or nearly so — victims of an insane cultural and political battle. Their love affair, their mutual search for refuge from the troubles that are tearing apart their country and their lives, is doomed from the outset. That the novel's conclusion will bring each of them grief beyond anything they have previously known is inevitable, and the more agonizing because it is inevitable, because their future together is without hope. Both characters are portrayed with great sympathy, Marcella in her struggle to find a new life for herself in the aftermath of her husband's murder, and Cal in his pitiful, damned yearning for love and a normal existence. It's an utterly heartbreaking book.

146. McLaverty, Michael. *Three Brothers.* New York: Macmillan, 1948. 213p. London: Cape, 1948. (Other editions.)

In this novel of an Irish family's struggles and achievements, Brendan Caffrey is a young public librarian. He wanted to go into banking, but his father urged him into library work. Brendan seems to be a capable librarian, if a touch reticent (he is afraid to tell a vagrant snoozing in the library to take his boots off the furnishings). Brendan is a dutiful lad, toward his parents as well as to his fairly worthless gambler uncle, who at one point steals books from Brendan's library to sell for gambling funds. Brendan has doubts about climbing the administrative hierarchy in the library, "for it has made the head librarian like a machine." Mr. Dunne, Brendan's boss, does have a penchant for the short order, but Brendan, ever accommodating, believes "that an honest innocence was hidden by the old fellow's abruptness" and displays a conscientious loyalty to the head librarian. Brendan's major conflict is with his brother, Frank. Frank is faking attendance at medical school and wasting his tuition money on self-indulgence. Brendan, the only one in the family who knows of Frank's ruse, often scolds Frank for putting his family at emotional risk should they discover his duplicity. Brendan does not play a major part in the book, but his character — earnest, loyal, dedicated — is well developed in an economical manner.

147. MacLeod, Charlotte. *Rest You Merry.* Garden City, N.Y.: Doubleday, 1978. 182p. London: Collins, 1979.

During the Christmas holidays, Professor Peter Shandy finds his best friend's wife, college assistant librarian Jemima Ames, dead in his house, apparently from a fall as she attempted to rearrange some holiday decorations. Shandy had no more use for her than most: "Everyone else thought she was a pest, too." A campus security man concurs: "Only thing surprises me," he says, "is that she bashed her own head in, when there were so many people around who'd have been glad to do it for her." Ames's death sets Shandy into motion when he notices discrepancies of detail suggesting foul play. As he pursues the case, further facts about the dead librarian come to light. She drank excessively; she was belligerent, a busybody, and a compulsive blabbermouth. As her husband puts it, "She could handle everybody's job but her own." Ames, in effect, appointed herself assistant librarian for management of a nearly forgotten bequest of books, the Buggins Collection. The college president "did not know Mrs. Ames's total inability to stick to anything she was really supposed to do, so he hired her."

Much the opposite of the lightly mourned Ames is her relative by marriage, Helen Marsh. Marsh, introduced well into the novel, is an attractive, quick-witted woman in her 40s with a Ph.D. in library science. Her exclamations of surprise include the phrase "My stars and garters!" Marsh serves ably as Shandy's sometime-aide and love interest as he closes in on the truth and she steps capably into the suddenly vacant assistant librarian's position in the Buggins Collection.

148. McShane, Mark. *Seance for Two.* Garden City, N.Y.: Doubleday, 1972. 177p. London: Hale, 1974.

William Wilson, 38, is the assistant head librarian at the free library in Oxton, a London suburb. He lived a life of respectable and uninspired banality until he learned of the kidnap-killing of a child by a married couple. William becomes wholly preoccupied with the case. The prime mover in the killing is Myra Savage, a spiritualist-medium. William sends her letters of moral support during her brief manslaughter term in prison. Upon her release, he meets her at the prison door. She recognizes in him a gift for psychic powers. He invites her to share his house. Myra draws him into a bizarre relationship as he takes steps to help assure that her prognostications come to pass. In the process, he commits crimes ranging from vandalism to attempted rape to planned political assassination. This book features felicitous prose, a ridiculous plot.

Magoon, Carey. *See* Carey, Elisabeth and Marian W. Magoon.

149. Makarenko, Anton. *A Book for Parents.* Moscow: Foreign Languages Publishing House, 1954. 409p. Translation of *Kniga dliaa Roditelei.* Moscow: Gos. Uchebno-pedagog, 1954.

A curious novel composed of didactic parent-child stories cobbled together to make the whole. In one of them, Vera Ignatyevna is the 38-year-old head of a factory library. She is an "enthusiastic" and dedicated librarian who "thinks only of books and of her family." She "had never complained once in her whole life." She works as hard at home as at the library; she even enjoys washing dishes. She sacrifices all for her two spoiled children. She herself owns only a single skirt, while her modishly dressed daughter whines that her parents never have any money for her fashion needs. Vera Ignatyevna is honored at a conference for her "great work" in the education of the Soviet reader and receives a prize: material for a new dress. Her daughter promptly covets the material. A comrade helps Vera Ignatyevna awaken to the need to bring up her children in the proper Soviet manner. It's not much as fiction but interesting as an example of Soviet propaganda.

150. Mallea, Eduardo. *The Bay of Silence.* New York: Knopf, 1944. 339p. Translation of *La Bahía de Silencio.* Buenos Aires: Editorial Sudamericana, 1940. (Other editions.)

The prominent Argentinian writer Mallea follows the career of the writer Martin Tregua. The third book of three that comprise the novel, "The Defeated," devotes much of its space to Martin's relationship with public librarian Gloria Bambil. Gloria's eyes, notes narrator Martin, "showed deep and pained surprise.... She was very pretty." She is fond of the plays of Synge and discusses them critically with Martin. He soon finds her almost continuously present in his thoughts, although her presence is not an easy one to bear. "She lived silently immured within her own personality.... She gave the impression of being absorbed in thoughts and calculations incompatible with the world in which she was destined to live." Gloria is searching for something; in her search, she refuses to admit others into her vulnerable depths. She lives alone, with no friends and few acquaintances. She presents herself as a woman without interest or ambition in possessing anything pleasant or enjoyable. "That's the way I *am*," she asserts. "You can't imagine what lucidity living entirely alone gives you." She seems to be sure of her own beliefs and indifferent to others' opinions of her. Martin tries to grasp the source and meaning of the terrible isolation with which she surrounds herself, but she will not speak of herself because, he believes, she genuinely detests herself. In a gripping statement, she reveals to Martin the apparent roots of her emotional coldness; they lie in her late father's hatred of her.

Whether Martin and Gloria become lovers in the fullest sense is open to question, but Martin claims that he loves her and is determined to help free her from the despair and self-loathing that dominate her. His efforts appear to be only briefly rewarded, leaving him one of the defeated.

The depth of character and seriousness Mallea reaches here makes pale, thin stuff of the achievements of most novelists. Here one experiences the vault from ordinary fiction, even ordinary fiction graced by talent, to purposeful literature rising from the foundations of human experience. The reader shares with

Martin the frustration of being unable to pull Gloria from the cave of her hopelessness; that she is in many ways an attractive, appealing character gives the pathos a biting edge. "How I hated to see her suffer!" exclaims Martin — and the reader shares his sentiment. *The Bay of Silence* is not, of course, only about Martin and Gloria. She is but one of his concerns, or, perhaps, obsessions. Another is the unnamed woman to whom he addresses his narrative; another is Argentina itself. One could make much of what Gloria stands for, but taken literally, she is an affecting creation who anticipates many postwar fictional characters lost in the endless pain of an existence that seems to hold no promise for them and that offers no reason to look forward to the following day.

151. Merwin, Samuel. *Anabel at Sea.* New York: A.L. Burt, 1927. 314p.

Anabel Cayne, a bright and spunky 25-year-old Wellesley grad and public librarian in Coventry, Massachusetts, wants to get married. With the idea of catching a husband along the way, she embarks on a world cruise, featuring stops in Panama, Japan, China, and elsewhere. She tours the world without finding suitable matrimonial material, until returning to the United States, where a poor but honest man wins her hand. It's a fluffy and innocuous romance for daydreamers. Anabel is not an altogether unattractive character, but the novel as a whole is mere cotton candy.

152. Mojtabai, A. G. *Mundome.* New York: Simon & Schuster, 1974. 154p.

Mundome is a deeply troubling account of a young librarian's relationship with his schizophrenic, somewhat older sister. Cataloger Richard Henken occupies a shadowy corner in the department and labors in an obscurity matching his setting. His boss, MacFinster, is a bureaucratic idiot preoccupied with efficiency who makes such observations as "Is it the desk that makes the man, or the man that makes the desk?" The staff of the sagging, ill-funded library awaits in some terror the arrival of an efficiency expert "as if it were a Second Coming."

Richard's overriding concern is the mental health of his sister Meg, recently released to his custody after some 10 years in an institution. Richard cares for his sister intensely — too intensely for his own welfare, it seems. He works with her daily in an effort to help her reengage with the world; his patience with her is boundless, his hope great, and his reward dubious. The failure of his efforts to bring Meg back to life among the conventionally sane produces shattering effects on his own health. *Mundome* — the "meaningless" word is a construction extracted from a Latin phrase in the novel — is a painful, haunting novel that offers many opportunities for reflection on the meaning and purpose of work, of human relationships, and of life itself. Believable, strongly drawn and emotionally affecting characters trapped in an impossible situation make *Mundome* a standout among works of fiction featuring librarians.

153. Monahan, Brent. *The Book of Common Dread.* New York: St. Martin's, 1993. 336p. New York: St. Martin's Paperbacks, 1994.

The Book of Common Dread is a satisfying thriller and horror tale with good characterizations and a credible academic setting, Princeton University, chiefly the Princeton library. The novel's overall merits make one of its main character's wrongly identified status difficult to understand. Simon Penn, a gifted linguist, works with rare books and manuscripts in the library and is referred to by both the author and by other characters in the book as a librarian. Simon has, however, no evidence of formal library training; the text notes explicitly that although he completed his undergraduate studies, he has attended no professional school. He did work as a student assistant in the Princeton library for four years as an undergraduate.

The novel's real librarian at issue is the beautiful 24-year-old Frederika Vanderveen, a reference librarian with a taste for necromancy. She enlists Simon in translating a rare text on the topic, allegedly for a girlfriend's scholarly purposes. She also rents Simon a room in her house, a mansion in which she lives alone after her father's death. Frederika is reputed to have obtained her reference position by sleeping with an assistant dean. But "apparently the reference librarian wanted little tangible from any man." Simon's friend Neil, who carried on a brief affair with Frederika, says that he believes that she feels "compelled ... to drain attention and affection from each man as quickly as she could, then move calmly on to the next."

One night, Simon discovers Frederika conducting a black magic ritual in an attempt to bring her father back to life. She seeks out the novel's villain, Vincent DeVilbiss (who does indeed carry out the devil's business) to assist her in this quest. He in turn appeals to her for help in gaining access to some cabalistic documents that he covets for evil purposes. She renders assistance with this as well as with his need for erotic satisfaction.

Literate, entertaining, and fairly scary, the novel follows the struggle of Simon and Frederika to overcome the foul purposes of DeVilbiss. It's a pity that author Monahan could not have conferred a library degree on Simon; in the intellectually rarefied atmosphere of Ivy League libraries, it seems unlikely that a nonlibrarian calling himself a librarian would be considered anything but a quack.

154. Monfredo, Miriam G. *Blackwater Spirits.* New York: St. Martin's, 1995. 328p. New York: Berkley, 1995.

Seneca Falls, New York, librarian, women's rights activist, and occasional sleuth Glynis Tryon finds herself involved with the Temperance and spiritualist movements, and, most critically from the plot's point of view, the rights of Native Americans. Monfredo applies a formula to each of the Tryon mysteries: extensive historical research — complete with "historical notes" at the end of each book — coupled with lively plots and characters, frequently individuals drawn from history itself, wrapped up in important historical events. In addition to running the village library in Seneca Falls, Oberlin College graduate Tryon writes book reviews for the local paper and contributes articles in support of women's rights. Here she befriends the town's new woman doctor, Neva Cardoza, who observes that Tryon seems "so composed, so self-possessed." Tryon disputes the assessment: "If you only knew how hard I fight shyness! All the time." The major dramatic business in *Blackwater Spirits* is the murder trial of Jacques Sundown, the half–Iroquois deputy sheriff of Seneca Falls. Monfredo's formula works reasonably well, although this novel and the ones described in Items 155 and 156 too often bear the flavor of expository writing rather than fiction. The reader receives too much historical data in the guise of dialogue, although by this outing the offenses have become less frequent than in the series opener, *Seneca Falls Inheritance*. It would be easy for a reader to become a Glynis Tryon fan; Monfredo's research is careful, her recreation of mid–19th century New York is credible, and Glynis Tryon is the sort of person almost anyone would like to have for a friend. On the other hand, the sense of being lectured to that too often crops up in the series is an obstacle that requires a fan's tolerance.

155. _____. *North Star Conspiracy.* New York: St. Martin's, 1993. 322p. New York: Berkley Prime Crime, 1995.

North Star Conspiracy is a reasonably serious mystery that is also a good bit of fun, set in 1854. With her friends Susan B. Anthony and Elizabeth Cady Stanton, Seneca Falls librarian Glynis Tryon also works on such feminist issues as suffrage. Glynis is no dilettante; when she has an opportunity early in the book to marry a man she truly cares for, she turns him down. To assent would mean the end of her career. Fully involved in the life of the community, Glynis becomes caught in a web of intrigue that includes murder and shows herself a capable ratiocinator. Like other entries in the series, the novel features historical notes at the end detailing people, places, and things the reader meets or hears about in the course of the story. A bit too much late–20th-century sensibility manifests itself in Glynis Tryon's point of view, but the story remains enjoyable.

156. _____. *Seneca Falls Inheritance.* New York: St. Martin's, 1992. 254p. New York: Berkley, 1994.

The first in Monfredo's Glynis Tryon mysteries, the title of this one alludes to both a disputed estate and the 1848 Seneca Falls Women's Rights Convention. Elizabeth Stanton seeks the assistance of librarian Tryon in ascertaining would-be attendees at the proposed convention. Some members of the all-male library board do not take kindly to their librarian's participation in extracurricular political activities and suggest that her tenure on the job may not be overlong. Tryon's politics are soon overshadowed by murder when a local finds a woman's body in the canal behind the Seneca Falls library. Other foul deeds follow suit, and Tryon joins forces with local authorities to find a solution. The novel shows the results of Monfredo's trademark diligent research, but too many prosaic passages on historical topics, excessive use of dialog to explain things to the reader, some stiff recitation of background matters (Tryon's family history and career moves, for example), and unlikely coincidence (the "chance" manifestation of a lengthy quotation from de Tocqueville on women in America) make awkward going. There is some real fun here, however: It's fairly delightful and altogether surprising to see Tryon out playing golf. But overall, it's not the strongest entry in the series.

157. Monteilhet, Hubert. *Murder at the Frankfurt Book Fair: A Wicked, Witty Novel About the Publishing of an International Bestseller.* Garden City, N.Y.: Doubleday, 1976. 204p. Translation of *Mourir à Francfort.* Paris: Editions Denoël, 1975.

The subtitle has it wrong. This novel is about fraud and deception of a variety of sorts, chiefly intellectual and emotional. It is not wicked in any sense. It is, however, a witty work, often deliciously so. Told in the form of diary and journal entries, the story follows the relationship of young Parisian librarian Mademoiselle Cecile Dubois and her German teacher, Dominique Labattut-Largaud (a.k.a. LL). A little bibliosleuthing by Cecile reveals that LL has been a success at mystery writing under a pseudonym. He fears that Cecile will blow his cover; he thinks of her as "a rather curious mixture of namby-pamby naïveté and shrewd, discerning observation." The contrast between LL's opinion of Cecile and her impressions of his opinion of her is both comical and pathetic. However naive Cecile may be, she is no slouch in literature, and she quickly realizes that the smash bestseller LL has pseudonymously published is a plagiarism. LL is convinced that he must play the "ardent swain" to keep this "devout, serious girl" from revealing the truth to the world at large. The murder of the title occurs very late in the novel, by which time the reader is likely to say "It's about time" and perhaps even rejoice over the selection of the victim. A literate, amusing, readable suspense tale, the novel does provide some fizzy moments, not the least of which comes when LL refers to author Monteilhet, claiming that he "has always got on my nerves with that limping copulation of sanctimoniousness and smuttiness out of which he tries to concoct a style."

158. Moon, Lorna. *Dark Star.* Indianapolis: Bobbs-Merrill, 1929. 343p.

Andrew Morrison, town librarian in Pitouie, Scotland, is a secondary character here, although an important one. Nancy, the ill-fated young heroine, is his assistant. Andrew is cynical and flippant; from time to time "he would become this other person, drunk with epigrams, hurling piquant blasphemies upon the air." An intellectually gifted man, Andrew is physically malformed: he walks on his thighbones, his useless lower legs dragging behind him in a pair of wooden boxes. A terrible humiliation connected with his handicap drove him from the university in Aberdeen back to his home in Pitouie, the one place where people were accustomed to him. He and Nancy have a tormented relationship that might, one gathers, have been romantic had Andrew not been consumed by his deformity. As it was, however, "There was an impassioned current between them that was not unlike hostility." Impassioned or not, *Dark Star* is a laughable novel, full of earnest, overwrought intensity, jarring verbiage ("When she got home, she found Granny in the midst of her first heart attack") and general foolishness.

159. Moore, Doris Langley. ***All Done by Kindness.*** Philadelphia: Lippincott, 1953. 282p. London: Cassell, 1951.

Mrs. Stephanie du Plessis is a young British librarian from Rhodesia with a strong background in art history. She is on her own, her husband having been killed in the war. She is "clever and well-read, devoted to her work, obviously destined to be chief librarian.... She took up every inquiry as a challenge: that was her nature." She also expresses herself "with alarming honesty," but in her honesty is a considerable moral courage. All her fine qualities come to the fore in this suspense tale of discovery and dirty business in the art world. Stephanie's knowledge of Greek and art help her identify for their owner first a book that belonged to one of the Medicis in the 15th century and then an amazing stash of paintings by Renaissance masters acquired with the book. When an underhanded art appraiser dismisses the paintings as worthless for his own base motives, Stephanie resolves to do what she must to protect the treasures from nefarious forces. It's an enjoyable story for art aficionados, with a resourceful librarian as heroine.

160. Morgan, Kate. ***A Slay at the Races.*** New York: Berkley, 1990. 208p.

Horse fancier Dewey James was the town librarian in Hamilton for 30 years. She is retired and a widow, now, although still active as librarian emeritus in the library's enterprises, the current one a teach-prisoners-to-read endeavor. Most of the locals think Dewey is "mildly lunatic." As evidence of her lunacy, she nearly lost her job in 1970 for hanging an enormous peace symbol in the library. The mystery here hinges on the discovery of a dead man in a horse's stall. The obvious conclusion: The horse kicked the deceased to death. Dewey doubts it and undertakes an investigation to discover the truth. She is not the only librarian on the scene. In one passage, the new town librarian, Tom Campbell, reveals himself to be an officious twit. Dewey expresses hope that he will learn. "He's still young," she says. "He was born old," says a companion. It's a competent, if unexciting, mystery with a conventionally "eccentric" librarian sleuth.

161. Morris, Hilda. ***Landmarks.*** New York: Putnam's, 1941. 294p.

The Arrowhead Public Library has a fireplace at one end of its vast reading room and the librarian's desk at the other. Miss Ebbets has presided over that desk for two decades and knows nearly everyone in the midwestern town. She is gray-haired; her eyes "sparkled with interest. Humanity, to Miss Ebbets, was more enthralling than literature. She was well versed in both." She praises the work of main character Paul Ledge, who has been commissioned to paint scenes of the community's life in the library. Paul finds Miss Ebbets "surprisingly well informed" on artistic matters. As he works on his murals in the library, he regards Miss Ebbets as "a joy," a deft and reliable guardian of his artistic privacy against the many curious visitors who would see his work before its completion. When she and Paul go to lunch one day, Miss Ebbets delights in the attention she knows they will receive from town gossips. She has not been to lunch with a man in years. "She wore an air of triumph" as she and Paul left the restaurant after an intimate talk concerning their linked histories. Miss Ebbets is a most attractive character. It is a shame that she can claim no more than a dozen pages of the novel as her own turf, but her impact is out of proportion to her presence, considering her nurturing of a young painter who finally finds his own artistic voice in his work on the library murals.

162. Moynahan, Julian. *Pairing Off*. Morrow, 1969. 252p. London: Heinemann, 1969. (Other editions.)

Pairing Off is a witty, amusing, and compassionate novel of a librarian pushing into middle age with no plan, no idea, and no real prospects for a creative life. Myles McCormick (Harvard A.B. in Classics, '48), is a rare-books assistant in the Boston Free Library. Fresh from a long and fairly pointless psychotherapy, Myles is working on a huge, ghastly collection of 17th-century English pamphlets.

"McCormick would have liked to meet that man who, when faced with apparently identical copies of a work of no literary or human value whatsoever, demanded to know whether they were *really* identical down to the last semi-colon, so that he could hit this man in the stomach and rip down the panels of his sleazy double-breasted suit lapels."

If this yearning suggests that Myles is not quite cut out for the cataloger's life, it is hard to tell what life his particular form would fit. Myles is a bit of a whiner and plays for sympathy by denigrating himself— but is also genuinely hard on himself. Much of the book concerns his painful death watch over a female friend; much of the rest focuses on his inability to act decisively, in his career or in his relationships with women.

The title comes from a passage in Joseph Conrad's *Chance*: "Pairing off is the fate of mankind. And if two beings, thrown together, mutually attracted, resist the necessity ... then they are committing a sin against life, the call of which is simple. Perhaps sacred."

Bitter though *Pairing Off* occasionally is, it is also often funny and ends on a surprisingly positive note, nowhere else than on a graveyard wall outside an Irish village. Strong characters, supple prose, and the author's penetrating view of man and woman make it an enjoyable book. And, although Myles finally throws over the library profession, Moynahan writes of the work with evident knowledge, as well as approbation.

163. Murakami, Haruki. *Hard-Boiled Wonderland and the End of the World*. New York: Kodansha, 1991. 400p. London: Hamilton, 1991.

Translation of *Sekai no owari to hado-boirudo wandarando*. Tokyo: Shin-chosha, 1985. (Other editions.)

A surrealistic science fiction fantasy, even stranger and also a good deal funnier than its title suggests. The narrator is sent to "the Library" to read old dreams. The Library is in a village at the End of Time. It is a dusty and stale place. The narrator passes the attractive Librarian and is accepted as the one Dreamreader eligible to use the facility. "It is my job," she says, "to watch over the old dreams and to help the Dreamreader." The first old dream she presents comes in a small animal's skull, that of one of the town's unicorns. The Librarian demonstrates the proper dreamreading technique and is solicitous throughout the narrator's many visits to the Library. She brings him a cool towel for his tired eyes and warm milk to drink.

The narrator visits another library in Tokyo to find references on mammalian skulls. The young reference librarian, who is reading a biography of H. G. Wells during slack periods at the desk, has long hair and an "elegant backside." She provides astute assistance and allows the narrator to borrow a reference book; in his gratitude, he runs to a Baskin-Robbins store to buy her an ice-cream cone. He persuades her to hand-deliver to his apartment the library's materials on unicorns. She suspects that he is deranged but agrees to his request. After she delivers the books, he serves her dinner. "Never in my life had I seen such a slim nothing of a figure eat like such a terror." After the pair have a brief and unproductive tussle in bed, the librarian reads aloud passages from the books on unicorns. The librarian dresses with grace the next morning and leaves this parting encouragement: "If you have food to spare or want to get together or whatever, give me a call. I'll be right over."

The narrator continues his dreamreading with the Librarian's help. She even accompanies him on a dangerous mission in the woods. Later, with 24 hours to live, he makes a dinner date with his Tokyo reference librarian. They go to an Italian restaurant, discuss literature, and eat voraciously. Back at her place, they eat pizza and listen to Miles Davis, Bing Crosby, and Pat Boone (yes, Pat Boone!) and make satisfactory love. From there, the narrator returns to the Librarian and "reads out" her mind. In the end, he says, "I know she waits for me in the Library.... All that is left to me is the sound of the snow underfoot."

There may be less to this novel than meets the eye, but it is also possible that its convoluted, episodic story and eccentric characters would offer rich possibilities for further investigation. It is, at the least, wholly original and leaves an exhilarating sensation in the reader's mind.

164. Musil, Robert. *The Man Without Qualities.* Vol. 2. London: Secker & Warburg, 1954. 454p. Translation of *Der Mann ohne Eigenschaften*. Berlin: Rowholt, 1930. (Other editions.)

General Stumm, a secondary character in this huge three-volume novel, is looking for the finest idea in the world. In hopes of locating it, he visits the

Imperial Library in Chapter 100, titled "General Stumm invades the State Library and gathers some experience with regard to librarians, library attendants, and intellectual order." It is an amusing chapter, with the naive general first sure that if he reads a book a day, he'll find that one grand idea. The task looks daunting when the librarian informs him that the Imperial Library holds 3.5 million books. In a funny parody of a reference interview, the librarian seeks to help the general with his research. Would he care for some nice pacifist literature? Something on theological ethics? How about a bibliography of bibliographies? The librarian scampers "like a monkey" to fetch books for the general. Ultimately, the librarian astounds his patron by telling him that he himself never reads any of the library's books, "Only the catalogues."

General Stumm claims that the librarian left him ready "either to burst into tears or to light a cigarette." Luckily an old stack attendant happens by to help the general find some useful books that the librarian apparently could not. The attendant has his own insights on library patrons, especially professors from the university. A professor will complain that he has been requesting a book for weeks without getting it, "until it comes out in the end that he's had it at home for the last two years, and never brought it back at all." (That is obviously a fiction; professors never forget to return their library books, nor forget what is on their shelves at home or in the office.)

165. Naipaul, V. S. *Mr. Stone and the Knights Companion.* London: A. Deutsch, 1963. 159p. New York: Macmillan, 1964. (Other editions.)

Richard Stone is the head librarian with Excal, a company whose products and functions are vague. Mr. Stone is approaching retirement age. He is terrified of cats, is conversationally dysfunctional, is unable to live for the moment, dislikes children, and is so detached from others that when he receives an invitation to a New Year's party, the note's penmanship and suspect punctuation annoy him. In spite of his apparent aversion to humanity in general, he marries a widow recently bereaved. The marriage gets off to a stiff and formalistic beginning. Mr. and the new Mrs. Stone refer to one another as Doggie, in reference to the song "How Much Is That Doggie in the Window?" which Mr. Stone whistles daily. In spite of the inauspicious marital beginning, Stone's wife Margaret's "plasticity of character" soothes his adjustment to marriage and to the loss of his cherished privacy. Midway through the novel, Stone receives a promotion up and out of the library on the heels of his inspired suggestion that the company create a new department, the Knights Companion, a sort of public relations strike force composed of company retirees. He does not return to the library. The chief characters in this novel are without exception unappealing; Mr. Stone, a chilly, servile type, is the least attractive of the lot.

166. Norris, Kathleen. *Martie the Unconquered.* New York: Grosset & Dunlap, 1917. 376p. London: Morray, William Bredon & Son, 1917.

For its time and presumably its primary intended audience — young, middle-class women — this novel is a surprisingly candid treatment of a woman's coming of age, her trials, her dreams, her disappointments, and her perseverance. Martie Monroe, a small-town girl of modest means, overcomes a number of setbacks on her way to becoming a successful magazine writer in New York City. A small portion well into the novel takes place in Martie's hometown public library, where the kindly and energetic town librarian, Miss Fanny, hires Martie as an assistant. It is in the library, where Martie works as a reader's advisor, that her life begins to expand "like a flower in sunlight."

Although it might share shelf space in a 1920s home library with Margaret Widdemer's *The Rose-Garden Husband*, this is a stronger and more seriously written book. According to one passage, "Martie never dreamed that the youth and sex within her had as definite a claim on her senses as hunger had in the hour before dinner time, or sleep had when she nodded over her solitaire at night." It is a passage that no novelist whose chief concern is the reinforcement of conventional values would write.

167. Oliver, Jane and Ann Stafford. *Business as Usual.* Boston and New York: Houghton Mifflin, 1934. 304p. London: Collins, 1933.

Hilary Fane, 27, loses her librarian's position at the municipal library in Edinburgh, Scotland, as a result of the Depression. Although her parents are university people and her fiancé a physician, she chooses to make her own way. She takes a room in a residential hotel in London and lands a clerical job at Everyman's, a great department store. Told in epistolary form, the story blends discreet social criticism with an attractive heroine's rise from menial shopgirl to influential businesswoman. Hilary is bright, humorous, and a delightful letter writer. She is also observant, not only in the store but in the city. She comments on elderly women who sort through trash containers on the street looking for bottles or bits of food. In a letter to her fiancé, she notes the contrast between the poor of London and the customers in a teashop, who "seem quite pleased with things." Hilary recognizes that even though she has assumed a hard and spare way of life — she meticulously sets out her meager weekly budget, which consumes all of her 2 pound, 10 shilling salary — those around her do not have the option of running home to well-off parents or to marriage with a doctor.

Hilary works capably, and progresses from the book department to the store's busy subscription library. There she demonstrates her professional skills, much to the annoyance of the library's longtime head, Miss Sparling, a woman with "a nasty, pointed, rattish face." Hilary overcomes workplace narrow-mindedness and backbiting, shows compassion to her eventual subordinates, and achieves unexpected happiness. No one will accuse the book of advocating radicalism, but its steady undercurrent of awareness of economic and class inequity gives a little edge to a basically optimistic popular novel. It has lots of nice illustrations by co-author Stafford.

Olsen, D. B. *See* Hitchens, Dolores.

168. Ostenso, Martha. *The Stone Field.* New York: Dodd, Mead, 1937. 310p.

Librarian Laura Keefe lives with and cares for her partially-paralyzed older brother. Laura becomes a close friend of the book's main female character, Jo Porte.

Relatively little attention is given to Laura, but she stands in a generally positive light when on the scene. It would be more positive if Laura were not compelled to refer to herself as a spinster at a relatively young age and if Ostenso did not describe her as a "dun-colored bird of a woman."

169. Pearson, Edmund L. *The Secret Book.* New York: Macmillan, 1914. 253p. New York: Books for Libraries, 1972.

The Secret Book may be described as a novel only loosely, yet it's close enough for the present purposes. This collection of librarian Pearson's sketches and tales consists chiefly of his *Boston Evening Transcript* pieces laid end-to-end. The notion of a missing "secret book" of great value helps give the whole some novelistic continuity, as does Pearson's tactic of using meetings of the Hell-Fire Club to advance the narrative.

The Hell-Fire Club is a group rather less infernal than its name suggests: They're a gaggle of book lovers who meet regularly to tell each other stories with a close connection to books and libraries. Sayles, a librarian, is a member of the club and enjoys telling stories to the others. He even reads a poem, printed in full in the book.

Sayles also recounts a funny story of that ubiquitous author, Ibid, along with the Cit brothers, Op and Loc. The highlight of his recitations may be his account of a reference librarian's attempt to humor a patron who knows nothing of books or libraries and thinks it the height of hilarity to insist that the librarian has read all of the books in the reference collection.

The harried librarian demonstrates aptly his hard-won sense of the profession: "If someone insisted on having a book on old blue china by Jack the Ripper, past experience has taught him the wisdom of having a look in the catalogue before committing himself finally."

Pearson's gentle good humor combines with his knowledge of literature and a congenial style to produce work that is still readable and engaging.

170. Pearson, Peter. *Postscript for Malpas.* New York: Dodd, Mead, 1976. 158p. London: Macmillan, 1975.

Courageous librarian saves the world!—or a fair piece of it, anyhow. *Postscript for Malpas* is set in 1985, ten years after conflagration in the Middle East has radically altered the world's political power alignments. Alexander Cotton is a 30-something technical librarian who oversees Great Britain's nuclear power information in a library deep underground. It is the nation's nuclear capability that has enabled it to reclaim its eminence as a global power. On a vacation on the Scottish coast, Cotton finds himself in an intrigue that threatens to destroy the country in a radioactive holocaust. Thanks to his nuclear expertise, Cotton sees through the scheme. A serviceable mystery-thriller with a heroic librarian at the wheel.

171. Pedneau, Dave. *A.K.A. (Also Known As).* New York: Ballantine, 1990. 325p.

There's not a lot to recommend this hard-boiled crime novel, not because it's hard-boiled, but because the characters are not much more than stick figures walking through the plot. The book also contains ugly violence against women that seems present less because it is critical to the story than it does simply for its own sake. Eloise Weldon, an attractive widow and assistant librarian at Mill-brook College, picks the wrong night to substitute at the library for her boss, Julia Pynchon. After she locks the building for the night, someone hiding in the stacks beats her to death. Head librarian Pynchon is convinced that the killer intended her as the victim, and does, in fact, turn up eviscerated later in the novel. There is, as indicated, little in the way of real character development or revelation here, although Julia Pynchon is seen struggling with her relationship with her daughter, a high school senior. Eloise is described as "a nice lady." She also proves to have been carrying on an affair with a married man: Millbrook College president Willard Hardison.

172. Perec, Georges. *Life: A User's Manual.* Boston: David R. Godine, 1987. 581p. London: Collins Harvill, 1988. Translation of *La Vie, Mode d'Emploi.* Paris: Hachette, 1978.

We meet Gregoire Simpson, an assistant sublibrarian, at the Bibliothèque de l'Opéra in Paris, in Chapter 52. The chapter offers a ludicrously overdetailed account of Simpson's minionlike archival duties. When the library lays him off in a cost-cutting move, Simpson supports himself with a series of inane jobs and then declines into apparent madness, culminating in a sort of hibernation in his seedy apartment. At length he disappears: "The general opinion in the building was that he had committed suicide.... But nobody ever came up with the evidence." Simpson is not the only deracinated librarian featured, if briefly, in the novel. Chapter 91 succinctly details the lunatic preoccupation of one Marcelia Echard, "sometime Head of Stack at the Central Library" in Paris. Echard believed that Hitler survived World War II and that the Fuhrer's subsequent contacts with such figures as John Foster Dulles, Einstein, and Hubert Humphrey had led the world to the brink of World War III. To demonstrate Hitler's alleged postwar activity, Echard spent many years compiling a vast collection of sources relating to Hitler's "false" death.

173. Peters, Elizabeth. *Die for Love.* New York: Congdon & Weed, 1984. 274p. (Other editions.)

Jacqueline Kirby has moved on since her work in books in Items 174 and 175. She is now assistant head librarian of Coldwater College in Nebraska. She has lived in what she calls this backwater for three years; when the novel opens, she is restless for some action. In her 40s, she is slim and fit and engaged in an affair with the head of the Coldwater English department. She heads off to a conference of the Historical Romance Writers of the World, in New York City, hoping for both amusement and a business-related tax deduction. Jacqueline demonstrates a humorously cynical attitude at the conference. Her "incurable tendency to interfere in other people's business" helps lead her to investigate the murder of an acid-tongued gossip columnist whom many of the conference attendants fear and loathe. *Die for Love* is funnier and more readable than *The Murders of Richard III*; Jacqueline Kirby is a witty, attractive character. Peters's own ideas about librarians are reasonably enlightened, as she indicates early in the novel (even if she makes it sound as though there are no male librarians): "Contrary to popular opinion, librarians are not prim, unworldly spinsters, isolated from the modern world; nor are university librarians unacquainted with what is loosely termed popular culture. If you prick them they bleed, if you drop in on them unexpectedly you may find them engrossed in a soap opera or a copy of *Playgirl*."

174. _____. *The Murders of Richard III.* New York: Dodd, Mead, 1974. 244p. Bath: Chivers, 1990.

Jacqueline Kirby works in a university library in the eastern United States. At her desk in the library she is given to "glowering impartially ... from behind her heavy glasses." She has a "quick unorthodox mind and weird sense of humor." In spite of the thick glasses, she is attractive. A mystery buff, she is fond of Josephine Tey's work. On vacation with her male friend, a lecturer at an English university, she becomes wrapped up in strange goings-on at an English country mansion. There, among a cast of eccentrics playing the parts of contemporaries of Richard III, a practical joker is recreating notorious crimes of the period, eventually with fatal consequences. Jacqueline is portrayed as the one level-headed, truly perceptive character on the scene, and she plays amateur sleuth with elan. The novel will probably amuse fans of English history, in spite of its dialogue-heavy style.

175. _____. *The Seventh Sinner.* New York: Dodd, Mead, 1972. 243p. London: Coronet, 1975.

Librarian Jacqueline Kirby is on vacation in Rome when she becomes acquainted with seven young scholars there on fellowships; they have nicknamed their group the Seven Sinners. At the announcement that Jacqueline is a librarian, one of the group responds nastily: "I spotted her at once. Dull, dreary, and middle-class." Jacqueline proves anything but dull and dreary. Another of the Seven, having discovered that Jacqueline's personality is one of multiple facets, says she doesn't sound "like a librarian." "There are typical librarians," observes Jacqueline, "but not all librarians are typical. Any more than any other profession." When one of the Seven is murdered, Jacqueline works with the Italian police to bring the killer to justice. In a display of her ratiocination, she expounds on the crime, the motive, and the culprit in the penultimate chapter. It's adequate to hold the attention, but unfortunately typical of the mystery genre in its reliance on a long-winded exegesis of the matter, even if a librarian has the pleasure of delivering the oration.

176. Phillips, Stella. *Hidden Wrath.* New York: Walker, 1982. 191p. London: Hale, 1968.

Miles, a young cataloger, has been disinherited by his rich father, yet he seems to accept this presumably crushing blow with equanimity. Pleasant, mildly facetious, and talented (he plays guitar and sings well), Miles is helping a small college library team catalog an old collection of books. The county library head says of Miles "...a very charming, accomplished young man. He gets on well with everybody.... He appears to take nothing seriously, and one is constantly surprised at what a fast, intelligent worker he is." The supervisor on the cataloging job, Miss Grant, seems to be the source of most of the tension in the group. She is gauche and insensitive. "I always thought she was a bit of a nut," says Miles, "but there are so many in the library profession they don't get noticed." In the police investigation that follows Miss Grant's spectacular poolside demise, Miles presents a calm and composed response. When an inspector asks the county library head if another librarian might have been after Miss Grant's job, the old fellow hoots in ironic mirth: "It's such a delightful thought — people eliminating each other for library posts." Perhaps so. At any rate, as one of the characters in this slight but passable English mystery notes, quoting Seneca, "It is the hidden wrath that harms," and hidden wrath has its way here.

177. Pirandello, Luigi. *The Late Mattia Pascal.* Garden City, N.Y.: Doubleday 1964. 252p. London: Dedalus, 1987. Translation of *Il Fu Mattia Pascal.* Rome: Nuova Antologia, 1904. (Many editions.)

The Late Mattia Pascal is a provocative, often funny, and also often deeply unhappy adventure in personal identity. Mattia Pascal is appointed librarian of the rarely patronized town library in Miragno, Italy. He replaces a deaf, nearly blind old man who apparently does not realize he has been turned out of his position (he dies four months later). The library is almost wholly empty; from time to time a rat pushes a book or two from the shelves. The rats are so numerous that Pascal describes his two-year tenure as librarian as "rat hunter." After the old librarian's death, Pascal finds to his disconcert that he is aping the old man in that he reads the library's books on the job in lieu of serving patrons. In fact, there are many more rats than patrons.

One day Pascal is summoned from the library; his wife is giving birth to twins. One dies promptly, the other a year later at the same time as Pascal's mother. Grief overwhelms him. Aimless, he bolts the library and travels without notifying friends or family to Monte Carlo, where he gambles recklessly and wins again and again. After his winning streak, with 80,000 lira in his pocket, he picks up a newspaper and finds that he has been mistakenly identified as a suicide victim in his hometown. His initial anger at the careless error gives way to jubilation. He could now keep all his gambling winnings; "I had no debts now, no wife, no mother-in-law. Nobody! Free! Free! Free! What more could I ask for?"

Pascal gets a new haircut and manufactures a new name — "Adriano Meis" — from names he overhears in a chance conversation and constructs for himself an alternate life history, should anyone ask. Pascal's new life proves unsatisfactory. He has created a new identity, but it is without any footing in reality, and the only way to maintain it is to deny himself normal social contacts. Through a nicely ironic route he returns ("reincarnates") as his old self.

"Madman that I was!" he scores himself. "How could I have believed that a trunk can live when cut off from its roots?" His return home is not altogether triumphant, but he stays on, and from time to time he goes out to the local graveyard to visit the spot where the body once presumed to be his lies. At the grave is a stone reading "Mattia Pascal Librarian Generous Heart Noble Soul" and so on.

The novel is a brilliant examination of the meaning not only of personal identity but of freedom and choice, and its tone of sustained irony and Pascal's own readiness to laugh at the absurdity of his situation never allows it to descend to the pop culture level of such thematically-related works as the film *It's a Wonderful Life*. There's nothing pat or sentimental about Mattia Pascal's story.

178. Poole, Ernest. *His Family*. New York: Macmillan, 1917. 320p. (Other editions.)

Young Isadore Freedom has a bit part in this novel; a Polish-Russian Jew, he changed his last name to Freedom upon his immigration to the United States. He first earned his living in a New York City sweatshop while attending night school and studying himself to sleep. At the time of his appearance, he works as a librarian in a New York public library "on an ill-smelling ghetto street." He greets a pair of visitors with enthusiasm; they note "a springiness in his step, vigor and warmth in the grip of his hand, in the very curl of his thick black hair, in his voice, in his enormous smile." Isadore takes his visitors for tea at a workers' restaurant whose denizens are happy to see him. There, Isadore gives a spirited speech on the value of books and reading for the struggling masses, on the way the knowledge in the books on the library shelves can constitute "a new god for the world." "In five years," thinks one of the visitors, "Mr. Isadore Freedom will either tone down or go stark mad." The reader does not learn which, but this glimpse of a true believer in the power of books and reading is tantalizing.

179. Provines, Mary V. *Bright Heritage.* New York and Toronto: Longmans, Green, 1939. 261p.

Bright Heritage is a library career novel. Fresh from high school graduation, Una Gregory takes a job as page in California's Calamento County Library system. She finds that library work is quite her cup of tea, and she decides to work her way through college and then go to library school. It's a standard novel of its kind, with nothing very unpleasant happening and even the less appealing characters hiding hearts of gold. Library work (circa 1939) is accurately represented, and librarians fare well, to be sure. Mr. Danby, the system head, is "not very tall, comfortably rounded, with clear rosy cheeks and a mop of iron-gray hair." He gives Una a serious but affable lecture on the importance of books and reading on their first meeting. Miss Allen is the assistant librarian, adored by all. The reference librarian, Mr. Warrington, has "a string of letters after his name ... and he wears the most beautiful clothes!" in one female page's opinion. Mr. Danby is "here, there and otherwhere," taking care of the countless business details of the system. As fiction goes, there is nothing compelling here.

180. Pym, Barbara. *An Academic Question.* London: Macmillan, 1986. 182p. New York: Dutton, 1986. (Other editions.)

Head librarian Evan Cranton plays a part of some importance in this novel of collegiate intrigue. Cranton, two years short of retirement, comes and goes through the course of the story, seldom leaving a good taste behind. Narrator and part-time library assistant Caroline Grimstone "suspected that Evan Cranton had no interest in books for their own sake and did his best to discourage visitors to his library from taking books out of the shelves and reading them." Ever humane, Cranton is convinced that euthanasia is a good solution for the "old and senile, or even the old and apparently useless." Variously cold, sarcastic, and contemptuous, Cranton would not make a good poster child for library school recruitment brochures. Nor is he the only unpleasant librarian in sight: minor character Heather Armitage, another part-timer in the library, is snide, quite likely racist, and "one of those people who do not expect their own experiences to be met with an account of one's own."

181. _____. *An Unsuitable Attachment.* London: Macmillan, 1982. 256p. New York: Dutton, 1982. 256p. (Other editions.)

An Unsuitable Attachment is a gentle and enjoyable story of romantic hopes and frustrations. One of the most important characters is Ianthe Broome, a 30-something librarian trained for the profession because her mother thought it a "ladylike" occupation that would allow Ianthe to meet "a refined, intellectual type of person. She had never seen Ianthe handing out books to the ill-mannered grabby students and cranks of all ages who frequented the library of political sociological books where she worked." Ianthe initially impresses one as of the stereotypically timid and reticent "librarian" sort. She does not like men, "except the clergy" and finds young women "alarming." She likes to help out with church business, and she reads poetry, although apparently no author more current than Tennyson. One of her friends tells her that it's difficult to imagine her falling in love: "You're so cool and collected and I'm sure a man would have to be almost perfect to come up to your standards." But it hardly matters, for, as another character says, "Librarians aren't really very lovable sort of people, are they?"

Ianthe's superior, head librarian Mervyn Cantrell, is an irritable fussbudget, forever spouting about some poor typist's errors on catalog cards. Without intending, he puts in motion a huge change in Ianthe's life when he hires young John Challow, five years' Ianthe's junior, as an assistant librarian. John immediately finds Ianthe attractive. One thing leads to another, and, as the two part after tea before Ianthe leaves on a church trip to Rome, John kisses her with more than valedictory intentions. "One did not behave like that in a public place with a young man, suitable or otherwise," thinks Ianthe, "and John was so very much otherwise." When she returns from Rome, Cantrell astounds (and revolts) her with something like a marriage proposal, and Rupert Stonebird, a pleasant anthropologist, makes a sincere pass at her. Ianthe has other hopes, and they are not dashed.

Well-imagined characters, effective dialogue, and frequent flashes of humor make *An Unsuitable Attachment* a very suitable day's reading.

Queen, Ellery. *See* Dannay, Frederic and Manfred Lee.

182. Raymond, Ernest. *A Chorus Ending.* London: Cassell, 1951. 330p.

A Chorus Ending has a refreshing change of pace for a crime novel: instead of librarian as murder victim, it features librarian as ax murderer. London reference librarian Everett Armidy is somehow shy and smugly proud of himself at the same time. His patrons see in him "a pleasant, smiling, soft-voiced man with fine features, blue eyes, a sad expression, and the stoop of a scholar." He seems to be a capable librarian, but he is at heart "solitary, shy, and nervous of intercourse with others." He lives with his aged mother, serves in his church, and in general lives a life without blemish. At the age of 50, he becomes caught up in an unlikely romance with Elfreda Du Cray, some 15 years his junior. Both Everett and Elfreda have experienced nothing meaningful in the way of romantic involvement; although their relationship begins haltingly, it progresses to a point where Everett seems to love Elfreda. Both are in high hopes when Everett goes for an interview for chief of another library. He prepares extensively, with little note cards he plans to place on his knees, out of sight of the interviewing committee. The interview is a disaster, an appalling exercise by Everett in nervous braggadocio. "And he had his dear little notes on his dear little knee," observes one committee member.

Reeling from the interview fiasco, Everett retreats into the works of Nietzsche and self-consciously adopts a new way of life. He rejects his mild manner and assumes the character of what he presumes to be the Nietzschean overman, free from the constraints of weary Christian ideals. In his new personality, he frequents pubs, where he attempts to ingratiate himself with the backslapping crowd. He'll gladly sing a lascivious song — "after fifty years as a nice, clean little librarian," notes a drinking companion. His tavern mates decide that Everett's remarkable change "probably has something to do with the prostate."

Elfreda's unpleasant mother stands between Everett and his beloved, but a man beyond good and evil is not beyond dealing with obstacles in a decisive manner. Everett is not, alas, a competent criminal, and the authorities have little difficulty in identifying him as the culprit in the hatchet slaying of the old woman, a crime for which Everett faces execution.

As long as *Crime and Punishment* is available, *A Chorus Ending* will have nothing new to say about the psychological ramifications of murder. The prospect of a librarian's launching himself into a life of pseudo–Nietzschean dissolution through the catalyst of a botched job interview is enough to strain any reader's credulousness. Author Raymond does not himself like Everett; he often mocks him, a tactic that does not help enlist the reader's sympathies. Yet the book, in spite of a painfully slow opening, acquires a certain momentum, and one watches Everett and Elfreda steamrolled by the inevitable with a certain grim amusement.

183. Rio, Michel. *Archipelago.* New York: Pantheon, 1989. 117p. London: Quartet, 1990. Translation of *Archipel.* Paris: Editions du Seuil, 1987.

Sixty-year-old Leonard Wilde is the librarian of the venerable Hamilton School, a well-endowed prep school. He observes the book's narrator, a student, with an "oblique, piercing eye, like that of a bird incapable of frontal vision turning its head to fix on you from the top of its perch." Although Wilde is not popular, the community of the school holds him in high regard. He possesses "an extraordinary competence" and a "monumental, encyclopedic, almost monstrous" knowledge of the library and its collections. He combines an "inhuman efficiency" with a biting wit, "always on the edge of cynicism," and an autocratic bearing. Wilde is a profoundly ugly man, physically, and exacerbates the effect with perverse neglect of his clothes. Says Alexandra Hamilton, the beautiful overseer of the school, "He is a misanthrope who despises solitude."

Wilde's face is one of "hideous incongruity, but of an expressiveness so singular and novel that it was difficult to take one's eyes off it." When the narrator visits the otherwise empty library during a term break, Wilde quietly assails him with an astonishing recitation of the young man's reading through his entire time at the school.

Wilde and Hamilton are emotionally close; he owes his job to her. The narrator discovers that the brilliant librarian is a window peeper: He climbs a tree outside Hamilton's house and observes her by night through the windows of the upper floors. Hamilton is aware of her librarian's arboreal voyeurism and accommodates it.

This short novel's high point is Wilde and the narrator's wild and ironically hilarious nocturnal sailing trip along the seacoast, during which Wilde is intent on drowning himself, the narrator equally intent on denying Wilde his fatal ambition. The "dazzling and deformed image of Leonard Wilde," as Hamilton puts it, is the center of this work and the major influence on its other characters. A more eccentric or more memorable librarian would be hard to find in fiction or anywhere else.

184. Rossner, Robert. *The End of Someone Else's Rainbow.* New York: Saturday Review, 1974. 191p.

The End of Someone Else's Rainbow is a delightfully and surprisingly unconventional crime tale that enlists the reader's sympathies completely on the side of the criminals, ex-con Wiley Bridger and town librarian Francine Pennypack.

Nearing 40, Miss Pennypack has settled into a stale routine in the town of Oak Hollow. After eight years of running the library, she finds that nothing much changes from day to day. A painter, she went into library science as a way to pay the bills while working on her art. She found her job through an ad in *Library Journal.* But her artwork has fallen aside, and she rarely enters the little room in her house that she set up as a studio. Her paint has dried out on the top of her dresser; "Me, too," she thinks, and she berates herself for her self-pity. She is "a quiet librarian in a dull little town" and none too happy about it. Her frustration does not seem to extend to her treatment of her patrons: She demonstrates an easy tolerance for the not-too-serious high school students who chit-chat away their study session and carries out her responsibilities as a reader's adviser with some aplomb, even as she chafes at the narrowness of her life.

Her curious friendship with Wiley Bridger, come back to town after nearly two decades in prison, is the beginning of a new career for Pennypack. Bridger went to the penitentiary for a bank job that netted $170,000, money whose whereabouts he has kept to himself. Pennypack and Bridger find parallels in each other's lives, and Francine, to Bridger's confused agreement, becomes his accomplice in retrieving the bank loot. It is a job she carries out with bravery and brazenness. "They can always find another librarian," she assures Bridger.

Amusing and suspenseful, the novel wastes no space on pat moralizing. Pennypack (whose surname is a fittingly funny commentary on her fortunes) is an appealing character, as is Bridger. In a story with many high points, librarians will appreciate one scene in particular: Francine refuses to let a girl take some noncirculating newspaper clippings out of the library because "a library runs by the rules"—an irony in the context of her *sub rosa* activities that she immediately recognizes. "Hang the rules" is the novel's credo, and one may be excused for wishing that hanging the rules would work to one's advantage as well as it does for Pennypack and Bridger.

185. Salamanca, J. R. *A Sea Change.* New York: Knopf, 1969. 501p.

A Sea Change is an overlong but often engrossing tale of obsession and loss. Michael Pritchard, who works in the Manuscript Division of the Library of Congress, addresses the reader three years after his wife Margaret has left him. There has been no subsequent communication between the two. He remains in their

Georgetown house, where he takes care of her possessions in the hope of her return. His recollections cover the entire span of his life with Margaret, beginning with the time he met her as a college student and rapidly fell in love with her. He also "fell in love" with the Library of Congress, while writing a paper during his work toward an M.A. in English. "I think libraries and bakeries are the two most wonderful-smelling institutions in the world," he observes. He describes himself as "a man in his early forties ... [with] a soft academic style of speech, and the rather humble and abstracted air of a man who has been brought much more recently than tradition normally requires in a man of his age to the contemplation of his own infirmities."

Michael and Margaret's marriage stumbles over her disappointment in what she believes is its excessively American nature. Michael loves her greatly but is obtuse about her needs. When she attempts to talk seriously with him after he has had a long day at the library, he can barely acknowledge the depth of her concerns. He seems in many ways more comfortable with his work than with his wife. He is not unhappy with his professional performance, which he judges "no worse than any other government employee, and better than many that I know." He finds in his work "a sense of peace, seclusion, and warm eternal conversation with the past that I drank in like wine or firelight."

The book, as noted, is too long. Vast plains of dialogue alternate with acres of description. But there is a compelling and tragic quality to Michael's obsession with Margaret that sustains interest in the story.

186. Sallenave, Daniele. *The Phantom Life.* New York: Pantheon, 1989. 245p. Translation of *La Vie Fantôme.* Paris: P.O.L., 1986.

The Phantom Life is a challenging account of a long affair between Laure, a young librarian, and Pierre, a teacher. As the novel begins, the affair has lasted four years. The couple try to be discreet; both want to hide their relationship from Pierre's wife and children. Laure and Pierre contact each other by telephone to arrange their meetings; it is always Pierre who initiates the calls and who ends them, sometimes with an air of false and irrelevant boisterousness to mislead those who may have wandered into range of his voice. Laure dislikes these moments but tolerates them.

Her job in a municipal library has lasted for the same period as her affair. She is uncertain whether she likes her work. She senses the gap between library-goers' views of her as a quiet woman and her emotionally draining and intellectually wearing affair. "A secret lay hidden in her, shining beneath her smooth surface." During a library conference in a distant city, Laure is in torment over the affair. Is it a beautiful secret or simply one more tedious example of commonplace faithlessness and desire stealing their tawdry moments of satisfaction in the midst of a life otherwise devoted to convention? In the final of the book's three parts, Laure believes that "their love seemed cold and artificial, a phantom life." Yet it is the life they have chosen and continue to lead.

In the novel's middle portion, the story traces some of the history of the two lovers. It was with Laure that Pierre rediscovered his love of books. She had studied for a doctorate but became disenchanted with academia and earned credentials for a career in librarianship. In spite of her ambivalence about the job, she does find satisfaction in it. Still, she is not unaware of the condescension directed toward her by neighborhood teachers who use the library: "It was obvious to her that privately they found her occupation inferior and her skills limited."

Laure's life, then, in both her profession and in her private existence, is a struggle in which she contends either directly (for example, with condescending faculty) or indirectly (with Pierre's family) for acknowledgment of her value. More crucially, perhaps, she struggles with her own sense of herself as a woman who persists in such a wracking way of life. Moving, adroitly written, and insightful regarding both the main characters, the novel is a quiet yet gripping examination of an affair.

187. Saroyan, William. *The Human Comedy*. New York: Harcourt, Brace, 1943. 291p. (Many editions.)

In Chapter 28, "At the Public Library," little buddies Lionel and Ulysses visit the "humble but impressive" local library in Ithaca, California. Neither boy can read, but Lionel especially likes to look at books. "He just liked to see them — the thousands of them." When Mrs. Gallagher, "the old librarian," sees the boys wandering around, she addresses Lionel sharply: "What you looking for, boy?" On discovering that the boys cannot read, she softens. "I have been reading books for the past sixty years, and I can't see as how it's made any great difference. Run along now and look at the books as you please."

188. Sawyer, Corrine H. *The J. Alfred Prufrock Murders*. New York: Donald I. Fine, 1988. 266p. New York: Ballantine, 1988.

When former librarian "Sweetie" Gilfillan turns up dead on the beach at the Camden Sur Mer retirement community in California, the residents lose one of their quietest and least offensive neighbors. That is how it seems, anyhow — and when Sweetie's death proves to be a murder, the result of multiple stab wounds, there is widespread astonishment. True, Sweetie could get on one's nerves with her habit of passing on information she gleaned from her reading, but she was a harmless sort. "A complete *nothing*," as one acquaintance remarks.

She was not quite nothing, it seems, for as a few of Sweetie's intrepid elderly acquaintances play amateur detective, they find a remarkable amount of valuable jewelry in her quarters. Sweetie seems in retrospect a hypocrite for so frequently referring to her straitened financial condition while sitting on this loot. Worse than a hypocrite, Sweetie is revealed as a vicious blackmailer. Using her skills as a librarian, she ferreted out the dark secrets of both neighbors and staff in the community and made them pay for her silence.

It's a good mystery with an unusual setting and characters and one of the nastiest librarians to ever draw fictional breath.

189. Sayers, Dorothy. *Gaudy Night*. New York: Harper & Row, 1960. 469p. London: Gollancz, 1935. (Many editions.)

Gaudy Night is a collegiate mystery featuring Lord Peter Wimsey and Harriet Vane. At a party early in the novel we learn about librarian Miss Gubbins, a very minor character. She is "an excellent soul, but rather earnest, and an appalling bore at College Meetings," says one of her old acquaintances. Another agrees: Miss Gubbins has "an unfortunate knack of making any subject dull. It's a great pity, because she is exceptionally sound and dependable. However, that doesn't greatly matter in her present appointment; she holds a librarianship somewhere...." It isn't enough that Miss Gubbins bears such an uneuphonious name; at the party she displays untidy hair, ill-kept skin, and a flair for tasteless dress. College librarian Miss Burrows, however, is seen, if briefly, as a diligent, well-organized worker, although she does come under suspicion herself. She is not, unfortunately, the guilty party.

190. Sayle, Helen. *The Blue Smock*. No place: Arcadia House, 1958. 220p.

Columbia graduate Katherine Merton, "assistant chief" at the Rutherford Public Library, is beautiful — "a stunner" — devoted to her work, and engaged to be married. She also suffers from a pathological aversion to "cripples," and when her fiancé loses an arm in a car wreck, she breaks off the engagement. She finds her own feelings almost as repellent as her fiancé's empty sleeve: "I am not a whole person at all, not a complete human being." Kathy is, however, proud of her work. She contributes an article to the local paper on the history of the library, hoping that it will attract a reader or two to the profession. She secures a free time slot for the library with the local radio station, "The Library Hour," no less. Happiness cannot be hers, however, until she conquers her irrational attitude toward the physically infirm. A rather odd blend of career-advocacy novel and psychological study, the book falls far short of serious or even compelling literature, in spite of the good intentions from which it came. The title refers to the quasi-uniform the librarians wear at the Rutherford P.L.

191. Seeley, Mabel H. *The Crying Sisters: A Mystery Story*. Garden City, N.Y.: Doubleday, Doran, 1939. 292p. (Other editions.)

Narrator Janet Ruell describes herself as "a respectable small-town librarian" whose life has been "openly humdrum and secretly desperate — the way life in a small town is for a girl who's still unmarried at twenty-nine." During a vacation in northern Minnesota, she agrees to accompany a surly highway engineer and his toddler son to a resort at Crying Sisters Lake. Her task: to take care of the boy for a month. As vacations go, it proves a memorable one, with murder foremost and suspicion everywhere. Janet Ruell is in the thick of it all, and she is a commendably strong character. It is no shock that she gets her man at the end of this middling mystery.

192. Shields, Carol. *Swann*. New York: Viking, 1989. 312p. Toronto: Stoddart, 1987. (Other editions.)

Early in this "mystery," a character describes Rose Hindmarch, librarian and township clerk of Nadeau, Ontario, as "a little turtle of a woman with a hair on her chin ... quintessentially virginal, mid-forties, twinkly eyed, suppliant, excitable." Rose has a nervous laugh, a "whinnying" voice, a "lachrymose" bearing and is given to "feeble meditations and moony recollections." Rose is "moist" and "repulsive." She does, however, have an entire chapter of the novel named after her, and there she takes on different colors. She is not only an efficient township clerk and by afternoons an effective public librarian, but she serves as curator of the town's local history museum. She has quietly adopted atheism, although she continues to serve on the board of the Nadeau United Church, and has been a member of the village council for 15 years. Rose is very proud of the history museum, where she has developed the Mary Swann Memorial Room. Swann, a local poet and passing acquaintance of Rose, died at 40, a murder victim.

Rose's chapter is an intimate and sympathetic account of a woman of considerable abilities, as well as disappointments. Of the latter, the greatest must be her lack of a life partner or even an occasional roll in the hay for the sake of good healthy lust. One of the most touching passages describes the one night when she shared her bed with the woman from the apartment downstairs. Rose invites the woman in for shelter from a row with her husband. The two sleep together, and Rose is filled with wonder at the woman's proximity, realizing "that a body was more than a hinged apparatus for getting around."

Much of the plot concerns Rose's attendance at a symposium on Swann in Toronto. There she hears her library dismissed as a "substandard" rural outfit that could not have nourished the mind of a poet. Mysterious events at the symposium lead to an even more mysterious conclusion.

Many readers will find it hard to accept the author's exaggerated presence in the book. Shields's intrusive narrative technique too often prevents the story from slipping naturally into a credible world-as-if-true. Her ultimate ploy, jerking the novel into the form of a screenplay, may cause whiplash in the unprepared. In spite of the author's overobvious hand, she creates in Rose a convincingly complex major character.

193. Simenon, Georges. *Maigret's Mistake*. New York: Harcourt Brace Jovanovich, 1988. 188p. London: Hamilton, 1954. Translation of *Maigret se Trompe*. Paris: Presses de la Cité, 1953.

Described as "a typical old maid" by her sister, Antoinette Ollivier is a 50-year-old librarian in a municipal library in Paris and is a relatively minor but still-significant character in this Inspector Maigret mystery. She possesses "the rather disdainful assurance of women who think they have penetrated all the great truths of life." Maigret interviews her at length about a case involving her sister's husband, a professor. She hates him "and all his kind"—hates him enough, apparently, to become an accessory to murder.

194. Skom, Edith. *The Mark Twain Murders.* Tulsa, Oklahoma: Council Oak, 1989. 277p. New York: Dell, 1990.

Set at Midwestern University (which sounds curiously like Northwestern University), this multiple-murder mystery contains considerable library action. The librarians themselves are not major characters but are sufficiently evident that they give the scenery some verisimilitude. The most prominently mentioned librarians are Marjorie ("Marge") Westwood, who presides over a noncirculating collection intended for undergraduates, and head librarian Coleman Lenites. Marge impresses as a businesslike individual with a wry view of library life. To a simple "How's it going?" she responds with a recitation of the day's absurdities. They range from a patron's threat to sue after his three-ring binder sets off the gate alarm to an apparently specious claim by the online catalog that all 14 copies of *Walden* are lost, to hectoring by Coleman about the need to shake down patrons for illicit thermoses. Where Marge seems reasonable and down-to-earth—she's studying karate to equip herself to deal with the scoundrel terrorizing the campus—Coleman seems to have lost all firm connection with practical reality. He has an especially large bug in his ear about forbidden food and drink. Late in the book he fairly pounces on a major character, quivering with outrage upon deciding that she has been smuggling coffee from the lounge into the library proper. He follows her to her carrel, "rattling out regulations about consumption of hot foods and beverages." Well-written and entertaining, the novel is a good addition to the list of fiction featuring murders on the library premises.

195. Smiley, Jane. *Duplicate Keys.* New York: Knopf, 1984. 305p. London: Cape, 1984. (Other editions.)

Duplicate Keys is a very fine and literate mystery by a Pulitizer Prize–winning author. Divorced, 31-year-old Alice Ellis is a cataloger with the New York Public Library. One day she discovers two of her friends, rock musicians, murdered in her friend Susan's apartment. The effects of the murder on the circle of friends that includes Alice and Susan is as much the subject of the book as the revelation of the killer.

Susan became a librarian to support her former husband, an up-and-coming poet. "On her own," however, "she would never have become a librarian, never in a million years." In spite of this assertion, Alice finds relief in her work from the emotional intensity following the murders. Her cataloging was "rather peaceful, impersonal work that gave her a spurious sense of distance" from the tragedy and its aftermath. Yet her work, of which we see enough to understand that she is more than a librarian in name only, is escape from her personal problems, yes, but something else, too: "In the library, Alice felt detached from the rest of her life, and more than that, permanently, immortally treading the aisles of the stacks.... Alice embraced her routine, the spar that would float her out of trouble into a healthy old age. At home, she worried, at work, she hummed."

The novel's consistent intelligent focus on human relations is its greatest strength. Alice's affair with a botanist and her deep feelings for her friend Susan receive particularly effective attention. But the mystery component of the story is not to be sniffed at. There are twists and turns and surprises, and a passage late in the book, with Alice fleeing an intruder in her apartment by walking along the narrow ledge outside her fourth-floor apartment, should be enough to leave any reader's heart pounding and mouth dry. Smiley's treatment of Alice Ellis is most satisfying, for Alice is a complete and complex human being in her hands.

196. Smith, Bradford. *American Quest.* Indianapolis: Bobbs-Merrill, 1938. 597p.

Surveyor Walter Quest grabs his hat one day and sets out to look for America. He drifts into the little New England burg of Abbottstown on his travels, there to make a striking impression on Katherine Jeremy, the town librarian. Katherine, a widow for eight years, has a daughter named Faith. Katherine is the sort who attends church as "one of the duties of the town's librarian"—but who finds relief from her civic religious obligations by roaming the hills above town when the service is over. She finds in Walter "a man in whom her womanhood could flower again" after the long years of widowhood. "You make me feel like a young girl again," she tells Walter, who cannot linger long in Abbottstown. On his ensuing wanderings, however, thoughts of Katherine return to him, and he does, near the conclusion of this seemingly endless, overearnest novel, turn back to Abbottstown to take Katherine in marriage.

197. Stephenson, Neal. *Snow Crash.* New York: Bantam, 1992. 440p. London: Roc, 1993.

Stephenson's prose can be a little dense, but he writes with a keen intelligence and dark humor. Here the U.S. government has collapsed, and the Library of Congress, now simply "the Library," has gone commercial, serviced by countless hackers who upload endless data to its innards. The librarian of *Snow Crash* is not at all human, merely the illusion of a man in the form of a "geeky daemon" of computer creation. From time to time, "the Librarian" helps the story's main character, Hiro Protagonist, gather information. "Like any librarian in Reality, this daemon can move around without audible footfalls." When the Librarian hands a hypercard to Hiro, Hiro "can hear the white noise of his trousers sliding over his leg." Thus Stephen King's Ardelia Lortz (*The Library Policeman*) is not the only nonhuman librarian to be found in fiction — although Stephenson's computer daemon is a good deal more polite and service oriented than King's just-plain demon.

198. Stevenson, Dorothy E. *Miss Dean's Dilemma.* New York: Farrar & Rinehart, 1938. 371p. Also published as *The Young Clementina.* New York: Holt, Rinehart, Winston, 1970. (Other editions.)

The narrator, Charlotte Dean, is an English librarian, a reader's advisor, in a library specializing in geography books. She addresses her story to a woman she "knew" for only ten minutes, a woman she met on a bus, whom she has manufactured into her "only real friend." At the age of 35, Miss Dean has led "the life of a hermit in the heart of a city." Although written with considerable facility, the novel seldom rises above the level of literate romance. Its concern is the manner in which Miss Dean loses and finally regains her early childhood sweetheart. (Clementina is his daughter's name.) There are some nice passages; notable among them is Miss Dean's description of her reaction at the age of 18 to the Great War, which she greeted first with incredulity and then a belief that came with terrible weight. At somewhere short of the novel's middle, Miss Dean abandons her modest career as a librarian and her life as a "hermit" in the city, to live in a country mansion (the oldest story in the book).

199. Stevenson, Robert Louis. *Prince Otto.* New York: Scribner, 1905. 298p. London: Chatto & Windus, 1885. (Many editions.)

Set in the imaginary German principality of Grunewald. Dr. Gotthold, who describes himself as "an old celibate, an old monk," is librarian to his cousin, Prince Otto — librarian and a good deal more, for as Otto agonizes over the burdens of office in a state edging toward revolution, Dr. Gotthold advises him candidly and incisively. Gotthold, a man of about 40, begins work before 6 A.M. He devotes his life to two things: erudition and Rhine wine. He is "the virgin priest of knowledge." Prince Otto describes Gotthold as a man of "interminable industry" possessing "a keen mind," a scholar who serves mankind, "scorning pleasures and temptations." As they become caught most awkwardly in affairs of state, Gotthold and Otto argue, accuse each another, and ultimately resolve their conflicts while under arrest. A strained, unnatural prose makes *Prince Otto* awkward reading, but Dr. Gotthold is a complex and interesting character.

200. Storey, Gail D. *The Lord's Motel.* New York: Persea Books, 1992. 212p.

Thirty-one-year-old librarian Colleen Sweeney works in a Houston public library. Her boss, the head librarian, is "not that great an administrator but she is a great bully." Colleen is productive and bright but sometimes cries for no apparent reason. Her main endeavor involves setting up library service for prisoners in the women's jail. Her choice of project is not, perhaps, coincidental; she herself feels confined in ways not unlike those of the incarcerated women she wants to serve. "I'm imprisoned and can get out only by some violent act against myself," she laments. "If I were a planet, I'd blow myself up."

Colleen lives in the Lord's Motel, an apartment building. She met her boyfriend Web when he was being auctioned as Most Eligible Bachelor at a Friends of the Library fundraiser. Web shows Colleen a lot of smart moves but no real tenderness. Does Colleen seek in him something of the cruelty that her father visited on her mother in regular beatings? Is it the memory of her parents' violent relationship that leads to her overwhelming desire to help Dolores, imprisoned for killing her abusive husband, straighten out her life?

Struggling to please Web, Colleen blunders into an arrest for prostitution in Galveston. She consults an attorney. "Maybe more librarians are arrested for prostitution than I thought," she notes. Out on bail, she consults a psychologist, who helps her recognize some of the psychological dynamics of her situation. Often grindingly unhappy, *The Lord's Motel* salves the reader's sensibilities in the end by allowing Colleen, a strong and resilient character for all her problems, to clamber out of the emotional cesspool she has long occupied. Everything is not "all better" in the end, but one has reasonable hopes that Colleen will prove to be more than a survivor.

201. Summerhayes, Prudence. *Girls in Green; A Novel of Library Life Between the Two Wars.* London: Hutchinson, 1949. 272p.

Girls in Green is a numbing story of two young women who hire on as student assistants at the Kingsteeple Municipal Library. Here "student assistants" are understudies, learning librarianship through on-the-job instruction. The students, who wear overall uniforms at work, come in contact with a variety of library staff members, including chief librarian Mr. Mundy. Mundy has a "quick, nervous gait," and, except to his intimates, seems "a very desiccated, pedantic sort of person." Mundy writes for an antiquarian journal and is working on a bibliography of "lost books," whose existence can only be surmised by surviving fragments. His assistant librarian, Miss Hide, is efficient, no-nonsense, and crabby. Miss Mitchell, head of reference, keeps to herself; younger staff members are inclined to laugh at her. She has her heart set on Mundy, a fact to which Mundy is oblivious. The novel is sufficiently somniferous that the reader's search for stereotypes runs neck-and-neck with the efforts of the Sandman to bring a merciful end to the business.

202. Swaim, Don. *The H. L. Mencken Murder Case: A Literary Thriller.* New York: St. Martin's, 1988. 171p.

The H. L. Mencken Murder Case is an engaging mystery set in 1948 New York City, where Howard, a lightly educated used book dealer, consorts with an aging Mencken and gets into trouble. Howard is also carrying on an affair with Ann Elkin, who studied library science at Hunter. Ann's past is colorful, if unfulfilled: She tried unsuccessfully to become a coal miner after her father died of black lung; she also tried to hire on as a firefighter and then as a cop after a pimp knifed her morphine-addicted alto-sax-playing lover. When she tried to sign up as a longshoreman in Jersey City, she was roughed up by roustabouts. Now she works in the public library, smokes Pall Malls, and is busy writing an historical romance. She seems unaware that her editor at Macmillan is jerking her about like a puppet, demanding major changes in her book without so much as pin money up front for it and with no promise of publication. The novel features the usual book-world intrigue, with an allegedly valuable 18th-century manuscript coming into Howard's possession. Ann's purpose is chiefly that of second banana (at most) to Howard. It is Mencken's sensibility that dominates the book, and an afterword that purports to be a retrospective glimpse of the major characters' fates is fully in keeping with his jaundiced worldview. Ann Elkin does not fare better than the rest.

203. Symons, Julian. *The Colour of Murder.* Anstey, England: F.A. Thorpe, 1988. 399p. London: Collins, 1957. (Other editions.)

One more librarian suffers the ultimate crime in this psychological mystery. John Wilkins meets Sheila Morton, an attractive new librarian, and tells her, falsely, that he is not married. Sheila, "a simple, honest and innocent young girl," in John's words, is caring for her invalid father. Initially attracted to John, she declines further involvement with him when she learns that he is, in fact, married. She becomes engaged to another man after her brief flirtation with John. When she turns up dead, murdered, on a Brighton beach at the book's halfway point, John is the prime suspect. Although crucial to the plot's main issue — John's arrest for murder — Sheila Morton is otherwise little more than incidental in the story.

204. Thomas, Ross. *No Questions Asked.* (Pub. under pseud. Oliver Bleeck.) New York: Morrow, 1976. 228p. (Other editions.)

The librarian in this mystery serves primarily as a means of explaining to the reader the basics of the case. This case is the theft of a valuable edition of Pliny's *Historia Naturalis*, on loan to the Library of Congress. In a passage of several pages early in the book, the narrator questions the chief of the Rare Books Division about the matter. The chief, with the ponderous name Hawkins Gamble Laws III, "was probably one of the politest men I ever met in my life." A thoroughly civilized and considerate sort who wears his Phi Beta Kappa key without a sign of affectation, Laws "spoke a kind of mandarin English, touched up with plenty of commas and semicolons, which you don't run across too often in the United States unless you subscribe to *The Economist*." Laws impresses the narrator, and the reader, as a skilled professional, and — yes — as a scholar and a gentleman, even if he does part his hair in the middle and wear a bow tie.

205. Thompson, Jim. *The Getaway.* New York: Vintage, 1990. 185p. New York: Signet, 1959.

When we meet Carol McCoy early in this hard-boiled crime novel, her library days are long gone. She has taken up with prominent crook "Doc" McCoy and has a serious record of her own: three arrests, suspicion of complicity in murder, armed robbery, and bank robbery with her husband. Before she met Doc, she worked as a librarian, "living with her stodgy, middle-aged parents and daily settling deeper into the pattern of spinsterhood." She was not unattractive, but "people saw only the dowdy 'sensible' clothes and the primness of manner, and thought of her as plain and even homely." Doc helped her change all that. There is no need to linger here on the exploits of Doc and Carol, for she has renounced librarianship and every other aspect of her former life — but should the question "What happens when librarians go bad?" come up at the reference desk, the tale of Carol McCoy might serve as an answer.

206. Timperley, Rosemary. *Suspicion.* Long Preston, England: Magna Print Books, 1983. 309p. London: Hale, 1978.

London librarian Ronald Lakely is, by the consensus of much of the rest of the library staff, the culprit in the murder of 20-year-old library assistant Anne Marlow. Lakely, of a working-class background, cut all ties with his family after his library training. Now not only does he lack family, but his professional associations have crumbled. "I was accustomed to being despised and unwanted," he says, "but now it's all taken a step farther and I'm positively hated." Ronald attempts suicide, repeatedly. Narrator Anna Lake, in her 50s, comes to Ronald's aid. He confesses to her that he raped Anne but contends that he did not harm her otherwise. The truth remains at bay until late in this tale of murder, lies, betrayal, and a librarian-gone-balmy. Timperley does evoke some sympathy for the much-plagued Ronald, but it is sympathy that may not be well taken. It's a fairly lurid potboiler.

207. Torday, Ursula. *Dewey Death.* (Pub. under pseud. Charity Blackstock.) London: William Heinemann, 1956. 285p. Also in her *The Foggy, Foggy Dew and Dewey Death.* New York: London House & Maxwell, 1959. (Other editions.)

Several cuts above the average mystery, *Dewey Death* is set for the most part in a British interlibrary loan operation. As it opens, it appears that several of the characters are close to open war with one another. One of the library functionaries, Mrs. Warren, is the source of considerable aggravation, for as a sharp-tongued busybody, she delights in making her colleagues miserable. The novel's most important character, 28-year-old Barbara Smith, is a reasonably successful author of swashbuckling romances; she is not above banging out a few pages of her current novel on work time, but she declines to let the staff know her pseudonym. When one of the staff is found dead in the elevator, stuffed into a book sack with a broken neck, the suspicions and animosities rife in the facility make for a satisfying investigation. Also satisfying is Torday's grip on office politics and the messy emotional involvements of people who work in close quarters with one another. She has insights, as well, into library administrators. Deputy librarian Latimer is a dignified man, careful of both his behavior and his clothes ("he was a constant reproach to the other librarians, who looked like undergraduates in a left-wing book-shop"), but the murder catches him completely flat-footed: "Which only went to prove that Mr. Latimer, like a great many executives, had no idea whatsoever of the life that smouldered beneath the office routine." A good plot and enjoyable characters, particularly Mark Allan, who is cynical, ironic, and ready to shock with his candor, place *Dewey Death* high on the library mystery ladder. Torday's tart humor helps, too. She pulls off a number of effective scenes, not the least of which is the dreaded Mrs. Warren's ferocious consumption of a cream bun.

208. Tully, Jim. ***Biddy Brogan's Boy.*** New York: Scribner, 1942. 300p.

Librarian Alberta Rowan plays only a small part in this novel, but it is an important one. In charge of the Hollywood, California, public library, she spends a good deal of time discussing contemporary authors with aspiring writer Biddy Brogan. "Near to sixty, she was beautiful as a sunset" in Brogan's eyes. She introduces the young man to a veteran author, Simon Lalend, who takes Biddy under his wing and gives him valuable critical advice. Rowan is as good hearted as Lalend, although her judgment of literature is routinely conventional. "I don't know what writing is coming to," she laments of a new novel. "This man runs the gutters of his mind through a book. Surely a distorted view of life — it isn't like that." It falls to Rowan to inform Biddy of Lalend's death, at the point when Biddy is on the verge of success as an author, a success in which Rowan is instrumental through her introduction of Biddy to Lalend. (Title note: Biddy is named after his mother, also Biddy Brogan.)

209. _____. ***Emmett Lawler.*** New York: Harcourt, Brace, 1922. 315p. London and New York: Melrose, 1922.

There is little of libraries or librarians in this novel of a poor young man going to meet the world, but what there is, is more than positive. When Emmett Lawler hits New York City with 50 cents in his pocket, he finds the metropolis "a wanton with a heart of ice." He seeks refuge daily at the Cooper Union Library, where he reads by the hour and where "the kind-hearted librarians helped him to find books worth while." The librarians referred to here come close to having wings: "There is more real democracy in an American Public Library than in any other institution in the land. There the woman of refinement waits on the outcast." Author Tully praises the librarians who assisted Henry George and Jack London. "Even to-day, perhaps, a library worker in some far corner of the land is instilling courage in a future George or London." Later in the novel, Lawler buys some stationery and returns to the Cooper Union Library to write a letter.

"One of the kind women, who had been his friend in the library, came up to talk to him — a rare human angel she was — who has spent the best years of her pulsating life in a wilderness of dead dreams." One can speculate on what that statement means, but there is no mistaking the reverence that Lawler, and presumably Tully, felt for the idealized librarians the novel invokes.

210. Valin, Jonathan. *Final Notice.* New York: Dodd, Mead, 1980. 246p. London: Futura, 1987. (Other editions.)

An apparent psychotic — the "Hyde Park Ripper" — has been busy mutilating expensive art books at the Hyde Park public library. Director Leon Ringold ("one of those angry little men who've never forgiven the rest of the world for looking down on them") has brought in detective Harry Stoner to nab the culprit. Stoner makes friends with the aging, "owl-faced" librarian Jessie Moselle, who dabbles in genealogy, takes astrology seriously, and favors Bushnell's Irish whiskey. Jessie provides some useful assistance in producing a list of suspects. And why not? She has "a little something" on most of her clientele, including what the stars allegedly reveal about their characters. Her take on librarians' experience of the world and the nature of their bravery, such as it is: "We haven't seen much of life, outside of what a few great minds have written about it…. But I think there is a certain courage that comes with education … not a physical courage … but an intellectual one." The novel's title comes from Miss Moselle's suggested moniker for the end-game move on the perpetrator, Plan Final Notice. A readable mystery-thriller whose dirty work extends well beyond slicing up photos of the Venus de Milo.

211. Van Vechten, Carl. *Nigger Heaven.* New York: Octagon, 1973. 286p. New York and London: Knopf, 1926. (Other editions.)

Mary Love, a young black librarian in a Harlem public library, is one of the central characters in this novel of life in that community, especially as it concerns the arts scene. Mary's reading taste ranges from prominent white authors — Jean Cocteau, Aldous Huxley, Sherwood Anderson — to such black writers as Jean Toomer, Claude McKay, and W. E. B. Du Bois. She's smart, restrained (too restrained, probably), and in love with an aspiring writer. Mary's life as a librarian is, unfortunately, all but invisible, although it figures prominently in an astute comment by one of her friends. When Mary confides that she doesn't know if she wants to be married, her friend dismisses her reservations: "Now what else can a coloured woman do? You're a librarian, but you'll never get as much pay as the white librarians. They won't even put you in charge of a branch library. Not because you're not as good as the others — probably you're better — but because you're coloured."

About that title (which comes from two of the characters' references to Harlem): Coupling its use of the ultimate term of racial opprobrium with the novel's dialect-drenched prologue, it is easy to be put off by the book at the beginning. Van Vechten is sincere, however, and if his use of dialect or indeed even his attempt to identify with his black characters is somewhat awkward, he was at least far ahead of most white writers of his time in his view of black Americans as complex (that is, human) individuals. He actually states in a footnote, some distance into the story, that a white person's use of the term nigger "is always fiercely resented," and his grasp of the burden racism lays on the everyday lives of its victims can scarcely be faulted. The book is interesting today chiefly as an early example of a white writer's determined effort to depict black urban life in a sympathetic and realistic way. The effort is not altogether successful but neither is it inept.

212. Wallace, Irving. *The Seven Minutes.* New York: Simon & Schuster, 1969. 607p. London: New English Library, 1969. (Other editions.)

The Seven Minutes is an occasionally interesting but creaky novel in defense of intellectual freedom, with a few stops along the way for a little gratuitous titillation. The book's title is that of a French novel almost universally considered "obscene." Attorney Mike Barrett helps present the defense of a California bookseller arrested for selling the offensive work. In the course of building his case, he visits Rachel Hoyt, a 40ish Los Angeles librarian, head of the Oakwood Library. She is "a great gal," in one character's opinion; she has stood up to the local censors for years. Barrett finds her "as colorful as a psychedelic poster." He asks her to refrain from adding *The Seven Minutes* to her collection so that the defense of the book can focus on a single "martyr," the bookseller whose trial is approaching. He also asks her to serve as an expert witness. She assents readily and offers what is, with a few narrative breaks to provide the illusion of a story being told ("She gulped down her coffee"), a speech of several pages on the virtues of intellectual freedom and the challenges a librarian faces in trying to encourage and protect it. Rachel Hoyt largely disappears from the novel after serving as the mouthpiece for the politically correct librarian's point of view according to Wallace. (She even recites passages from the *Library Bill of Rights.*)

213. Wallis, Ruth S. *Too Many Bones.* New York: Dodd, Mead, 1943. 232p. London: Hammond, 1947.

In this tolerable mystery, budding anthropologist Kay Ellis begins her career in a private museum, where DAR member Alice Barton has been the longtime librarian. "Miss Alice" fills in Kay on the background of the Proutman Museum, with particular attention to benefactress Zaydee Proutman, a thoroughly unpleasant sort. Proutman disappears, and Barton proves to be her murderer. Her complacent confession of the deed — "I had a pleasant evening, but I was a little anxious" — is almost comical. The title refers to the museum's large collection of human bones, including at last, a little ironically, those of Zaydee Proutman. Although Barton demonstrates some of her capabilities, her library skills do not come into play.

214. Walpole, Sir Hugh. *The Cathedral.* New York: Doran, 1922. 459p. London: Macmillan, 1922. (Other editions.)

Set in England in the late 1890s, this novel of a proud man's ruin features one of the most spiteful, evil-minded librarians one could meet in a work of fiction. The victim-to-be is Archdeacon Brandon, of Polchester. Brandon occupies an important role not only in the Church but in his own eyes. He is "satisfied with himself, his appearance, his abilities, his wife, his family, and above all his position…. This last was very splendid."

Alas for Brandon, his satisfaction is a lamb for slaughter at the hands of Miss Milton, the town librarian. Milton appears in a relatively small share of the book's pages, barely three dozen, but she is the deciding factor, aside from the man's own pride, in Brandon's fall.

Milton is a dreadful librarian who has managed to cling to her post for two decades. She literally sits on new novels to save them for her favored patrons. She hates children and is an insufferable snob. She lies to patrons in her disfavor about which books are out and knits "endless stockings" while on duty. Her physical appearance is the equal of her conduct: she has "little red-rimmed eyes," a "freckled and flushed complexion," and a "clumsy thick-set figure." At last her performance — "incompetent, utterly incompetent" — gets her sacked. She blames her dismissal on Archdeacon Brandon. A quirk of fate gives her a route to vengeance by revealing the affair that Brandon's wife has been carrying on with another local clergyman. Milton's reprehensible action has the desired effect, on the chief parties and on the area citizenry: "The Town was bursting its fat sides with excitement over it all!"

Walpole's attack on small-town complacency, small-mindedness, and self-satisfaction makes good reading. His characters are not simple two-dimensional types. Their fleshed-out humanity invites sympathy, even in their self-induced misery. Miss Milton is the exception; she possesses a single dimension, one of absolute wretchedness, and is beyond sympathy. She is every ill will and petty malevolence in Polchester blended and boiled down into a single character. In that role, she shines, albeit darkly.

215. Weisbecker, A. C. *Cosmic Banditos.* New York: Vintage, 1986. 193p.

Cosmic Banditos is a truly lunatic and quite amusing novel concerning the narrator's search for the meaning of life. The search extends from the jungles of Colombia to Sausalito, California, and features the narrator's preoccupation with quantum physics. The librarian here comes wrapped in a blanket and occupies a few pages approximately a third of the way into the story. The aging and frail Señor Rodriguez is the director of the University of Barranquilla Research Library. One day the narrator sends his bandito buddies from their lair to procure books on physics from the library. They seize the books, hundreds of them, in a violent biblio-raid. They also bring Rodriguez back into the wilds, bound, gagged, and blindfolded, in a blanket. The librarian was saved from death under a counterassault by government troops when a bandito hauled him out a bathroom window. The narrator unties the librarian and attempts to explain to him "why he was sitting in a shack in the wilds of the Sierra Nevadas, instead of running the University of Barranquilla Research Library.... Señor Rodriguez stared at me wide-eyed as I gave him a crash course on the Underlying Nature of Reality." The poor librarian then collapses into unconsciousness without saying a word; the banditos tote him back to town to dump him in front of the medical center. The narrator notes that he "had grown quite fond" of the librarian during their brief encounter.

216. Wharton, Edith. *Summer.* New York: Scribner, 1917. 216p. London: Macmillan, 1917. *McClure's* 48 (Feb. 1917–Aug. 1917). (Other editions.)

Young Charity Royall is the town librarian of North Dormer, a little backwater where "it's enough to make people hate each other just to have to walk down the same street every day." The lawyer Royall rescued Charity some years earlier from "the Mountain," where the area's poorest folk live, and has since served as her guardian. Charity has no real education and no real clue how to run a library. She was appointed to the job, which she sought as a way to earn enough money to leave the town. On duty in the library, she feels "dead," and thinks of it as a "prison house." Her ignorance of life and literature bear down on her, making her feel inadequate. She considers her life desolate, ugly, and intolerable. Her fortunes turn with the arrival in town of a young architectural expert, Lucius Harney, on assignment for a publisher. She and Lucius engage in a fairly torrid affair. Serious fiction of the first order, *Summer* posits no easy solutions to complex human problems and in fact defies what might be many readers' building expectations about the resolution of Charity's fate. Charity is a very nicely drawn character, who, although full of loathing for what she sees as her mean background, refuses to disown herself from her heritage or from "her people" on the Mountain.

217. White, Nelia Gardner. *The Bewitched Spinster.* In her *The Merry Month of May, and Two Other Short Novels.* New York: Viking, 1952, pp. 87–160.

Kate Kinney is the 54-year-old librarian in the village of Old Huxley. She is "tall, long-faced" and has "perfected the art of spinsterhood." The lending library is attached to her house, where she earns a little money providing room and board to a young writer, Reggie Jones. Kate has often served as an effective amateur counselor for the townsfolk, listening to them talk through their problems in the library. She covers her own problem, a failure to engage in any genuinely loving relationship, beneath a veneer of efficiency, uprightness, and no-nonsense character. Reggie, however, has a way, unlike anyone else in town, of penetrating Kate's well-practiced defenses. As he writes a novel, they become friends, in spite of Kate's initial suspicions about his seriousness. Through the catalyst of her friendship with Reggie, Kate realizes that for all her courage, competence, integrity, and steadfastness, she has subsisted through her life not on love but on pride. "I have been bewitched by pride," she says, and goes on from that realization to begin a new life. In spite of some shallow ties to the theme of the stereotyped librarian, the novel is one of effective insight and realistic observation. Kate is a complex character, and one sympathizes with her as she looks within herself to find the truth that she has long denied.

218. White, Patrick. *The Solid Mandala.* London: Eyre & Spottiswoode, 1966. 317p. New York: Viking, 1966. 309p. (Other editions.)

After leaving high school in Sydney, Australia, Waldo Brown took a clerical job with the Sydney Municipal Library. Now in his 30s, he is still there, although not for much longer. And although his activities in the library receive only brief attention in the novel, his view of his superior, Mr. Crankshaw the Librarian, is scathing. For several pages in midbook Waldo's jaundiced evaluation of Crankshaw makes it plain why Waldo is on the verge of resigning. Several years younger than the slender Waldo, Crankshaw is obese and subtly vicious: "He had the hands of one who had felled timber, without having known the feel of an axe, except the one he used, by law of gravity, on those beneath him."

219. Widdemer, Margaret. *Rose-Garden Husband.* Philadelphia: Lippincott, 1915. 208p.

Miss Phyllis Braithwaite, Assistant for the Children's Department, Greenway Branch, City Public Library, is "a twenty-five-year-old young woman with reading glasses and fine discipline and a woolen shirtwaist." Known to the children who frequent her department as "the pretty one who laughs," Miss Braithwaite's wants are simple: she wants a lot of money, a rose garden, and a husband. "I'd marry *anything* that would give me a rose-garden," she says, "so long as it was a gentleman — and he didn't scold me — and — and — I didn't have to associate with him!" In 1915 young women certainly felt greater pressure to marry young than today, and Miss Braithwaite senses her prime time beginning to expire. Answering her ambition and her anxiety, she leaves the library profession to enter an arranged marriage with a rich young invalid.

Chiefly interesting as an example of the embodiment of prevailing values in popular romantic fiction, *The Rose Garden Husband* advances a number of ideas that have since fallen into disrepute. They include not only the most obvious, the notion that a young woman's life is hopeless without marriage, but casual racism (for example, in the stereotyped portrayal of a black housekeeper) and blatant ethnocentrism ("Poor little wop," Miss Braithwaite thinks of one of her Italian patrons). The novel's prose is adequate, although incessant childish references to Miss Braithwaite as "the Liberry Teacher" quickly wear thin.

220. Wiesel, Elie. *The Fifth Son.* New York: Summit, 1985. 220p. London: Viking, 1986. Translation of *Le Cinquième Fils.* Paris: Grasset, 1983. (Other editions.)

Alphabetical order is an indispensable tool, but it does, sometimes, place works of wildly disparate nature and quality shoulder-to-shoulder. There is, really, none but an arbitrary aesthetic sense in following *The Rose-Garden Husband* with *The Fifth Son.* Wiesel's novel is a powerful, memorable story of love, history, and the search for self; it deserves lasting regard and will surely earn it. The narrator's father, Reuven Tamiroff, is a librarian, "a loner," who "feels at ease only among dead or invented characters who, locked into or liberated in thousands upon thousands of volumes, live in his imagination." Tamiroff lives in Brooklyn and works in a public library in Manhattan. An omnivorous reader, he takes particular pleasure from his religious studies: "He looks as if he is in pain, so intense is the joy he derives from reading."

Tamiroff, a survivor of the Holocaust, wrestles with thoughts of good and evil. "I know that he sees everything," his son says, "that he is aware of everything, that nothing escapes him." Tamiroff cannot bear to speak of the war, even though he fought heroically with the Polish army against the Nazis. He also served with courage as president of the Davarowsk ghetto's Jewish council during the war. As such, he could have demanded a relatively comfortable dwelling, but chose, from a sense of justice, to live in a dingy apartment. He is a logical man who "dissects thoughts like a surgeon" but reveals little of himself in his daily affairs. His intense letters to his dead son are scattered through the book; they give insights not afforded by Tamiroff's routine conduct: "The silence within me at times becomes so heavy that my heart comes close to bursting," he confesses in one letter. The narrator does not completely grasp his father's nature: "Try to understand: My father likes solitude and silence; in fact, that is why he chose to be a librarian." Does Tamiroff like solitude and silence, or are those the conditions he requires to maintain his sanity?

Major plot developments in the novel are the narrator's discovery of his father's participation in a postwar guerilla execution attempt on the Nazi overseer of the Davarowsk ghetto and the revelation of the true identity of Ariel, the son to whom Tamiroff has written his impassioned letters.

Rich characterization, a beautifully organized story line, and a deep sense of shared feeling with those in extreme emotional stress are among the qualities that make *The Fifth Son* such a potent work.

221. Wills, Garry. *At Button's.* Kansas City, Mo.: Andrews and McMeel, 1979. 174p.

When the story opens in 1977, Gregory Skipwith is a reference librarian at the New York Library. He took his job "to avoid dealing with people" (a strange choice of specialization for someone trying to avoid the public). He becomes acquainted with Marcia, a student researching life among the city's prostitutes.

He confides in her that he is trying to break from his past, especially the portion involving Button's, a club of 18th-century fanatics, a place to which his "friend," the sinister Wingate, pleads for him to return. The novel jumps back to 1974, and we learn the truth about Button's, Wingate, and Skipwith. The truth has something to do with spies and the CIA. Although it is possible, perhaps even likely, that this bibliographer's faculties were by this point fogged badly by a surfeit of mystery-suspense-thriller exercises, it is also possible that this novel, with its frequent tracts of tedious dialog, is as dull as it seemed and Gregory Skipwith as colorless a character as he appeared.

222. Wilson, A. N. *Wise Virgin*. New York: Viking, 1983. 186p. London: Secker & Warburg, 1982.

Giles Fox, a cynical British librarian and philologist specializing in medieval studies, loses his sight and two wives and becomes romantically involved with his research assistant. It's an interesting novel of ideas (on love) and intense characterization that quickly strays from any real concern with libraries or with Fox as a librarian. Nevertheless, Wilson organizes this comic if not especially funny story with admirable skill.

223. Wodehouse, P. G. *Leave It to Psmith*. London: Barrie & Jenkins, 1976. 240p. London: Herbert Jenkins, 1923. New York: Burt, 1924. (Many editions.)

Leave It to Psmith is typically hilarious Wodehouse fluff. Miss Eve Halliday comes to Blandings Castle to catalog the large private library presided over by "that amiable and boneheaded peer," the Earl of Emsworth. Miss Halliwell proves to be attractive and cheerful, with "a general effect of valiant gaiety, a sort of golden sunniness." She is also loyal, hardworking, and smart. No wonder Blandings hanger-on Freddie Threepwood ("the human limpet") is crazy in love with her. She considers Freddie a nuisance. Aside from her positive qualities, Miss Halliwell is also in financial distress. She "invested" her last spare pounds on a horse race. Her pick, Bounding Willie, bounded to a sixth-place finish. At Blandings, she becomes involved with the entire riotous crew, including title character Psmith. Psmith immediately develops warm and tender feelings for the castle "cataloguist" and masquerades as her best friend's husband as a ruse to worm into her good graces. Ridiculous situations, preposterous characters, and language laughable by its deliberate elegance make the book an airy delight.

224. Wright, Laurali R. *The Suspect*. New York: Viking, 1985. 217p. Toronto: Doubleday Canada, 1985. (Other editions.)

Sechelt, British Columbia, librarian Cassandra Mitchell is 41 years old and has recently gone shopping for a man by advertising in the personals section of the local paper's classified ads. "Books are my work, my comfort, and my joy," read her ad. Results have proved poor to unspeakable until a response from police staff sergeant Alberg. Mitchell's involvement with Alberg runs into complications as a result of her friendship with the elderly George Wilcox, the prime suspect in the murder of an equally aged acquaintance. Alberg is investigating the case; as suspicion mounts against Wilcox, Mitchell is torn between her loyalty to her old friend and her feelings for Alberg. It's a better-than-average crime novel, thanks to good characterizations, including that of Mitchell, whose faithful attention to a friend proves more important to her than romantic desire.

225. Yates, Elizabeth. *Nearby.* New York: Coward-McCann, 1947. 276p. Chicago: Peoples Book Club, 1948.

Town librarian Miss Patch plays a minor but significant role in this story of Mary Rowen, a conscientious, liberal young teacher struggling to overcome the provincial assumptions governing her rural school in the New England community of Nearby. Miss Patch, who has been on the job for many years, embodies some contradictory values of a sort not unknown in library traditions. Her approach to librarianship leans well toward the idea of the library as a preserve of knowledge, rather than a source, and that of the librarian as guarantor of "the best" in literature and protector of her clientele's morals. To the latter objective, she goes so far as to decline to buy a copy of Thomas Hardy's great novel *Jude the Obscure*, because of what she considers some dubious conduct on the part of its characters. "In the eyes of the town fathers she was a good librarian. Culture was safe in her hands, though not dynamic."

Yet Miss Patch is by no means wholly devoted to the inertia that this view suggests. She does have "a slightly uneasy feeling at times that the library should be functional or it could not hope to receive its annual appropriation. She knew that she could not let it become a morgue, though the authors of most of its books had long since left earth's sphere of activity." Miss Patch also welcomes the opportunity to put her own perceptions to a challenge. She "was always glad to see Mary Rowen — partly because her opinions about books were invariably more stimulating than those of the villagers." Miss Patch also lobbies effectively for an increase in the library's acquisitions budget to help provide Mary Rowen's students new books, and she offers Mary some sympathetic attention when the schoolteacher's relations with some members of the community run afoul. Overall, *Nearby* is an engaging, idealistic novel populated by believable characters — including Miss Patch.

226. Yorke, Margaret. *The Small Hours of the Morning.* New York: Walker, 1975. 180p. London: Bles, 1975. (Other editions.)

Margaret Yorke's background as a library staff member shows to good effect in this blend of thriller and psychological study. Yorke takes pains to show what one of the story's ultimate victims, Cecil Titmuss, is like. He serves as an unassuming deputy librarian in the provincial English town of Felsburg. Every time he enters the building he feels a thrill, even a sense of ownership, although he is in no way a self-important man. Much of his time must go into behind-the-scenes administrative work, but he knows many of the library's patrons by name. He makes the extra effort for patrons, even delivering in person a book that an elderly and ailing woman desires. He is irritated by other staff members' rule-bound officiousness, yet he is extremely patient, a quality revealed in his hobby of building models of famous cathedrals with matchsticks. At home, he revels in reading to his two young children, whom he adores; he likes to assume the personalities of the characters in such books as *The Wind in the Willows*. He is a kind man and a capable librarian. "He thought himself a happy and fortunate man." And so he seems to be. One of the strengths of this novel, advertised as a thriller, is that it shows how the effects of criminal acts ricochet wildly, damaging the lives of those who would at first glance appear to be quite immune to them. Titmuss proves to be one of these individuals, as does a socially awkward young woman who, she believes, wishes only to protect the librarian's happy family life when she learns that his wife is having an affair with a taxi driver. Yorke demonstrates a grasp of human folly and sorrow considerably beyond that suggested in the routine thriller, and achieves here a story that sustains suspense while provoking genuine pity for those caught up in events they cannot control and emotions they cannot understand.

II. Short Stories

227. Amis, Kingsley. "Moral Fibre." In his *My Enemy's Enemy*. Harcourt, Brace, World, 1963, pp. 119–148. *Esquire* 51 (March 1959): 114+ (Other sources.)

Reference librarian John Lewis and his wife, with the intervention of a social worker, take on a part-time cleaning woman, 19-year-old Betty. Betty may not be precisely "fallen," but she is "inadmissably inclined from the perpendicular." The social worker, an unbearable, officious bore, contends that Betty's problem is a lack of "moral fibre."

A very funny story initially, "Moral Fibre" evolves into John's serious reflection on the conflict between "doing good" for (or to) people and the basic human need for freedom. The story is better when it's being funny. The dialog is sharp, and John's conversations with Betty are particularly so. She, by the way, leaves the housekeeping trade and assumes a lucrative position as a prostitute down by the docks. She urges John to visit: "You ought to come down there one night and have a couple of drinks and a bit of fun."

John Lewis, witty and thoughtful, is not seen at work, though when Betty asks if he's "still working down that old library," he assures her that, yes, he "gives them a hand" occasionally.

228. Anderson, Poul. "Wolfram." In his *Homeward and Beyond*. Garden City, N.Y.: Doubleday, 1975, pp. 153–158. First publication.

Karl Georg Johann Friedrich Augustus Wolfram is court librarian to the margrave of Oberhaus-Blickstein, "or whatever the place was called." He presides over a collection of "astoundingly unimportant books and documents" and works at cataloging them. His social standing enables him to mix with the local intellectuals. Outwardly, Wolfram is staid and ordinary. Among his conservative virtues were that "he did not make financial speculations, frequent the taverns, or pinch servant girls." In his other life, he is a mineralogist, discoverer of wolframite, a composer, a folklorist (if an inept one), and a scintillating correspondent. He exchanges letters with such eminent scientists as Linnaeus and Lavoisier. A good-humored imaginary biography.

229. Angoff, Allan. "A Matter of Character." *North American Review* 248 (Dec. 1939): 345–365.

Leo Concannon, head of the local public library's periodical department, has always been a cooperative and accommodating sort in his relations with the public. He has over three decades in library service and is well respected by other library staff as well as by the public. He does sometimes bore his subordinates a bit with his reminiscences about his brief fling with theatrical work in New York City some years earlier, when he shared an apartment with a young actress for a few months.

One day an old friend from New York visits Leo. Thrown into a fit of regret by recalling the lost opportunities of his life in the big city, Leo takes his unhappiness out in uncharacteristic ill treatment of his patrons: "The whole bunch of you in here are a bunch of loafers," he informs his reading room habitués. The library director calls him on the carpet (literally) and delivers an humiliating upbraiding. Leo's career seems on the verge of disintegration. The story does concern a matter of character, but the character that is wanting is the library director's, not Leo's. The director, who has "the ease and deliberate manner of an old librarian of the upper strata," cannot understand the reaction that an old emotional disappointment can provoke when suddenly stirred, even many years after the fact. It's an effective story; the reader readily sympathizes with Leo.

230. Armstrong, Charlotte. "The Case for Miss Peacock." In *Ellery Queen's Crime Carousel: 21st Annual.* New York: NAL, 1966, pp. 1–13.

Miss Mary Peacock, a retired librarian from Philadelphia, is window shopping on a California street when a shopkeeper accuses her of robbing her that morning at gunpoint. The balance of this amusing little story shows how Miss Peacock, who lives quietly and alone, nevertheless has made a significant, positive impression on many of the people in her neighborhood.

231. Asimov, Isaac. "What's in a Name?" In his *Asimov's Mysteries.* Garden City, N.Y.: Doubleday, 1968, pp. 40–56. London: Rapp & Whiting, 1968. Published as "Death of a Honey-Blonde" in *Saint Detective Stories* 5 (June 1956): 110–125. (Other sources.)

One of two pert "girl librarians" at the Carmody University Library has been murdered with cyanide. Suspicion focuses on the dead librarian: Did she mistakenly poison herself with a cup of tea intended for her co-worker as a result of a conflict over a boyfriend? Asimov describes the two librarians as "fixtures like bookshelves," scarcely noticed by the patrons. The plot turns on the presumed familiarity a chemistry librarian would have with the Beilstein organic chemistry encyclopedia, but from the point of view regarding librarians' images, the story is one more example of the diminution of the job. The librarians, after all, are "girls" and blend in so thoroughly with their setting that they are almost invisible.

232. Austin, Josephine. "Miss Cynthia's Last Night." *Wilson Library Bulletin* 14 (June 1940): 764+.

Austin, herself a librarian, is forthright in her stereotyping: "Miss Cynthia was an old maid," reads her first sentence. In spite of the unfortunate opening, this little story of a veteran librarian's last night on the job before retiring is nicely written and rather touching. Miss Cynthia (who does not receive the courtesy of a last name) has spent 35 years as librarian of Vicksburg, a small midwestern town. She has handpicked her successor and now reads encomiums to herself in the local paper. She goes through the old, familiar routine of her closing duties with "a sense that in some glorious unpredictable manner" life would bring much to her that she has not already claimed from it. Embarkation for Cynthia upon retirement is the end of a way of life, but her outlook suggests that it is the beginning of another that will also prove rewarding.

233. Babel, Isaac. "The Public Library." In his *You Must Know Everything: Stories, 1915–1937*. New York: Farrar, Straus & Giroux, 1969, pp. 17–20. London: Cape, 1970.

One of Babel's earliest works, "The Public Library" first appeared in a Petrograd newspaper. Not really sufficiently developed to warrant designation as a story, the piece is nonetheless an interesting character sketch. The narrator observes the denizens of the local library, from students enjoying deferments from military service to a "worn out" old Jewish man who dozes at his table, to a loud middle-aged woman "frankly and ecstatically voicing her astonishment at the printed word and engaging her neighbors in conversation." As for the librarians, or "the assistants," as Babel refers to them, "they are dowdily dressed and extremely thin.... Altogether, they have been debilitated by books, by not being able to have a good yawn every now and then."

234. Bacon, Josephine Dodge Daskam. "A Little Brother of the Books." In her *Whom the Gods Destroyed*. New York: Scribner, 1902, pp. 159–187. Freeport, N.Y.: Books for Libraries, 1970. *Scribner's Magazine* 32 (Oct. 1902): 400–407.

Treacly sentiment suffuses this story of Jimmy, the little crippled boy who makes himself indispensable in the town library. Miss Watkins ("I am Miss Watkins, the new librarian, and when I give an order here it must be obeyed") first finds Jimmy, a lad of ten, perhaps, sitting in the closed stacks with a volume of mythology. She sends him packing, crutch and all, into the reading room. She is professionally aghast when she learns that her predecessor permitted Jimmy routine access to the stacks, and, worse, actually allowed him to assist in readers' services, selecting books for the patrons. Miss Watkins' sense of propriety weakens in the glow of little Jimmy's sweet temperament and ready helpfulness. There isn't a dry eye in the library when "the poor little feller" succumbs to scarlet fever, allegedly contracted from contact with a book taken from a sick room.

Jimmy, by the way, shows some penchant for censorship: he refuses to let an adolescent borrow work by Poe, convinced that the youth's aim is to scare his little sister silly with it.

235. Beeman, Robin. "A Parallel Life." In the author's *A Parallel Life, and Other Stories.* San Francisco: Chronicle Books, 1992, pp. 1–55. (First publication.)

The narrator is a reference librarian in the Walnut Grove, California, public library. She likes her work: "It's funny how much I like the job." At 39, she's married with two children. Her husband Bill is a gentle mathematician whom she claims to love, but during their marriage she has been through a half-dozen affairs. Bill hasn't a clue to her extramarital activities: "It had never occurred to Bill that I might have a parallel life." Her current affair, conducted during her lunch hour, is with Jack, an insurance salesman with whom she has "nothing in common but our time together and a certain bald lust."

The origin of her approach to marriage seems fairly evident in her father's behavior. He moved out when she was ten, leaving her, her mother, and her sister behind to pursue his own indulgences. At one point in the story, she stumbles upon him trying to put the make on a young woman outside a bar. It is an unseemly discovery, yet she rationalizes her own faithlessness with some facility: "If you live in a big city, you could probably spend more time looking for a parking space than I spend in these trysts."

When Jack's wife receives a cancer diagnosis, he becomes both increasingly despondent and increasingly dependent on the narrator. Apparently overwhelmed with the burden of what has become a very gloomy affair, she yields to illness herself, at least long enough to revert to a childlike status for a brief time.

There is a bit too much of the obvious to the story (like father, like daughter), but the narrator's observations are not without interest or acuity, particularly her concluding remark: "We don't need to know everything."

236. Bellow, Saul. "Him with His Foot in His Mouth." In his *Him with His Foot in His Mouth, and Other Stories.* New York: Harper & Row, 1984, pp. 1–59. *Atlantic Monthly* 250 (Nov. 1982): 114–119+. (Other sources.)

Professor Shawmut, a 60-year-old music historian living in exile in Vancouver, British Columbia, narrates this story, which comprises a long letter to Carla Rose. Miss Rose is a retired librarian living in Orlando, Florida. Shawmut offended her some three decades earlier. He recreates the scene at Ribier, a New England college where he first taught in the 1940s. There he made a ghastly wisecrack to Rose one day in front of the library in response to an innocent compliment she paid him. "The nasty little community" of the college was soon in a state of mirth over Shawmut's cruel remark. Rose was "a pale woman with thin arms" who was "never pretty." Yet Shawmut does not think ill of her: "Allow me to presume," he writes, "that you are old-fashioned enough not to be furious at having led a useful life." He uses his idea of Rose (who may quite possibly never think of Shawmut and may also never see his letter) as a sounding board for the selective story of his life, a life rich with unfortunate, spontaneous quips. That Carla Rose appears but very briefly in the story yet serves as the means for the entire tale's unfolding is curious and a neat bit of technique by Bellow.

237. Belzer, Sophia. "The Substitute Librarian." *Wilson Bulletin for Librarians* 11 (Oct. 1936): 102, 103.

The substitute librarian in the branch, Miss Eckhardt, is "a timid maiden lady" whose presence is dour and appearance severe. The restless adolescents in the library on a June evening feel her eyes on them, eyes "hard and dry like a stick pointed at them." Eckhardt is unhappy with herself and cannot understand why she cannot get along better with the library's young visitors. At one point she orders some unruly youths out of the library and is nearly amazed when they obey her. She returns to her seat, where "she took up her tools like one in a good dream," to slip books and file the day's circulation. Poor Eckhardt manages material things well; human beings seem too much for her. The story's reinforcement of negative stereotypes is mitigated by references to the regular librarian, Miss Donohue, as exuberant, energetic, and with a "ready Irish wit." No doubt her patrons will be happy to see her return.

238. Berriault, Gina. "Who Is It Can Tell Me Who I Am?" In her *Women in Their Beds: New and Selected Stories.* Washington, D.C.: Counterpoint, 1996, pp. 15–33.

Alberto Perera, a librarian nearing retirement, is responsible for book selection in poetry and literary fiction in the San Francisco Public Library. He is a librarian "who did not look like one," with his Borsalino hat, his Bogart raincoat, his English boots, and his black silk shirt. He lives in the Tenderloin district among addicts and prostitutes. One day a homeless man engages him at his desk in discussion of a poem; another day, the same man argues with him about staying the night in the library. The man is ill with tuberculosis; in the end, his death leaves Perera stunned, attempting to sort out the vagrant's legacy. It's a good story, with Perera a librarian of ambiguous and arguable qualities.

239. Betts, Doris. "Miss Parker Possessed." In her *Gentle Insurrection, and Other Stories.* New York: Putnam, 1954, pp. 197–223. London: Gollancz, 1955.

Forty-year-old town librarian Miss Agnes Parker is "possessed by a devil." Alone in the stacks, she confides to the silent shelves, "I really am quite mad." She fears that she will "do all sorts of horrible things," and has "scandalous thoughts" about library council member Mr. Harvey. She is "possessed," one gathers, by an internal uprising of her long-suppressed self. She yearns to breathe freely and to run wild, especially where Mr. Harvey is concerned. After nearly 20 years on the job, her patience with the stale pace of the town's life and her place in it has nearly run dry. She can no longer bear the meetings of the book club; she has caught herself about to do "absolutely monstrous things" during its gatherings. At one point, she feels overwhelmed during a library council meeting and rises to demand the addition of a good sex manual to the collection. "'Sex,' she croaked between clenched teeth" but is thought to be saying "sick." Someone brings her a glass of water.

Although occasionally very funny in its opening pages, the story shifts its tone. A long and not-at-all-funny passage midway through illuminates the parched confinement of Parker's life, as well as her sorely limited grasp of her professional existence. The story takes a hard turn to the sorrowful when Miss Parker overhears council members' remarks about her before a meeting. Her bewilderment and disillusionment are most affecting, and Betts does a good job of softening the reader's defenses with the story's initial comical effects.

240. Blochman, Lawrence G. "Murder Walks in Marble Halls." In *Chapter & Hearse: Suspense Stories About the World of Books.* Edited by Marcia Muller and Bill Pronzini. New York: Morrow, 1985, pp. 103–169. *The American Magazine* 134 (Sept. 1942): 121–139.

A murder in the New York Public Library's south reading room causes a stir. The dead man, a trustee of the library, clutches a fragment of paper bearing cryptic writing. Shortly afterward, a young library assistant turns up dead on the stairs. The mystery's solution owes much to librarian Phil Manning, who displays not only a gift for detection but physical courage. The story is, however, a little short on characterization and a little long on explanation.

241. Borges, Jorge Luis. "The Book of Sand." In his *The Book of Sand.* New York: Dutton, 1977, pp. 117–122. London: Lane, 1979. *New Yorker* 52 (Oct. 25, 1976): 38, 39. Translation of the title story in *El Libro de Arena.* Buenos Aires: Emece, 1975.

A man, evidently a librarian, retired from the Argentine National Library, receives a caller at his door. The caller specializes in Bibles but also offers the librarian a marvelous tome, the *Book of Sand,* which has neither beginning nor end. Indeed, it is impossible to find the first or last pages of this book. The librarian becomes a "prisoner of the book," so obsessed is he with its fantastic properties. He devises a simple scheme to rid himself of "the obscene thing," a scheme that will inevitably leave it in some other victim's hands, perhaps with terrible consequences. The stark, brief economy of the story stands in contrast to its flirtation with eternity, an idea also essayed in Item 242.

242. ____. "The Library of Babel." In his *Ficciones.* New York: Grove, 1962, pp. 79–88. London: Weidenfeld & Nicolson, 1962. Translation of

"La Biblioteca de Babel." In the author's *Ficciones*. Buenos Aires: Emece, 1956. (Many sources.)

This 1941 story, an exhilarating depiction of the universe as a library (or the Library, as Borges calls it), both dazzles and baffles with its language and ideas. There are librarians here ("I know of a wild region whose librarians repudiate the vain superstitious custom of seeking any sense in books"), but they seem to be less the managers of a bibliothecal realm than clueless scouts situated at random points in an infinite terra incognita: "There are official searchers, *inquisitors*. I have observed them carrying out their functions: they are always exhausted." More than enduring a long afternoon at the reference desk, they pass their time in eternity: "the Library will last on forever: illuminated, solitary, infinite, perfectly immovable, filled with precious volumes, useless, incorruptible, secret." The librarians here are shadowy servants of a world of knowledge beyond knowing. It's an amazing tale. (Borges was for a number of years director of the National Library of Argentina.)

243. Boucher, Anthony. "QL696.C9." In *Chapter and Hearse: Suspense Stories About the World of Books*. Edited by Marcia Muller and Bill Pronzini. New York: Morrow, 1985, pp. 223–239. *Ellery Queen's Mystery Magazine* May 1943: 16–28. (Other sources.)

This World War II–vintage story relies on the concern about fifth columnists in the United States for the basis of its plot. It seems that sinister agents are using a sleepy Los Angeles Public Library branch as a drop-off point for coded messages. The murder on the job of branch librarian Miss Benson leads the authorities, with the help of a down-on-his-luck-but-still-brilliant ex-cop, to crack the case. The most important clue is the Library of Congress call number that composes the story's title. It's a tidy little mystery, with a red herring or two for the reader's pleasure, along with a junior librarian who might better have stuck to her legal profession.

244. Bradbury, Ray. "Exchange." In his *Quicker Than the Eye*. New York: Avon, 1996, pp. 207–219. (First publication.)

Miss Adams has worked as a small-town public librarian for 40 years, and she is tired. The whole business is, "All in all, too much." Shortly after closing one evening, a man in military uniform begs entry to the library. Recalling him from years before, Miss Adams admits him. He was a favorite patron as a boy; she still has the stamped book cards from the books he borrowed so long ago. "Librarians save everything," she says. He tells her that because of the kind treatment she gave him as a child, including her leniency in letting him use the adult section, he used to think of her as Mrs. God. Adams helps her visitor reclaim his past, and, as she does so, loses some of her own fatigue. It's a gentle story and a good one.

245. Breen, Jon L. "The Dewey Damsel System." In his *Hair of the Sleuthhound: Parodies of Mystery Fiction*. Metuchen, N.J.: Scarecrow, 1982, pp. 50–52. *Wilson Library Bulletin* 45 (April 1971): 770–771.

This first of the author's many contributions to the *Wilson Library Bulletin* reads now, he notes in the Scarecrow volume, "like a Sam Spade radio show"—close enough. The story, a flyweight parody, puts librarian and private investigator Ev Millweedy ("How many private investigators are there with library-science degrees?") on the case regarding stolen pages from a library's rare-book room. The culprit proves to be a library staff member. It's mildly amusing and thoroughly silly. Breen, by the way, has been a diligent bibliographer of crime and legal fiction, in such books as *What About Murder? A Guide to Books About Mystery Detective Fiction* (Scarecrow, 1981), and *Novel Verdicts: A Guide to Courtroom Fiction* (Scarecrow, 1984).

246. Brewster, Elizabeth. "It's Easy to Fall on the Ice." In her *It's Easy to Fall on the Ice: Ten Stories*. Ottawa: Oberon, 1977, pp. 45–56. Also in *Stories from Atlantic Canada*. Edited by Kent Thompson. Toronto: Macmillan of Canada, 1973.

"It's Easy to Fall on the Ice" is an effective treatment of a character chafing at routine but not fully awake to the fact. Margaret Estabrook is a cataloger in a Canadian government library in a large city. She's 39 and keeps careful track of her weight (113 pounds) and the encroaching lines on her skin. The story follows her through a single, ordinary day, in almost cinema verité fashion, moving from one banal moment to another. She has a dull breakfast, puts on old clothes to contend with the dust from construction in the library, has a tedious conversation with her gossipy, none-too-bright secretary, and closes the day with routine relief in the arms of her lover. The moment that sharpens the entire story comes early, when Margaret is waking up that morning from a dream involving a vacation on the moon. There is a strong sense that although present, Margaret is not really here.

247. Brown, Gladys A. "Come Back with Me." In *Anthology of Best Short-Short Stories*, Vol. 5. Edited by Robert Oberfirst. New York: Fell, 1957, pp. 212–214.

Cora, a librarian, narrates this account of her decision to move to California after her mother's death. She spent many years caring for her invalid parent and denied herself numerous opportunities. She intends to leave her apparent lover, Jim, and does, at least temporarily. It's told in a curiously flat, emotionless tone, until the story's final paragraph, which gives the whole piece a wrenching twist that brings Cora's unhappiness into sharp relief.

248. Burns, Grant. "A Note from Sonora Sector." *Library Journal* 109 (June 1, 1984): 1096–1098.

The unnamed narrator is a college librarian attending the ALIAS (American Library and Information Assimilation Society) annual meeting in Aspen-Co, Sonora Sector. It is sometime in the 21st century. Federal law controlling print materials is strict; those who break them may find themselves "mind-vacked." Much of the story concerns the background of the present regime. War, environmental disaster, and economic upheaval have fractured the nation. The narrator lives a double life: He's also a low-level player in the underground movement against the Feds and their authoritarianism. He has an ally in Sheila L., a village librarian from Dakota Sector, with whom he exchanges banned 20th-century books. The story's pessimism finds some relief in its streak of black humor and hope for a future that will eclipse the dreary present.

249. Butler, Ellis P. "The Gnat." *American Magazine* 107 (Feb. 1929): 28–31+. *World's Best Short Stories of 1930.* Edited by Paul Palmer. New York: Minton, 1930.

Miss Mary Gatlett is the librarian in the Denton Public Library, a building erected thanks, as far as the public knows, to the late Japheth Strone's philanthropy. Gatlett, now in her 40s, was assured a lifetime position as librarian-in-chief by the terms of Strone's endowment. Her salary is $4,000 a year, a large sum in 1929. She earns it through effective service highlighted by her knowledge of the whole town's reading tastes. In an amusing way, and without knowing it, she owes her post to the town's most pitiful case, Flin Werster. In his lifetime, Flin had only one good memory, that of ten-year-old Mary Gatlett rushing to his aid when he was being beaten by schoolyard bullies. He worshipped Mary from then on, in obscurity. Acting on his gratitude, Werster, like an annoying gnat, pestered Strone into building the library and installing Mary Gatlett in the librarian's office. It's light stuff but worth it for the illustration of brave little Mary stepping in to thrash the bullies.

250. Campbell, Ramsey. "The Enchanted Fruit." In his *Demons by Daylight.* Sauk City, Wis.: Arkham House, 1973, pp. 128–141. London: Star, 1975.

Derek, a Catholic librarian in his late 20s, is taking a week off from work to move into his new flat. Shortly before attending a housewarming party organized by his new acquaintance, Janice, he goes for a drive in the nearby country. There he finds in a remote glade a tree bearing a strange and wonderful-tasting fruit. He returns to town with plans to revisit the tree. Over the next few days, he finds himself feeling increasingly out of sorts; food becomes repellent, all of it bearing the rank flavor of decaying fruit—the fruit of the tree in the glade. Derek decides that his distress can be corrected through the rite of communion. Indirectly, perhaps, it is. A strange but interesting story by this British master of psychological horror, it is concerned with the ability to identify with another's pain (a capacity Derek may need to enhance) and with the importance of finding salvation not in the ethereal but in other human beings.

251. _____. "In the Shadow." In his *The Height of the Scream*. Sauk City, Wis.: Arkham House, 1976, pp. 193–201. London: Star, 1981.

The male narrator, evidently an assistant librarian, has little time to prepare the Halloween show for his young audience in the public library. Anxious about the quality of his production, he ad-libs a story as he casts shadows in the light of a film projector. The shadow play goes dreadfully wrong. Far from an artistic success, it scares the children badly, as the librarian's earnest efforts are swallowed by one of Campbell's characteristically insidious manifestations of evil. The narrator seems (and there needs to be a little emphasis on that verb) an innocent tool of the dark force. His supervisor, branch librarian Mrs. Sim, is a dark enough force herself. When the narrator asks her permission to do the shadow show for the youngsters, she reveals her sensitive management technique: "So long as they don't disturb anyone else, I don't care what you do." She also "glowers" at children coming in for the show — a sweetheart!

252. Canfield, Dorothy. "Avunculus." In her *Hillsboro People*. New York: Holt, 1915, pp. 209–231. London: Cape, 1915. *Everybody's Magazine* 20 (Feb. 1909): 259–270.

J. M. Atterworthy has been the librarian of Middletown College for four decades, almost from the day he completed his studies there. He lives in three rooms in the library tower and has passed a life of quiet scholarship. He fears, however, that he has missed out on something, somewhere. On a summer vacation trip to his old hometown, an errant baseball fells him, and he recuperates in his childhood room, now part of a house shared by several immigrant families. Over some weeks, "Old J.M." becomes a trusted member of the families. He becomes an "uncle" to their rag-tag gaggle of children. He adjudicates their games; he arranges for one of the girls to attend a school of design; and he ultimately takes back to his college a Russian immigrant youth. It's a thoroughly sentimental tale of a reclusive man's blossoming into the world of human fellowship through healthy exposure to the working class.

253. _____. "Hillsboro's Good Luck." *Ibid.*, pp. 187–206. *Atlantic Monthly* 102 (July 1908): 131–139.

In the town of Hillsboro, tucked away in the Green Mountains, there had always been a public library. It was a humble affair, though, with a haphazard collection and without a librarian. One day a rich businessman stumbled upon the scene. Eager to do good, he blessed the village with the funds for a new library building and a librarian "in perpetuity." The librarian proves to be a Miss Martin, fresh and crisp from Albany. She wears fashionable dresses and performs her job with "missionary fervor." She sets out "to practice all the latest devices for automatically turning a benighted community into the latest thing in culture." Miss Martin's estimation of the villagers does not augur well for her tenure in the library. In short order she alienates, offends, or bewilders every would-be reader in town, child or adult, with her rigid notions of what constitutes effective library practice. It is a fitting finale that the library goes up in flames, inadvertently torched by the building's drunken janitor. Martin lights out for more familiar territory, to marry "the assistant to the head of the Department of Bibliography in Albany." The Hillsboro dwellers return gladly to their benighted ways. It's a funny story with some sharp edges; the villagers fare little better, and perhaps worse, than Martin in Canfield's satire. The story may not stand close comparison with some of Mark Twain's skewerings of provincial ways, but it is somewhere in the neighborhood.

254. Chappell, Fred. "The Lodger." In *The Year's Best Fantasy and Horror: Seventh Annual Collection.* Edited by Ellen Datlow and Terri Windling. New York: St. Martin's, 1994, pp. 116–130. First published as a chapbook: West Warwick, R.I.: Necronomicon, 1993.

"The Lodger" is a wonderfully funny story in which a librarian fights off the soul of a deceased poet. Robert Ackley, a connoisseur of arcane literature, is a young cataloger with a North Carolina university. He awakens one morning after reading the work of a "marginal versifier" from Cleveland, one Lyman Scoresby, with a terrible craving for nicotine — an odd feeling for a nonsmoker. The craving is a harbinger of Scoresby's attempt to take over Ackley's life; he has already taken up lodgings in Ackley's mind. Ackley spares himself no anguish in trying to drive the Cleveland poet from his head. His tactics include consumption of copious quantities of beer, junk food, and junk reading, and close attention to televised dreck (from sitcoms to C-Span). From there he moves on to immersion in ghastly contemporary poetry, followed by current literary criticism of the most pompous, incomprehensible, and jargon-laden sort. The results of Ackley's campaign against his unwelcome guest within are outrageously ironic.

The story does contain a technical blunder: Ackley's assignment is the "recataloging" of books in the library to prepare them for inclusion in the facility's long-awaited online system. The transfer of catalog information from paper to machine-readable form does not entail recataloging — a mildly annoying hiccup in an otherwise delightful story.

255. Chilson, Robert. "Written in Sand." In *Isaac Asimov's Worlds of Science Fiction.* Edited by George Scithers. New York: Dial Press/Davis, 1980, pp. 74–89. London: R. Hale, 1983.

It is not altogether clear whether the main character here is a librarian. Let us assume so, however, for what he does is what a librarian would do, if it were possible to return in time to ancient Egypt to oversee the salvaging of thousands of volumes from the great Library of Alexandria. The story describes 21st-century bookman Paul Enias's ten-year sojourn in the past, where he assumes a Grecian identity in the course of attempting to spare for his own time the volumes that would otherwise have been lost forever. One can only wish that it were possible!

256. Chizmar, Richard T. "Like Father, Like Son." *Ellery Queen's Mystery Magazine.* March 1997, pp. 78–83.

A middle-aged county librarian in Pennsylvania reflects on his family's once-happy life since gone to pieces. His mother is dead, his siblings scattered, and his father is a lifetime guest at the state pen. The librarian knows that some folks in the community believe him as addled as his father, "spending all that time in a house full of stinky old cats. Just like some blue-haired spinster." But he has no regrets, and when he feels his "family" gather around his ankles, purring, he claims that he has "all the answers I'll ever need."

257. Dabrowska, Maria. "Miss Vincent." In *Russian and Polish Women's Fiction.* Edited by Helena Goscilo. Knoxville: University of Tennessee, 1985, pp. 282–302.

In this story written in 1929, Polish author Dabrowska portrays two librarians of polar opposition. Miss Vincent, the librarian in charge of a little library in an army post, has permitted "a multitude of flaws" in the library's operation. Miss Vincent is "an unusually tiny and mobile person similar to a little spider." She plays piano, dotes on her dog, and knows nothing about literature. She is garrulous, vague, and indifferent to the demands of her work. Natalie Sztumka, a supervisor from the central administration, has come to step in and help Miss Vincent clean up the mess in the library. Natalie is sharp, efficient, and task oriented. Miss Vincent tests Natalie's self-control to the maximum with her rambling, self-centered, and pointless observations. During her review of Miss Vincent's frightfully inept work, Natalie's attitude shifts from anger and contempt to pity. Her experience with Miss Vincent seems to lead her to a reconsideration of her attitude toward humanity at large: The helpless stumbling of men and women deserves not condemnation, but sympathy and even sorrow. It's a well-written tale; the reader will identify readily with Natalie's offended sense of professional propriety, as well as with her internal struggle with her evolving perceptions of Miss Vincent and the inevitable haplessness of human endeavor for which Miss Vincent stands.

258. Deagon, Ann. "Reading the Chocolates." In her *Habitats.* University Center, Mich.: Green River, 1982, pp. 95–101.

Miss Grover, in the neighborhood of 50 or so, has been systematically stealing books from the college library. Most were published in the late 1920s. Associate librarian Mr. Stromberg seems to be suspicious of her; at one point, he follows her partway home in his car. He pleads a "mutual interest" in books and asks to visit her house. There he interviews her, ostensibly for an article on her effort to restore the house and its contents to a condition contemporary with the time her father committed suicide. As he takes notes, she feeds him chocolates. Mr. Stromberg does discover a great many of the library's books, but by the time he does, it hardly matters. Another librarian-as-victim tale, this one has a definite pulp-fiction air about it.

259. De Camp, L. Sprague and Fletcher Pratt. "No Forwarding Address." In their *Tales from Gavagan's Bar* (expanded edition). Philadelphia: Owlswick, 1978, pp. 65–74. New York: Twayne, 1953. (Authors' names in reverse order on the Twayne edition.)

Keating, a public library reference librarian, recounts in a neighborhood bar a tale about Laban Mestor, "one of the most wonderful reference librarians in the world on history or geography, or language or philosophy." The odd thing about Mestor is that the duration of his various sojourns, including a whaling voyage to Greenland and life among the Tlingits, adds up to over 200 years. It's an amusing story, well told by both the authors and Keating.

260. Derleth, August W. "The Sandwin Compact." In his *Mask of Cthulhu*. Sauk City, Wis.: Arkham House, 1958, pp. 99–129. New York: Ballantine, 1971. *Weird Tales*, Nov. 1940. (Other sources.)

For the reader in the mood for one of Derleth's rococo horror tales, "The Sandwin Compact" should do nicely. The narrator, Dave, is a librarian at Miskatonic University. One evening, as he sits down to supper with some fellow librarians, he receives a cryptic call from his cousin, Eldon. Strange happenings are afoot at the Sandwin House, the old manse where Eldon and Dave's Uncle Asa live. The odd phenomena include peculiar noises, odors, and wet doorknobs. Dave shows his mettle with his prompt response to Eldon's call for help, but neither his good intentions nor his knowledge of recondite histories of evil — "I recognized the connection between Eldon's narrative and certain ghastly and forbidden accounts hidden in the library at Miskatonic University" — can save old Uncle Asa from fulfilling his end of the dreadful bargain alluded to in the story's title.

261. _____. "The Slayers and the Slain." In *The Nightmare Reader*. Edited by Peter Haining. Doubleday, 1973, pp. 277–286. In the author's *Lonesome Places*. Sauk City, Wis.: Arkham House, 1962. *Weird Tales*, Sept. 1949.

A great library houses the record of human folly and arrogance. The narrator, a periodical librarian in the Wisconsin Historical Society Library, also believes that it contains "something more ... something sentient in the very atmosphere ... something that lies in wait for sensitive souls." Working alone in the

Historical Society stacks by night — especially the newspaper stacks, with their endless, terrible record of cruelty and suffering — poses dangers far too great for the impressionable. It's a very effective story, easily read not as simply a literalistic ghost tale but as a metaphoric parable of history's crushing weight as it lies upon those sensitive to its enormities. The narrator tries but fails to protect an innocent young student from the dangers of the stacks.

262. Draper, Hal. "MS Fnd in a Lbry." In *Laughing Space; Funny Science Fiction Chuckled Over by Isaac Asimov and J. O. Jeppson.* Edited by Isaac Asimov and J. O. Jeppson. New York: Houghton Mifflin, 1982, pp. 515–519. London: Robson, 1982. *Magazine of Fantasy & Science Fiction,* Dec. 1961.

In the distant future, the great "liebury" no longer exists, nor do books, now referred to as "bx." The narrator traces the decline of a "biped civilization" overwhelmed by the written word. Attempts to control the flood with "files of files of files of files" contained in a "catalog of catalogs of catalogs" helped for a while: "Everybody now knew how to find out anything." Inevitably, a seemingly routine breakdown in the retrieval systems resisted the repair efforts of a "bibliothecal mechanic." Not even the efforts of His Bibliothecal Excellency, Mlvl Dwy Smith, solved the problem, and the dominos of this unfortunate culture began to collapse. It's fluff but fun, and anyone who has manipulated computer files will be able to identify with the plight of the helpless bibliothecal technicians.

263. Eisenberg, Frances. "The Horse in the Apartment." In *The Bear Went Over the Mountain: Tall Tales of American Animals.* Edited by Robert B. Downs. New York: Macmillan, 1964, pp. 315–332. *Story* 17 (July–Aug. 1940): 27–39.

Miss Piper, a "rather peculiar looking" public library cataloger closing in on 40, has been a confirmed animal lover her whole life, even though the animals she loves do not fully return the sentiment. Miss Piper doesn't like change, and the idea of having a whole apartment of her own frightens her. Nevertheless, circumstances lead her to a stay in a large apartment. It's a good thing it is large, for Miss Piper falls in love with a horse, a weary milk-wagon puller whom she steals and hides in her rooms. Their life together does not equal Miss Piper's dreams; for one thing, the horse enjoys only classical music on the radio, while Miss Piper prefers lighter fare. Miss Piper is a stereotype, but her emotional obtuseness over the horse is a good example of how cheap sentiment can end in hardheartedness.

264. Eliade, Mircea. "Nights at Serampore." In his *Two Tales of the Occult.* New York: Herder and Herder, 1970, pp. 1–60. Translated from the Rumanian "Nopti la Serampore."

The narrator recalls a terrifying event in Bengal that occurred when he was a university student. The event involved a Tibetan scholar and Calcutta resident, Van Manen, who was the longtime librarian and secretary of the Asiatic Society of Bengal. A Dutchman "in the second half of life," he had come to India as a youth. He had a deep grasp of the Tibetan language, as well as a taste for hard liquor and a covert inclination toward the occult. He planned to write a manual of Buddhism for the general public, and he was noted "for his kind heart and his good nature." With Van Manen and another scholar colleague, the narrator often visited a friend's bungalow at Serampore, a few miles from Calcutta. During one of the visits, an encounter with the long "dead" past thoroughly frightened all three men and left Van Manen a victim of melancholia. Van Manen seems throughout the story a confident, capable man, but he proved no match for the supernatural. It's an effective story, aided by its exotic setting. (Eliade states in his introduction that Van Manen was an actual person, Johan van Manen, a prominent Tibetan scholar in Calcutta between the world wars.)

265. Emmett, Elizabeth. "Enchantment." In *The 6th Annual of the Year's Best S-F*. Edited by Judith Merril. New York: Dell, 1962, pp. 160–174. New York: Simon & Schuster, 1961.

The central character in this fantasy is a librarian hired to catalog an estate library before its sale. "To her, books were kinder than life. She found her acquaintances, forged her friendships among the people created by man instead of God." She moves into the castle where the library is housed and soon becomes consumed in the setting's mysterious atmosphere. Lured from her workroom to a tower several floors above, she reads a book written and privately published by the late owner, and she looks in rapt wonder from a tower window at an otherworldly view. The story proceeds to illustrate a mystical bond between the librarian, who has a severe birthmark on her face, and the late owner, a deformed, gnomelike man with a brilliant mind and ideas about heaven. It's an atmospheric story that does a good job of showing how the librarian's emotionally susceptible nature yields to exotic circumstances.

266. Emshwiller, Carol. "The Circular Library of Stones." In her *The Start of the End of It All: Short Fiction*. San Francisco: Mercury House, 1991, pp. 36–46.

An elderly woman describes what she perceives to be her unearthing of a great circular library of white stones, the knowledge repository of some ancient race. Her own daughters question her pursuit, yet as she digs, she sees "the librarians dancing on the beach in front of the sacred circle of the library. And they were all old." She is convinced that the librarians meet her eyes with theirs. It's an interesting, if not altogether successful, effort to find reason in what would otherwise pass for madness, with the reason lying in women's thoughts and writings.

267. _____. **"If the Word Was to the Wise."** *Ibid.*, pp. 83–93.

In an unnamed place, the library is the most important building: "No other building is ever to be as tall or as magnificent." "Princes" guard the two safes in the library's subbasements. One safe contains the sacred laws of the library and the land; the other contains the banned books of lewd and antilibrary writings. The male narrator has devoted nearly 20 years of service as a prince of the library. Behind their backs, those in authority refer to the princes as "rats from the cellars." The wife of the head librarian bans the narrator from the book stacks of the library when she finds that he and her daughter Josephine are having an affair. The unfortunate couple dare to enter a place in the library where "the elite of the library" scorn the sacred word and live out the secrets of the forbidden safe. It's another of Emshwiller's fantasies, this one an unsettling peek into the contrast between hypocrisy and good faith.

268. Ferguson, Neil. "The Second Third of C." In *Interzone: The 2d Anthology; New Science Fiction and Fantasy Writing.* Edited by John Clute, et al. New York: St. Martin's, 1987, pp. 3–15. *Interzone* no. 19 (Spring 1987).

Roger Morse, a librarian of the future specializing in lexicography, is compiling a new dictionary for his library employers. While laboring over the second third of the c section (from cat to cozen), he becomes acquainted with a young woman, Sharon, who escorts him through her anarchic neighborhood as he does his field work. In exchange for her guidance, he brings her coffee, news, food—and books. Sharon has worked as a prostitute in exchange for books, which have become difficult to obtain. Her customers' temporary excitement is "nothing, nothing alongside the slow enduring pleasure" she derives from the books they give her. Sharon finds the scholarly Morse attractive, even though he's bespectacled, plump, rumpled, and seldom shaves. "Well, you know what they used to say," he tells her. "You don't want to judge a book by its cover!" Although Morse is literally a gentleman and a scholar (and a considerate lover as well), his boss is "a third-rate academic" who toadies to the authorities. They are not happy with Morse's field work; it costs too much. His boss orders him to abandon his careful methods. Outraged at his superior's truckling, Morse quits his job and repairs to the urban wilds with Sharon. "He had crossed a divide, exchanged the familiar babble of librarians for a wary incommunicability." To say that things do not go well from this point is not too extreme. It's a chilling story of an episode in a world too easy to imagine being real.

269. Flynn, Michael. "Mammy Morgan Played the Organ; Her Daddy Beat the Drum." In *The Ascent of Wonder: The Evolution of Hard SF.* Edited by D. G. Hartwell and K. Cramer. New York: Tor, 1994, pp. 937–966. London: Orbit, 1994.

Dr. Riessman, a physicist who specializes in ghost detection, tries to discern what it was that startled librarian Hilda Schenckweiler one dark night as she worked overtime, alone, in the old public library. The library has long been associated with tales of hauntings; the remains of its founder, Mammy Morgan, lie interred in the library grounds. Below the library driveway, the remains of 88 departed lie at rest, having been relocated from a graveyard disturbed by the library's construction. As Schenckweiler shows Riessman the grounds, she exhibits what to him seems a troubling and callous humor about death and its possibilities. Schenckweiler, however, fears that her perceptions of ghostly business may have been nothing but her imagination at work. In the climax, Schenckweiler saves Riessman's life, not from an apparition, but from a mental ghost of his own. It's ironic that a story focusing on hard science fiction — there's a lot of technical mumbo-jumbo here — should save itself as fiction through its grasp of human nature, a nature that Schenckweiler understands well.

270. Folsom, Elizabeth I. "Natural Selection." In *As We Are: Stories of Here and Now*. Edited by W. B. Pitkin. New York: Harcourt, Brace, 1923, pp. 47–72. (First publication.)

Marcia May, assistant librarian in a Chicago branch library, lives next door to a steel mill family newly arrived in the neighborhood. The Quoids are upwardly mobile, thanks to the war production going on at the mills. Larry Quoid, however, is frustrated that he cannot attract the attention of the librarian. Staring at her and striking poses on the streetcorner does not cut it with her as it does with the young women of his own class. Mrs. Quoid hates Marcia, because she represents a level of cultural attainment that is beyond her. Larry believes that Marcia has "class" and is wholly uncertain how to approach someone with that property. A powerful force draws them together in spite of their cultural differences, and, on a night when Marcia comes to warn Larry not to attend a labor rally where trouble waits, they embrace in passion. Their romance progresses. Even Larry's mother swallows her dislike of "that stuck-up girl" to please her son. But when Marcia discusses her job, Larry chuckles. "Gee, but that's funny work.... Just handing out books and taking them back again. Sort of like taking tickets at a theater, isn't it?"

The story's title says it all: It is a Darwinian tale of the propagation of, if not species, then cultures, and in the world author Folsom envisions, there can be, ultimately, no common ground but that of physical attraction between a laborer and a librarian.

271. Frank, Harriet. "The Girl with the Glow." *Saturday Evening Post* 227 (Feb. 5, 1955): 34–35+. Also in *Saturday Evening Post Stories, 1955*. New York: Random House, 1956.

Pop fiction of the girl-gets-boy genre. Hollywood Branch Library librarian and narrator Miss Baker claims that she knows "as much about life as the next person." Her main interest, however, is not in further expanding her knowledge but in landing a man. The library is not a bad place for manhunting: "Men come and go all day long through the library." Pete, a movie executive, comes into the library one day hoping that Miss Baker will be able to help him locate a woman he has seen, the character of the title's story. Miss Baker gets down to her reference business and turns over every rock in the search. Meanwhile, she laments to herself over the singleness that haunts her in spite of her not-unpleasant looks and her many accomplishments: "It's true that I might not remind a man of a water sprite, but I make a wonderful fudge cake." In the end, it could be no other way: Miss Baker's hard work to find "the girl," coupled with her selfless sincerity, gets her the man.

272. Gabbard, Gerald W. "More Things." In *Nameless Places*. Edited by Gerald W. Page. Sauk City, Wis.: Arkham House, 1975, pp. 45–50. (First publication.)

"More Things" is a little tongue-in-cheek takeoff on Lovecraftian beings that slither and drool in the dark. Much of the action in this exercise occurs in the library of Northeastern Upper South Central Texas State Teachers College. (Rah, rah, rah for old NUSCTSTC!) Two English literature students discuss the "Pale Thing That Laughs, down in the library stacks." A bibliographer who bit off a tad too much to chew, perhaps? No librarian is directly observed in the story, but the observations on libraries as redoubts of gloom make "More Things" worth mentioning here. A Miss Pinkerton, apparently a librarian, evidently keeps an eye on contraband foodstuffs in the NUSCTSTC library. One of the students jokes that the Thing would, to survive in the deep, dark stacks, have to avoid snacking "on those who might be missed: janitors, librarians, student assistant librarians, and so forth." It's passably amusing fare.

273. Gale, Zona. "The Cobweb." In *U.S. Stories: Regional Stories from the 48 States*. Edited by Martha Foley and Abraham Rothberg. New York: Hendricks House / Farrar Straus, 1949, pp. 415–429. Also in the author's *Bridal Pond*. New York: Knopf, 1930. *Atlantic Monthly* 103 (May 1909): 640–649.

In Timber, Wisconsin, a corner of the village store serves as the public library. Lissa Bard, the librarian, is habitually late for work, although "no one seemed really to care that when the librarian reached the City Library, the clock above the cheese pointed to fifteen past seven." Not long out of school, Lissa lives with her hardworking but untutored older sister, Kate. Kate resents Lissa's reputation for intelligence and scholarly ability. Kate might sweep the dust and cobwebs from the books in the library, but some of the local women laugh at her inability to remember the author of *The Pathfinder*. "She's the otherest from me that a person can be," reflects Kate on her sister. The cobweb of the title hangs from a corner above the bed where Kate convalesces from a long illness. Its fate connects directly to a moment of insight on Kate's part and a secret act that allows her to resume her formerly motherly attitude toward Lissa. Lissa Bard emerges as an admirable character, however distant her reality may be from Kate's understanding of it. It's a thoughtful psychological tale.

274. Giovanni, Nikki. "The Library." In *Brothers and Sisters: Modern Stories by Black Americans.* Edited by Arnold Adoff. New York: Macmillan, 1970, pp. 141–146. (First publication.)

"The Library" is an interesting period piece by a developing writer. A young black girl describes how she first learned of her African-American heritage in the local "Colored-Only" Carnegie library. After pleading with the black librarian for more and truer books, she follows the librarian to a secret, fantastic vault, the Black Museum, where the African-American history and future lie in books, some yet to be published. The librarian metamorphoses into an African woman with bare feet and a strange, long gown.

275. Granit, Arthur. "'Songs My Mother Taught Me That Are Not in Hamlet,' or, 'Come Into My House, Horatio! There Are More Things under the Mattress Than Are Dreamt of in Your Philosophy!'" In his *I Am from Brownsville.* New York: Philosophical Library, 1985, pp. 221–238. *Brooklyn Literary Review* 4, 1983.

In the opening pages of this story set in the 1930s in the Brownsville section of New York City, the action takes place in a Carnegie library, the First Free Public Library for Children in the World. The library "squatted there, although with great dignity, among a vast sea of tenements and an endless array of clotheslines." The narrator is in the reading room on a winter night shortly before closing when a series of voices booms out in the facility. The first claims to be that of Karl Marx, the next Lenin, followed by Stalin, Freud, and God. The librarian, an Irish hard case who will drag talkers from the room by the scruff of the neck, first assumes that the narrator, a Jewish boy, is responsible: "In the second she spent looking at me suspiciously, I knew she was deciding whether or not I had killed Christ." She finally identifies the offender, a youth practicing ventriloquism. "As the furious librarian dragged the culprit down the aisle, I realized her motive was not all books, but included the destruction of Soviet America. That was the way it was with the Irish in those days!"

276. Greenberg, Joanne. "Gloss on a Decision of the Council of Nicaea." In her *Summering: A Book of Short Stories.* Holt, Rinehart and Winston, 1966, pp. 81–97. (First publication.) London: Gollancz, 1967.

"Gloss on a Decision of the Council of Nicaea" is a fine story in which a sheltered librarian takes a moral stand and goes to jail for it. Myra, county librarian of the southern community of Tugwell, has begun giving library privileges, in violation of the local laws, to a young black man. She refuses to accept the belief that the ideas residing in the library are government property to be distributed according to racial lines. Myra, who came to Tugwell three years earlier in response to "a wildly exaggerated ad in the *Library Journal*," leaves her office one day to take even more direct action. She joins a demonstration protesting the discriminatory treatment of black readers. The story's main dramatic conflict concerns Myra's jail-cell confrontation with Delphine, the acknowledged leader of the protest group. Greenberg demonstrates a penetrating psychological awareness of both Myra, a "toy librarian in this toy white town of antimacassars and mint tea," and Delphine, whose intense anger leads her to harsh treatment of her own sisters-in-protest. The story's title refers to the connections Myra draws between ancient historical events and those of the present.

277. Howland, Bette. "Public Facilities." In her *Blue in Chicago*. Harper & Row, 1978, pp. 67–94. *Commentary* 54 (Aug. 1972): 45–55.

The unnamed narrator has taken a part-time position at the Borglum branch of the Chicago Public Library. Situated north of the Loop, the branch caters to a regular clientele of the broken-down, the aged, and the derelict. It is in this regard an inner-city library like many others. "At Borglum the level of tolerance for individual extremes was very high. It had to be — the facts were too peculiar." The narrator, who works in the reference department ("the backwater of backwaters") describes her co-workers. There seems to be no one at the branch with either real initiative or a true sense of public service. The head librarian is an authoritarian sort with a taste for assigning pointless tasks; her second-in-command is a timid soul afraid to apply for a better job. The branch's real stars, such as they are, are its elderly and down-and-out patrons, studying the *Wall Street Journal* in dreams of riches or simply coming in to escape the bitter Chicago winter. The story concludes with a closing-time scuffle between a young punk and a half-dozen of the regulars, a scuffle that would be comical were it not so pitiful. It's a believable slice of downtown library life.

278. James, M. R. "The Tractate Middoth." In his *The Ghost Stories of M. R. James*. 2d ed. London: E. Arnold, 1974, pp. 209–234. Also in his *More Ghost Stories of an Antiquary*. London: E. Arnold, 1911. (Other sources.)

Librarian William Garrett, upon his errand to retrieve a book, *The Tractate Middoth*, from the university library, suffers a mysterious "attack." He is found lying unconscious on the floor among the Hebrew materials. Garrett later reports that on his errand, undertaken for a Mr. Eldred, he saw a very disturbing patron: an old parson, with cobwebs across his face, sitting at a study table. A call number plays an important part in Garrett's pursuit of a missing will and a new life as a manor holder. It's a ghostly tale told with James's usual restraint. The library is modeled after that at Cambridge University.

279. Jemison, Karen. "Identity Crisis." *New Zealand Libraries* 38 (Dec. 1975): 310, 311. Also in *Revolting Librarians*. Edited by Celeste West and E. Katz. San Francisco: Booklegger, 1972.

"Identity Crisis" is a funny vignette set, apparently, in the 21st century, after the 2005 copyright law has left underground photocopying in the hands of a few "renegade" librarians who have "succumbed to the glamour of easy minimum wage." They use ancient copiers, "running on toner and guts." Librarian hero Ranganathan Phlox struggles to avoid entrapment by the Space Corps: "If he didn't, he might end up on Penal Colony 6, reading spine labels to retired librarians."

280. Kaufman, Sue. "Summer Librarian." In her *The Master, and Other Stories*. Garden City, N.Y.: Doubleday, 1976, pp. 18–43. London: Hamilton, 1977.

Twenty-year-old Maria, home from college for the summer, is substituting for the village librarian. It's not a demanding job, with traffic light in the little library, and it gives Maria opportunities to reflect on her past, part of it spent curled up with a book in this very library. The comfortable routine of the job is upended one day when Maria sends a group of ball-playing adolescents away from the library yard. One of them, 16-year-old Harry, develops a serious crush on her. Maria treats the young man's interest with contempt but finds herself drawn to him in spite of herself.

Maria has been able to attend college only by virtue of her determined work at part-time jobs; Harry, a bright boy from a poor family, strikes a note of sympathy in her. The story also suggests some parallels between Maria and her mother, a superficially superior woman who is secretly despondent over having to sell her home of four decades. Maria's own shaky sense of superiority to Harry collapses when they finally embrace, dangerously, in the library, as a squirrel runs crazily "across the slippery roof above their heads." The story features nice attention to character and the unspoken needs of the heart, whose protection from the elements is slippery, indeed.

281. Kees, Weldon. "The Library: Four Sketches." In his *The Ceremony, and Other Stories*. Port Townsend, Wash.: Graywolf, 1984, pp. 65–75. *Direction* 1 (no. 3, 1938): 21–31.

A cold, humorless librarian intimidates a new clerk and sees to it that a patron goes away empty-handed; a young woman chews her nails while mutilating a copy of Whitman's *Leaves of Grass*; an old man working as a library custodian refers to the head librarian, in a letter to his son, as "the meanest woman God ever let draw breth and why He dont strike her dead is a mistery to me." In the concluding sketch, a bitter librarian complains to one of her colleagues that an attractive young clerk "just better watch her step." Kees wrote these vignettes of library life — in a library where no one in his or her right mind would want to work — shortly after he began his tenure at the Denver Public Library, where he stayed six years.

282. _____. **"Public Library."** *Ibid.*, pp. 62–64. *Diogenes*, Oct./Nov. 1940.

Librarians are present chiefly by implication in this series of brief impressions, most of them statements by patrons, of public library life. Any public services librarian would obtain ironic amusement from a number of the entries revealing patron ignorance, bad taste, impatience, and moral superiority. Samples:

"'I imagine you people that work in the library have lots of time to read all the good new books.'"

"'I'm a taxpayer and a property-owner and it seems mighty funny to me that I can't get a card, just because I don't have any identification.'"

"'Why must they write such books when there's so much that's unpleasant in the world already? That's what I'd like to know.'"

283. _____. **"The Sign."** *Ibid.*, pp. 112–118. *New Mexico Quarterly* 13 (Autumn 1943): 309–313.

Libraries — and librarians — are no more immune to fixation on stupefying trivialities than are other organizations and their functionaries. Here, Miss Quivey is a recent addition to the librarian staff at a public library. She observes a number of things very "wrong" with the library but is too timid to act forthrightly on them. Instead, she bides her time, looking for the golden moment when she might bring her concerns (invariably insignificant) to the attention of her superiors. Her chief worry is the lack of a sign over a stairway to advise patrons they cannot enter the closed stacks at the top of the stairs. Kees' portrayal of Miss Quivey's agonized rumination over this sign is a fine study of the way people who cannot identify or assert control over things that matter come to obsess over the "importance" of those that do not.

284. Koger, Lisa. "The Retirement Party." In her *Farlanburg Stories.* New York: Norton, 1990, pp. 171–193. (First publication.)

Assistant town librarian Miss Lucy McKewn, 36, lives in a three-room apartment over a garage with her invalid father. While Lucy labors under the supervision of the soon-to-retire head librarian Mrs. Worsham (an opinionated nitwit who possesses "a face like a book mite"), her father sits at home cracking hickory nuts and flinging the shells all over the apartment. Lucy would gladly trade her college education for a husband and a houseful of children. Her longing for a happy family is so pathetic that when a friend gives her a picture frame for her desk, Lucy leaves in the frame the smarmy "family" scene the manufacturer installed for display purposes. Lucy's father returns her devoted care with curses and feeble attempts at physical violence. When Lucy turns to her minister for consolation, he assures her, altogether fatuously, that God "never gives us more than we can handle." Mrs. Worsham retires from her position — and Lucy seems to retire from hope. It's a fine story of frustrated longing, with a passing airplane in the final paragraph symbolizing nicely the freedom that Lucy will probably never enjoy.

285. Lang, Allen. "The Trail of the Catfish." In *To Be Read Before Midnight: 21 Stories from Ellery Queen's Mystery Magazine.* Random House, 1962, pp. 206–226. (Other sources.)

Barbara Jordan, a young readers' adviser ("that little redhead") in the public library, helps the story's hero, library detective Max Holloway. Holloway is charged with trying to retrieve at least some of the library's "missing" 100,000 volumes. Jordan is eager to help; she is "still sore about being sugar-talked out of a batch of expensive books" by a biblioklept known as "The Catfish." Soon Barbara waxes romantic over Max. "What is this strange power I have over girl librarians?" he wonders. It's hard to say, but he and Barbara nail their thief. "Girl librarians" everywhere will probably not be amused at the patronizing tone directed toward Jordan.

286. LeGuin, Ursula K. "The Phoenix." In her *The Compass Rose: Short Stories.* Harper & Row, 1982, pp. 128–134. (First publication.) London: Gollancz, 1983. (Other sources.)

Noted science fiction writer LeGuin here envisions a vignette from some anonymous civil war. An aging actress who played many roles in the now-demolished Phoenix Theater assists a young librarian injured in a library fire set by partisans in the war. Considerable ambiguity marks the story. The librarian, a brave man who very nearly lost his life trying to extinguish the fire and then saving a few books, says very little. What he does say — "Not valuable" — might apply to the books for which he nearly died or to his own life. In the end, it seems, the librarian saved the books "not because he had opinions, not because he had beliefs … but because he was a librarian. A person who looked after books. The one responsible."

287. _____. "True Love." In her *Searoad: Chronicles of Klatsand.* New York: HarperCollins, 1991, pp. 73–87. London: Gollancz, 1983.

Frances, who teaches in a library school, has been a librarian since the age of 20. In the summers she volunteers in the small library in the town of Klatsand. She loves books, almost physically. "For me, sex is sublimation. Left to itself, in its raw, primitive state, my libido would expend itself inexhaustibly in reading." When a used book dealer sets up shop nearby, Frances is drawn to him. They have a satisfying summer of what she describes as "true love," but the truth dissipates as fall approaches and as Frances learns that their true love is not exclusive. In the end, her choice of loves — reading a book until twilight — reinforces her earlier claim about herself and makes it seem quite sincere. For her, the love of books is more durable than the love of people.

288. Lesins, Knuts. "Delicate Mission." In his *Wine of Eternity: Short Stories from the Latvian.* Minneapolis: University of Minnesota, 1957, pp. 143–150.

The mission referred to in the title concerns librarian Arnis Grant's setting straight his cousin Ilmars, who has formed an evidently unfortunate attachment to an "older" woman. She's 29; he's 25. Arnis, who possesses "the cleverest brain" in the family, goes boldly (or not so boldly, perhaps) to question the woman about her true intentions. The story's ending is a bit telegraphed, but it's an enjoyable bit of froth.

289. Lewis, Lucille. "The Man Who Talked with Books." In *Crime Without Murder: An Anthology of Stories by the Mystery Writers of America*. Edited by Dorothy S. Davis. New York: Scribner, 1970, pp. 173–176. London: Gollancz, 1972. *This Week*, Jan. 1956.

Mr. Spry, a retired public librarian, owns a huge personal library. He now lives in a rooming house and hankers after a larger room able to hold his collection in comfort. All he need do is persuade Miss Pringle, whose room he covets, to move elsewhere. Mr. Spry achieves his objective in a most ironic way. It's a humorous little story portraying the librarian as clever and imaginative.

290. Lindsay, Frederic. "The People of the Book." In *Streets of Stone: An Anthology of Glasgow Short Stories*. Edited by Moira Burgess and Hamish White. Edinburgh: Salamander, 1985, pp. 90–96.

This story is one of the few works noted in this bibliography about which there is some ambiguity concerning the profession of the character at issue — librarian or not? One could make and justify either assumption here, but the story survives the cut for its observations on libraries and librarians. The anonymous character of concern was once "a tall thin boy with eyes like a hare" who performed menial tasks in a public library. At the time of the story's telling, it is 30 years later, and the boy is now a man in a quiet room, examining a book he stole from the library of his youth. "Long before he had encountered Borges, the man at the desk in the quiet room had understood the great libraries, their shells and content, as being like a human skull and what it held." He meditates on the history of libraries, including the Library of Alexandria, where "the last librarian was torn apart by a mob of religious fanatics howling for darkness." People are not worthy of "the book," he believes, but their effort gives cause for some hope. The story may be a bit more elusive than necessary, but its depiction of a young man who cherishes literature and reveres libraries as places "where the truth lived or hid and tried to survive" makes it vivid and worthy.

291. Loran, Martin. "An Ounce of Dissension." In *The Pacific Book of Science Fiction*. Edited by John Baxter. London: Angus & Robertson, 1969, pp. 27–48. *Analog Science Fiction/Science Fact*, July 1966. (Other sources.)

In a craft displaying the insignia of the Library Service, Librarian Stephen Quist travels through space, where "there was no being in the whole huge bestiary of the universe weird enough to surprise a Librarian." Quist's mission, as it is the mission of the Library Service as a whole, is to carry ideas to civilizations in want of them: "Whether a race moves forwards or backwards, to glory or to the grave, is a decision that rests with you alone," goes the Library Service mission statement. On a planet the Library Service has not visited in many decades, Quist's welcoming committee burns every book on the ship. Unflappable, Quist contacts the local underground and, with the help of his onboard computer, Bookworm, sows the seeds of dissent from the local regime's repressive rule. It's a funny departure from the stereotype of the meek, ineffectual librarian and nicely accomplished.

Maartens, Maarten. *See* Schwartz, Jozua M.W. van der P.

292. McDevitt, Jack. "The Fort Moxie Branch." In *Nebula Awards 24: SFWA's Choices for the Best Science Fiction and Fantasy 1988.* Edited by Michael Bishop. New York: Harcourt Brace Jovanovich, 1990, p. 124–139. Also in *Full Spectrum 1.* New York: Bantam, 1988.

This charming fantasy will whet any book lover's appetite. In the little North Dakota town of Fort Moxie, a struggling novelist finds in an abandoned house a library holding unknown literary works by great masters and by the unheard-of. The librarian, a young woman named Coela, explains how these books came to be here in the Fort Moxie branch of the John of Singletary Memorial Library. As in much fantasy and science fiction, the emphasis is on the idea. Character development is a distant concern, although not as distant as Coela's headquarters!

293. MacDonald, John D. "The Reference Room." In *With Malice Toward All: An Anthology of Stories by the Mystery Writers of America.* Edited by Robert L. Fish. New York: Putnam, 1968, pp. 153–157. (First publication.) London: Macmillan, 1969.

A Los Angeles hit man finds himself transported not quite intactly into the distant future. There he becomes a living (more or less) resource in a most unusual reference collection. The agent of his acquisition is, of course, a reference librarian.

294. McKinlay, Mary C. "Like a Diamond in the Sky." In *Long Night of Waiting, by Andre Norton, and Other Stories.* Edited by Roger Elwood. Nashville: Aurora Publishers, 1974, pp. 49–60.

Librarian Simon Palmer performs his cataloging chores with methodical precision. He is aloof and uninvolved with others. "He had no interest in world affairs, people's problems, or other people individually." He wants nothing from life, until the development of the wondrous Sky Homes, domiciles that drift around the earth, high in the sky. Simon craves a Sky Home, and stops at nothing, including murder, to obtain the funds to buy one. At length, he quits his librarian's post and takes a lowly job in the stock market, where he uses his library research skills to amass information that allows him to multiply his ill-gotten nest egg. It's an undistinguished story that moves to a sophomoric climax.

295. Marz, Charles. "Lucy Wallis." In his *Centerville, USA.* Freeport, N.Y.: Books for Libraries, 1971, pp. 140–155. New York: Century, 1924.

In this collection of character sketches about denizens of Centerville ("There are more Centervilles in the United States than towns of any other name," the author informs us), Lucy Wallis is the town librarian. About 30, she is "a tall girl with ruddy hair ... her cheeks were thin; her lips were pale; her eyes were handicapped by thick round lenses that struggled with astigmatism.... Her dresses were a serviceable gray." The story's focus is on an amusing exchange between Lucy and a shy young high school teacher who haunts the library. Alone in the place one day, the two discuss their high regard for serious literature — philosophy and such. They identify each other as rather special cases in a town where tastes run to popular fiction of "the lightest sort." When they part, we see them returning to their preferred books of the moment, both works of popular fiction — of the lightest sort.

296. Mattison, Alice. "The Library Card." In her *The Flight of Andy Burns, and Other Stories.* New York: Morrow, 1993, pp. 11–20. *Mississippi Review* 17 (no. 3, 1989): 75–82.

A young couple, Robert and Shelley, take their infant and their five-year-old daughter to the library to get the older child a library card. A pleasant and talkative children's librarian approves the child's card application. The real issue in the story is the ominous foreshadowing of trouble ahead between Robert and Shelley: The children's librarian appears in a sudden absurd fantasy in which Shelley imagines her carrying on an affair with Robert.

297. Miller, Alyce L. "The Nature of Longing." In her *The Nature of Longing: Stories.* University of Georgia, 1994, pp. 87–105. New York: Norton, 1995.

Mr. Farrell, the town librarian, recalls his childhood, especially the role of Cousin Pearl. Pearl, who attended college and taught for a time at an academy for "colored" women, was an artistic individual, both a superb seamstress and an accomplished classical pianist. As a boy, Farrell envied her style and grace. He is now an adept librarian who assiduously nourishes the reading of his clientele: "I have tended the minds of our town as carefully as I tend my garden." He has exercised great discretion in his homosexual relationships and lives by himself in the house where Cousin Pearl once lived. One day he finds a vile message chalked on a wall in the library; it refers to both his race and his sexuality. The message unnerves him: "The security of all the years I have lived here, respected and considered, now teeters like a pane of glass on the edge of a cliff." Most of the remainder of the story consists of Farrell's further recollections of his childhood among a group of women, especially Cousin Pearl, whose own frustrated ambition and stifled romantic hunger find a responsive chord in both the boy and the man Farrell's own soul. It's a good story of a man's review of his life and of his accommodation of his own private needs.

298. Mitchell, Silas W. "The Mind Reader." In *Representative American Short Stories*. Edited by Alexander Jessup. Boston: New York: Chicago, and other places: Allyn and Bacon, 1923, pp. 821–849. Also in the author's *The Guillotine Club, and Other Stories*. New York: Century, 1910. *The Century Magazine* 74 (Sept. 1907): 655–678.

Dr. Alston has pursued a somewhat checkered career, including a stint as a prison physician, and has developed a notable ability to read lips, which sometimes allows him to pass himself off as a mind reader. When he lends assistance to a tight-fisted old man, the elderly miser, who happens to be a board member of a large library, rewards him with a position in the library. While serving in a modest capacity as a selector of scientific books, Dr. Alston helps solve a murder. It's unexceptional fiction and wordier than necessary, but Alston's actually being given living quarters in the library itself is a perquisite that many librarians might find attractive.

299. Moore, Lorrie. "Community Life." In *The Best American Short Stories 1992*. Edited by Robert Stone and Katrina Kenison. Boston: Houghton Mifflin, 1991, pp. 162–178. *The New Yorker* 69 (Sept. 30, 1991): 29–36.

At a relatively early age, Olena Resnick, a cataloger and sometime reference librarian with a major midwestern university library, lost her parents in a car crash. Her parents' sudden death seems to have placed Olena (whose name, treated as an anagram, reads "Alone") under a lasting shadow. She is bright and witty with a nice sense of the ridiculous, but she struggles to take real pleasure in her life. Her aloofness contrasts with the empty-headed enthusiasm of her new live-in boyfriend, Nick. Nick "cavorts" with community activists, whom Olena finds "small, awful, nothing people." Nick nags her, however, to "get involved with the community." Moore builds strong reader sympathy for Olena throughout the story; Olena's willingness to submit to the cloddish Nick perplexes but does not lessen this sympathy. The story closes with a hard turn that gives insight on the reasons for Olena's distance from "the community" as well as from Nick. It's a sad and painful story, whose effectiveness owes to the author's fine character building and careful revelation of details from Olena's past.

300. Munro, Alice. "Carried Away." In her *Open Secrets: Stories*. New York: Vintage, 1995, pp. 3–51. *The Best American Short Stories 1992*. Edited by Robert Stone and Katrina Kenison. Boston: Houghton Mifflin, 1991. *The New Yorker* 64 (Oct. 21, 1991): 34–46+. (Other sources.)

Skillful choreography of characters, viewpoints, and manipulation of time mark this story of a woman's life in a small Ontario town. We meet Louisa, the adept town librarian, in World War I, when a local boy on the front becomes "carried away" in his romantic correspondence with her. Louisa is a young, well-educated woman with a taste for whiskey: "It is for my health," she explains gravely. She lives in a boarding hotel. Her reputation is not quite spotless, but "she had her life to live, like anyone else." We last see Louisa in the 1950s, long after she has set aside the library profession to help manage her husband's factory. Munro has a finely tuned sense of the failures of communication and understanding that prevail even among those who try to be sympathetic with one another. Her complex and ambiguous portrayal of Louisa, a woman who "believed in the swift decision, the unforeseen intervention, the uniqueness of fate," invites immediate rereading and discussion.

301. _____. "Hard Luck Stories." In her *The Moons of Jupiter: Stories*. New York: Knopf, 1983, pp. 181–197. Toronto: Macmillan of Canada, 1982. (Other sources.)

Julie is a children's librarian in Toronto. Married with children, she hikes and makes her own yogurt, whole-grain bread, and granola. She's an outgoing woman who volunteers for numerous public service organizations. She also suspects that she has, in the matter of love, "missed out on every kind." She and her close female friend, the narrator (a bookmobile driver), share wine and their sad stories of romance that did not happen with a male acquaintance. It's another of Munro's penetrating character studies, with a stong undercurrent of guilty sorrow over lost opportunities.

302. Munro, Hector H. "The Story of St. Vespaluus." (Pub. under pseud. Saki.) In his *The Short Stories of Saki*. New York: Modern Library, 1951, pp. 185–193. *The Complete Short Stories of Saki*. London: Lane, 1930. (Many sources.)

Vespaluus is the young nephew of a pagan king. When Vespaluus adopts Christianity, the king calls in the Royal Librarian for consultation concerning the boy's correction and, ultimately, his punishment. The Royal Librarian bears the brunt of the king's displeasure over the unsuccessful effort to return the youth to pagan embrace. The librarian, among other assaults, is struck "repeatedly and promiscuously over the head with an ivory chessboard, a pewter wine-flagon, and a brass candlestick." It's not a particularly fine story, in spite of the librarian's slapstick treatment.

303. Nicholson, Meredith. "The Susiness of Susan." In his *Best Laid Schemes*. New York: Scribner, 1922, pp. 3–33.

Vassar graduate and "accredited librarian" Susan Parker takes a position with the public library in Indianapolis. "Susie was a small human package with a great deal of yellow hair, big blue eyes, an absurdly small mouth and a determined little nose." She is energetic and prankish; a classmate once suggested that a book about her might be titled *The Susiness of Susan*. Susan identifies this "susiness" as her customary lively character. A banker and his wife invite her to a dinner party. At the party, Susan engages in both witty "susiness" and in clever recollection of material in the Vassar library that helps a young archaeologist at the party defend his claims of discovery. A certain attachment looms between Susan and the scientist. Susan's performance at the dinner is the highlight of a story otherwise marred by a fawning view of the rich and presumably sophisticated.

304. Page, Richard. "First Night." *Wilson Bulletin for Librarians* 11 (May 1937): 595, 596+.

New librarian Jane is on her first evening duty in the library. Although she is responsible for the facility, she is not apprehensive. She sings a bit to herself, "feeling wonderfully free and untrammeled." Jane deals with a number of minor patron concerns, including the necessity of showing some firmness at closing when a man rapt in his research can scarcely believe the time has fled — a nice vignette.

305. Painter, Pamela. "Something to Do." In her *Getting to Know the Weather: Stories*. Urbana: University of Illinois, 1985, pp. 47–51. *Ms.* 15 (Aug. 1986): 58–60+

A young librarian with the Boston Public Library (her next door neighbor "could never picture me a librarian, what with no glasses, all that blonde hair") tells a series of fantastic lies to her boss, her family, friends, cab driver, and everyone else she meets, the whole of it focusing on an apparently spur-of-the-moment sojourn in New Orleans. The story is an edgy blend of the comical and the cruel, with the latter winning out, leaving the impression that this anonymous librarian harbors an advanced loathing for all the commonplace details of her life. It is not merely that she feels "bored," as she claims, but angry, fed up, and on the verge of pushing everything, herself included, over the brink in this imaginative character study.

306. Palencia, Elaine F. *Small Caucasian Woman: Stories*. Columbia: University of Missouri, 1993. 158p.

Local college librarian Blanche Callicoat Long introduces and narrates several of this collection's 17 stories. Blanche decries the decline in quality of local gossip, and she seeks to correct the matter with these pieces concerning the lives of her friends and neighbors in the eastern Kentucky redoubt of Blue Valley. It's an interesting tactic by the author, who has written romance novels under the name Laurel Blake. The stories, however, many of which originally appeared in small press magazines, do not always blend well into the thematic effort. Nevertheless, in such stories as "Blanche Long Tells What Keeps Shug Watson Going," and "Blanche Long Recalls What Lee Ann Hawkins Did with Her Life," Long reveals herself to be an observant student of the local scene.

307. Parker, James R. "Ex Libris." In his *Attorneys at Law: Forbes, Hathaway, Bryan & Devore.* Doubleday, 1941, pp. 237–247.

Mr. Bethune abruptly quits his post as librarian with the Forbes, Hathaway law library after 23 years. "It was a commonplace at Forbes, Hathaway that the firm's librarian knew more law than all the senior partners put together." Mr. Bethune, in fact, has left the firm to practice law himself. His departure leaves the firm in upheaval. It's a nice satiric tale of the long-subjected achieving due justice, with a most apt quote from Don Marquis's *archy and mehitabel.*

308. Pearson, Edmund L. *The Librarian at Play.* Boston: Small, Maynard, 1911. 307p.

The title of librarian Pearson's collection of stories of library life is well chosen. It is a playful group of pieces, written with a light hand and good humor. Most of the 14 entries appeared in the author's column in the *Boston Evening Transcript,* and for the most part they hold up surprisingly well, particularly in their depiction of librarians and other library staff doing their best to maintain their composure and to serve the public in busy settings. In "By Telephone," harried reference librarian Pansy Patterson has the dubious pleasure of answering the telephone on the Baxter Public's first day of phone reference service. She receives a steady stream of ridiculous questions, wrong numbers — "Hello! How are yer for pigs' feet to-day?" — and annoyed patrons who cannot, for example, fathom why she is unable to tell them the title of that book, "quite thick," with the "bright red cover."

In "The Crowded Hour" and "By-Ways and Hedges," librarians and other staff try gamely to keep up with the public in hectic circumstances. Pearson indulges himself comically with "Their Just Reward," in which a minion of Satan leads the librarian narrator on a tour of a corner of hell reserved for abusers of books and librarians. "The Boss," notes the minion, is most proud of the space devoted to genealogists, "the folks who have driven librarians to profanity and gray hairs." The "genies" are compelled to entertain at an interminable lawn party the very ancestors, many of them revolting, they sought so hard to claim in life.

Not every piece holds up as well as the majority, but the majority are good fun, and Pearson's sensibility as a librarian genuinely interested in both books and people comes through nicely.

309. Peele, David. "The Cataloguing on the Wall." *Wilson Library Bulletin* 45 (April 1971): 772–774.

Quellery Een is "a junkie-interpreter-rakehell-author-compiler-detective" now turned librarian. He has set up in the library a DOM (dirty old man) room next to the children's corner and has appointed his father the chief of same. Inspired by his reading in the *Viking Portable Mickey Spillane*, he shoots to death cataloger Slinki Porter. Soon 15 "dames" apply for the open position, drawn by Een's fame. All of the American Library Association knows of his "erect figure, lean and sensuous hips, muscular shoulders, insolent eyes, handsome, arrogant face — this was a man to make a woman forget the Dewey rules." Some actual chuckles, as opposed to polite smiles, reside in this little satire taking off from a remark in *McCall's* about athletes not looking like librarians.

310. Phillips, Robert. "Peckerman." In *The Arbor House Treasury of Mystery and Suspense*. Edited by Bill Pronzini, et al. New York: Arbor House, 1981, pp. 519–530.

Barry Peckerman is a successful 45-year-old university reference librarian. He drives a Buick, listens to opera on FM radio, and lives happily with his wife. His name once bothered him, but he seldom thinks about it any more. His life turns upside down when he learns that a hot new rock star shares his name. When the other Barry Peckerman's single climbs to the top of the charts, librarian Peckerman finds himself besieged with bad jokes and nonsensical requests; a student even wants him to autograph the rocker's record. Through a series of ludicrous events, Peckerman's existence slides into wretchedness over the name confusion. He forgets to shave, doesn't eat, and is rude to patrons. His humor improves when he starts dealing drugs and trading in white slavery. "Every day he left the house whistling, going about his job of debauching and debasing the young." The story follows librarian Peckerman's notorious alternative career to a delightfully ironic conclusion. It's certainly one of the funniest stories noted in this bibliography.

311. Plunkett, James. "The Eagles and the Trumpets." In *Modern Irish Short Stories*. Edited by Frank O'Connor. Oxford University Press, 1957, pp. 266–296. Also in the author's *The Trusting and the Maimed and Other Irish Stories*. Devin-Adair, 1955.

"The Eagles and the Trumpets" is a bittersweet story with the emphasis strongly on the bitter. A young small-town librarian, clearly very bright but "bored to death with the town" and who admittedly has no convictions about her life or her work, meets Sweeney, a young man on holiday from his work in a stultifying office. The two find common ground, and a romance seems to be blooming, but fate deals the pair an ironic, unkind hand. The sadness is tempered somewhat by the librarian's subsequent friendship with a commercial traveler who has also known hard knocks. There is no presence of library life here, but the unnamed librarian is a strong character and the story a touching one.

312. Porter, Hal. "The Daughter of the Late Bishop." In his *A Bachelor's Children: Short Stories*. Sydney, Australia: Angus and Robertson, 1962, pp. 130–140.

The narrator, recuperating from an illness, visits an unnamed Australian city. It is a terrible town that rattles the sensitive narrator. In a public library a functionary shrieks at him, insisting that the library is for members only. From behind her counter, "smiling from a long face like a pallid kangaroo's, was the daughter of the late Bishop." The narrator strikes an acquaintance with the librarian. One night, she asks him to supper. She lives along but for her "poor invalid Jo Jo." On his last visit to the librarian's house, the narrator learns the truth about Jo Jo. Floridly overwritten, the story features a pummeling atmosphere and a librarian with whom few would care to sup.

313. Prose, Francine. "Rubber Life." *North American Review* 276 (June 1991): 44–49. Also in her *The Peaceable Kingdom*. New York: Farrar, Straus, Giroux, 1993.

The library-science student narrator works in the public library in a resort town and house sits for an absent couple. The house she tends is allegedly haunted. She reads widely, from true crime to tennis to Henry James. Her interest in a patron, Lewis, becomes pronounced. She delights in finding good books for him. Although Lewis lives with another woman, he and the narrator become lovers. The ghost in the house intervenes unpleasantly. It's an interesting story marred by a forced conclusion.

314. Sage, Victor. "Obscurity." In his *Dividing Lines*. London: Chatto & Windus/The Hogarth Press, 1984, pp. 3–11.

A small, old librarian of Austrian descent presides over a chilly English county library. The story's young narrator has come to know the librarian slightly, but not as well as the librarian knows him. When the librarian invites him to share a bottle of Guinness in a back room one rainy day, the narrator is surprised to learn that the librarian knows he is an aspiring author. "You forget," says the librarian, "I have nothing else to do, but observe my few customers." The narrator has, in fact, tried to write a story about the librarian, but the effort failed for lack of knowledge of the man. The librarian alleges that "history is made by the obscure" and goes on to illustrate his claim with an engrossing story involving himself and Sigmund Freud.

Saki. *See* Munro, Hector H.

315. Schwartz, Jozua M. W. van der P. "The Library." (Pub. under pseud. Maarten Maartens). In his *Brothers All: More Stories of Dutch Peasant Life*. Appleton, 1909, pp. 81–105.

Following a visit to Scotland, where the peasants "all read Shakespeare, Carlyle, Emerson and Burns," Hilda, a young countess, returns to Holland intent on starting a subscription library. The peasants in her neighborhood could stand some uplifting: they savor nothing literary but tales of scalded babies in the local papers. The townsfolk agree, on the advice of Churchwarden Spottle, to set aside a portion of a building for the library that Hilda assembles, provided the collection contains nothing "immoral, improper, indecent, or unorthodox."

It's a funny, sometimes biting, account of "culture" coming to the masses via the earnestness of a young, self-appointed librarian.

316. Shibaki, Yoshiko. "Ripples." In *The Showa Anthology: Modern Japanese Short Stories 2: 1961–1984.* Edited by C. Van Gessel and T. Matsumoto. Tokyo: Kodansha International, 1985, pp. 317–336.

Takako, a university librarian in Tokyo, lives with and cares for her frail and elderly mother. "As long as she lived with her mother, it seemed, she herself would never enjoy any happiness." Takako has hopes of marriage, but her three-year affair with Tamura, a young researcher, seems at a dead end. Soon after a corporate developer's agent tracks down the family to offer a million yen for some land that Takako's late father bought during World War II, Takako's fears come true: Her family falls into greedy speculation and squabbling over their windfall. Her brothers and sisters reject her belief that the money should go to their mother's nursing home care as they fantasize about the many wonderful things they will be able to buy with it. The ripples of not-so-pleasant insight following the news of the land spread to Takako herself. When she sees the lot with Tamura, she realizes that even she is infected by greed and by the self-serving nature of her own imagination. Following the lot's sale, Takako takes a gift to the agent who spent months locating the family. "She would never see him again, and for her as for him, this moment seemed very precious." A sense of quiet resolution marks the story, thanks to Takako's considerate gesture toward the agent and to what seems her innate, if not unblemished, goodness.

317. Smither, Elizabeth. "Librarians." In her *Nights at the Embassy.* Auckland, New Zealand: Auckland University, 1990, pp. 55–66.

The narrator, a public librarian, reflects on the colleagues and library science students she has known in her career. There was Sabina, who loved books, had no patience for fools, and came to work in provocative outfits. She became a missionary, then a computer programmer, "and finally a socialite in the mould of Elsa Maxwell." For reference librarian Mercedes, "It was nothing ... to answer three questions at once and flirt with a fourth. She shone through sleeplessness, migraines that would have felled others, domestic upheavals, the death of parents." Louella is prone to disaster (she is the one pinned to the floor when a range of books topples), but she is a gifted wisecracker. Mary-Jane, beautiful and strong, had a truly upright character, and Daniel, a gifted schmoozer, affected a

Groucho Marx style. There is nothing here in the way of plot, but the anecdotal, impressionistic treatment is effective. The conclusion is quite nice, with the narrator, dressed as a witch for a library promotion, experiencing a moment of rich insight.

318. Taber, Gladys. "The Legend of Lavinia." In her *One Dozen and One: Short Stories*. Philadelphia: Lippincott, 1966, pp. 184–202. *Ladies Home Journal* 73 (March 1956): 82+.

Lavinia Brewster is the town librarian; she is "slender and really lovely." She moves in with bank worker Ella May Mott, in the old Mott house, where they live "a lovely life." "They loved each other," and were "generous and gentle in all they did." When a local minister expresses romantic interest in Lavinia, she refuses to leave Ella May: "She would be lost without me," she asserts, even though it is clear that Ella May is the boss in this house. A domestic dispute between the couple leads Lavinia to move out, into marriage with the minister, and to a satisfyingly ironic conclusion. Taber skirts the question of the story's lesbian relationship, although she is probably as straightforward as she could be in a mass-market "women's" magazine from the 1950s.

319. Tanasoca, Donald. "Affair at the Square." *Wilson Library Bulletin* 28 (Dec. 1953): 364–369.

Victor Hummingbird, a New York City librarian, solves a little mystery involving a purloined copy of Henry James's *Washington Square* bearing an inscription by the author. Although Hummingbird's actions are those of a deft sleuth, his character is pale and undeveloped.

320. _____. "Honeysuckle for Hummingbird." *Wilson Library Bulletin* 26 (Nov. 1951): 233–237+.

Hummingbird is working the information desk on a wintry Sunday evening. A mystery writer referred to Hummingbird by a friend presents him with a puzzle in the form of a poem. The writer hopes to solve the puzzle before the deadline for the column he contributes to a pulp magazine. Hummingbird agrees to help and ponders the stickler during a break that takes him out into the bracing cold. He solves the puzzle in an inspired fashion, and he and his admiring client go off for a late coffee together at "a little coffee shop where they grind the coffee before your eyes."

321. Tuttle, Lisa. "Lizard Lust." In her *Memories of the Body: Tales of Desire and Transformation*. New York: Severn House, 1992, pp. 129–146.

A London librarian who loved her life of books cannot believe that it is "lost forever," that now the only words she reads are those she writes herself. She has fallen into the company of a group of — women? female creatures? — who seem to be from another world, where the possession of a lizard gives a woman power and possibilities. The librarian's only friend now is a young woman, Maggs, who herself acquires a lizard and frees the librarian from her enslavement to another lizard-bearing woman. To what end? one wonders. One wonders a good bit about this story, including why it might not have been a little more amenable to comprehension.

322. Verlaine, M. J. "Teresa Forgives Herself." In the author's *A Bad Man Is Easy to Find*. New York: St. Martin's, 1989, pp. 83–97. (First publication.)

Teresa is a plain, intelligent, and honest young woman who "knew what job she deserved: she had long planned to be, and duly became, a librarian." She is so deeply involved in her work that she mentally assigns Dewey classifications to conversations she overhears on the subway. She lives with her parents, "undated, unmarried, unloved." She is alone in New York City, where "libraries are the refuge of the lonely." An opportunity to appear briefly on television gives Teresa a surge of confidence and determination, and she starts a relationship with a workman swept away by her new bearing. The portrayal of the librarian's life is, one hopes, through Teresa's eyes, not the author's; the story is sufficiently ambiguous on that point to warrant discussion.

323. Wagar, W. Warren. "A Woman's Life." In *Afterlives: An Anthology of Stories About Life After Death*. Edited by Pamela Sargeant and Ian Watson. New York: Vintage, 1986, pp. 161–177. (First publication.)

Sixty-year-old Bess Merton, shy, reliable librarian in the suburbs for 35 years, learns that she has serious heart disease. Hesitant to accept urgently needed bypass surgery, she tells her doctor that she must get back to the library: "I'm what they call a fixture." The story's positive qualities, involving a character study of an indecisive woman facing a life-or-death decision, are hobbled by a secondary fantastic theme concerning ethereal "bats" that swoop down to appropriate the lives of the gravely ill (although without the bats, the story would not have qualified for the anthology).

324. Walker, Augusta. "The Day of the Cipher." In *Prize Stories, 1954: The O. Henry Awards*. Edited by Paul Engle and Hansford Martin. Doubleday, 1954, pp. 242–253. *Yale Review* 42 (Dec. 1952): 199–211.

Perhaps a fantasy of universal fate, perhaps a faithful record of a mind coming unhinged, this study of a librarian with problems is memorable and disturbing. Lorna works in the city library, in "a darkish hidden place" where she peruses incoming books to assist in cataloging. Other librarians pass her as she works, with their "spectacles and pencils and humped shoulders." As the story opens, Lorna seems to be succumbing to paranoia. The women in her rooming house are, she believes, deliberately excluding her from conversation; other librarians are looking at her and "seeing" what she does with the books. Convinced that she must make a break from her routine, she seeks a room in another rooming house, only to find that her prospective landlord gleefully, so it seems, humiliates her. An encounter with a young man seems to promise relief, but as the story progresses, Lorna's conviction that she is isolated, an object of observation and derision, shades into an apparent belief that she is hopelessly alone in the crowd of humanity and that others, all others, share the same alienation. Even a once-familiar street now looks strange to her. It's a story whose considerable ambiguity allows plenty of room for discussion.

325. West, Jessamyn. "The Condemned Librarian." In her *Collected Stories of Jessamyn West*. New York: Harcourt, Brace, Jovanovich, 1986, pp. 423–440. Also in her *Crimson Ramblers of the World, Farewell*. New York: Harcourt, Brace, Jovanovich, 1970. *Harper's* 211 (July 1955): 45–53.

Miss McCullars, a teacher and fairly adept amateur painter, recounts how she left teaching to return to college in Oakland, California. There she sought treatment from Dr. Louise McKay, formerly a school librarian. Dr. McKay is "this little ex-librarian, a doll of a woman." When Dr. McKay botches Miss McCullars's diagnosis, she loses her position with the college and blames Miss McCullars for deliberately obstructing her work. Miss McCullars herself feels compelled to abandon her educational plans. Dr. McKay returns to the life of a high school librarian. "Don't you love books?" asks Miss McCullars. "I had better love books," says the former doctor, who from time to time sends Miss McCullars bitter postcards to remind her of the fate for which she blames her. "We can't all escape," reflects Miss McCullars, "some of us must stay home and do the homely tasks, however much we may haved dreamed of painting or doctoring." That may be, but something in McCullars's attitude suggests that she is not particularly pained at having been instrumental in sending librarian McKay back to the stacks and the high school.

326. Wetherell, W. D. "Why I Love America." In the author's *The Man Who Loved Levittown*. Pittsburgh: University of Pittsburgh, 1985, pp. 79–94.

Rufus, an aging and angry African-American, comes to the public library to retreat from the world while he feigns reading. His pretense is persuasive, for he finds himself pressed into service in the library as a "literacy volunteer." Miss Brint, the librarian who enlists him in this task, is well intentioned but oblivious: She hasn't a clue that Rufus thinks of her as "machine tooled" and a royal pain in the backside. She inflicts an Asian couple on Rufus, trusting that he will be able to help them master English well enough to write an essay, "Why I Love America." Miss Brint's sincere idiocy is, unfortunately, not quite beyond belief. The assignment she gives Rufus blossoms in a manner both ironic and dreadful. Although Miss Brint sets things in motion, it is Rufus who carries them to ends that Miss Brint could not foresee and could probably not understand.

327. Williams, Tennessee. "Something About Him." In his *Collected Stories*. New York: New Directions, 1985, pp. 213–220. *Mademoiselle* 23 (June 1946): 168+.

Miss Rose, assistant librarian at the Blue Hill, Mississippi, public library, becomes enamored of Haskell, a store clerk who visits the library to read modern verse while squirming in his chair. She falls in love with Haskell on a beautiful morning that reminds them both of the poetry of Browning. Rose is transported with the delight of romance: "What alacrity, what spontaneous good humor she displayed all that morning to the library patrons!" Haskell, who strives to be courteous and pleasant, still has "something about him," the townsfolk say, that puts them off. The outcome for Rose and her sweetheart cannot be sanguine, and Rose's concluding words ("Milk and a cream cheese sandwich") carry in them an ominous implication for her future. It's a nice story about the effects of mindless malice. Rose, who comes off well in contrast to her townfolk (including her snippy head librarian) is a gently realized character for whom one wishes well but fears the worst.

328. Wilson, Barbara. "In the Archives." In her *Thin Ice*. Seattle: Seal, 1981, pp. 33–40. Also in her *Miss Venezuela*. Seal, 1988.

In a self-serving career move, Sammy, an overweight female university librarian with an "almost obscene curiosity," has latched onto 30-something poet Nell Golden. Nell, who narrates the story, describes the life of the librarian as "dedicated to pigeonholing, to classifying, to saving for a rainy day." The archival collection over which Sammy presides is "a morgue for writers waiting to be reclaimed by posterity." Nell reaches some insights about her own ambition and needs, but Wilson displays few insights about librarians in her stereotyped and unpleasant treatment of Sammy.

329. Woolrich, Cornell. "The Book That Squealed." In *Women Sleuths*. Edited by Martin H. Greenberg and Bill Pronzini. Chicago: Academy Chicago, 1985, pp. 113–162. Also in the author's *Angels of Darkness*. New York: Mysterious Press, 1978. *Detective Story*, Aug. 1939. (Other sources.)

A not-bad mystery in which young public librarian Prudence Roberts solves a kidnapping case by cleverly piecing together a message derived from the missing page of a romance novel. A degree of stereotyping of librarians as timid, rule-bound monitors of library policies is offset in part by Prudence's determination, intelligence, and courage.

330. Wooster, Harold. "Machina Versatilis: A Modern Fable." *Library Journal* 94 (Feb. 15, 1979): 725–727.

A computer systems designer in a remote kingdom first assists the Royal

Librarians with effective ways of preventing the public — the annoying public — from bothering them with their requests for books. Then he tries to help the king with a program that will provide him a supply of satisfactorily nubile women. The story tries for comical irony but falls flat. Strangely, within the pages of a professional library journal, the story promotes some of the very stereotypes that have plagued the profession.

III. Plays

331. Ferris, Monk. ***Don't Tell Mother.*** New York: Samuel French, 1984. 104p.

Cinnamon Schmidt is a "desperately plain" Chicago librarian in her mid–30s who keeps a pencil in her hair bun. One afternoon she witnesses a bank robbery downtown, panics, and flees the scene. She is the only witness who can identify the robber. Cinnamon fears that if her mother hears about the robbery, she'll force her to transfer from the downtown Chicago Public Library headquarters to a neighborhood branch. Cinnamon describes herself as "a terrible klutz." She is also extremely nearsighted. As events demonstrate in this frantic farce, Cinnamon is not without a sense of the absurd or an ability to improvise. The script is difficult to read; the play would probably work better as nature intended, on the stage.

Franklin, Clay. *See* Hensinger, Franklin.

332. Frayn, Michael. ***Alphabetical Order.*** London: Samuel French, 1976. 66p.

Leslie, the new assistant librarian in the newspaper library, is "a shy, clever, violent" young woman. The librarian, Lucy, is an affable sort in her mid–30s. Everyone likes her because of her sympathetic attitude toward her staff and toward other newspaper employees. Lucy presides over an office that is anything but as neat as alphabetical order. It is a study in chaos, yet Lucy and her crew get the job done. When Leslie appears for her first day on the job, all do their best to impress her with their loony charm and lopsided wit. Lucy sees that Leslie is not amused; the newcomer is more interested in pigeonholing everyone according to a few simple personality traits. In short order, Leslie whips the library into a state of frightening efficiency, and she moves in on John, Lucy's new live-in mate, with the idea that she's doing him a favor. He needs to be "pinned down." "Preferably without anesthetics," notes Lucy. When the paper folds, Lucy and her staff return to their habit of comical anarchy, but they seem ready to follow the determined Leslie when she tries to rally them to keep the paper going on their own. The play has moments of mirth in the reading, although it is too sketchy to achieve any real character development.

333. Gagliano, Frank. *Night of the Dunce.* New York: Dramatists Play Service, 1967. 52p.

Night of the Dunce is set one dreadful night in the decrepit old Road's End Branch Library in an anonymous city. Mattie Vickers is the 60-year-old, fashionably dressed branch director. As the play opens, she is determined to sack her assistant librarian, Malcolm Supley. Though a good librarian, Supley has violated one of Vickers's edicts by speaking to the city commissioner. The play takes a quick, sinister turn with the introduction of David, a young, part-time staff member who has manipulated Vickers into firing Supley. He wants Supley's job. David is nasty to Supley and another library assistant while toadying reprehensibly to Vickers. As the unpleasantness continues into the evening, local oddball Max Kupreef takes Vickers aside and tells her what he thinks: "I've seen you change from a driving force in the community to some kind of hesitant, hat-wearing, hair-tinted, carefully made-up widow." Vickers breaks, then, and pours out her fears for the future of the library. She admits that she has been falsifying reports to the city commissioner, indicating a larger number of patrons than reality has provided, afraid that the library will not only be closed but demolished should the truth about its emptiness become known. Demolition is on order, but from an unexpected source: a gang of punks, the Dunces, terrorize the library staff and threaten to destroy the place. "'Christ, we're librarians,'" shouts Vickers at the punk assault (which the punks dub Project Library Raid), determined to stop it.

It's a frightening vision of society going to hell, with the library crew, at road's end for certain, about to take the ramparts in a defense of reason that is clearly doomed.

334. Guare, John. *A Day of Surprises.* In *Best Short Plays.* Edited by Stanley Richards. Philadelphia: Chilton, 1970, pp. 283–294.

A Day of Surprises is a two-character play set in the New York Public Library. Librarians Miss Jepson and Mr. Falanzano are working with paste pots when they notice one of the stone lions is missing from in front of the library. Miss Jepson realizes that this explains why there is a lion in the women's restroom, a lion that has devoured her colleague, Miss Pringle. Mr. Falanzano confesses that he and Miss Pringle were engaged. The play devolves into Mr. Falanzano's recitation of his clumsy and, we are to believe, comical lovemaking with Miss Pringle in the rare-book room and his subsequent sticky relationship with Miss Jepson. It's an annoying, unfunny, and stereotype-laden work by a now highly regarded playwright.

335. Hensinger, Franklin. *No Sweet Revenge.* In *Two for a Happening: A Dramatic Duo in Three Acts.* New York: Samuel French, 1969, pp. 59–72.

Hazel Evans, in her mid–30s, "is a disciplined spinster." In this two-character play, Keith Brady, her no-good former lover of sorts, stops in fresh from New Orleans. He ribs Hazel about her work as a librarian in a southern town. She assures him she finds "great satisfaction" in the job. For a long time she was bound to the town while she cared for her invalid mother. Keith calls her a "mistress of books — but never one in bed." Hazel admits, with Keith's prodding, that she leads something of a double life: When loneliness sets in, she goes to a nearby park, adopts the name Isabel, and strikes up conversations with strangers — male strangers, chiefly. This potentially embarrassing information in hand, Keith attempts to blackmail Hazel. Her response to his effort is the main focus of the play.

336. Lazarus, John. *Chester, You Owe My Bird an Apology.* In his *Babel Rap and Chester, You Owe My Bird an Apology.* Toronto: Playwrights Coop, 1972. 32p. (The two works are separately paged in the volume.)

Librarian Marjorie Hendershott visits her friend, 47-year-old Chester, and Chester's dominating older sister, Hattie. Shortly after their introduction, Hattie tells Marjorie "it doesn't take much in the way of brains to be a librarian." Marjorie, described as "elegant" and "poised," possessing "a youthful energy, enthusiasm and sense of humor," does her best to help Chester break free from bondage to his harpy sister and her repulsive pet cockatoo. The play is passably funny and ambiguous enough in its conclusion to amount to something more than mere popular time filler — but not much more.

337. Maggi, Carlos. *The Library.* In *Voices of Change in the Spanish American Theater.* Edited by W. I. Oliver. Austin, Tex.: University of Texas, 1971, pp. 105–169.

Uruguayan dramatist Maggi opens this play in 1917, with the young library director (the Director) fulminating over his speech on the laying of the new library's cornerstone, a speech to be attended by the Secretary General. He is also in a dither over a poem on which he is working, "The Low Blow of the Oboe," for a literary magazine and worries whether his frock coat will be ready for his weekend wedding. In the midst of these claims on his attention, he interviews a woman who wants to work in the library. "I love books!" she exults. "I've got one at home."

When the next act begins, set ten years later, the new library has not yet been built. Decades more pass, and still the "new" library remains a figment of the staff's imagination. They stumble through their pointless work as makeshift adjustments in the old library solidify into permanent features. The formerly young Director is pushing into middle age and not liking it. "My life's become meaningless, bitter," he complains. "I'm wasting my life, throwing it away on one stupidity after another." He can't stand his family. He hates his wife. "Life is so wonderful," he says, "I've thought of killing myself."

In the end, when the library is about to undergo demolition and the collection is in dead storage, a literary scholar engages the Director in a nonsensical, pompous argument over obtaining a manuscript. With the library about to come down around his ears, the Director laments, "All the days of my life. Coming to the same place, seeing the same people. And what for? For nothing. Absolutely nothing."

A play of merciless futility and hope that exists only to be defeated, *The Library* initially offers some space for laughter, but the joyless, bureaucratic absurdity that accumulates throughout leaves room for little but despair and pity.

338. Marchant, William. *The Desk Set.* New York: Samuel French, 1956. 90p.

Bunny Watson is the chief reference librarian at a major television network. She supervises a staff of several librarians, who work busy days dealing with a vast range of questions. Bunny combines terrific efficiency, thanks to an encyclopedic memory and almost superhuman arithmetical abilities, with a cheerful, "we're all in this together" approach to the job. She and her staff do seem united by a common desire to marry themselves off. Trouble arrives in the form of an efficiency expert who threatens to replace the reference crew with a computer. When the machine moves in, it's a monster: nine feet tall, eleven feet wide. Bunny and her reference colleagues prove that there is no substitute for the human touch in reference work — and Bunny gets her man. It's an amusing early exercise in computer phobia.

339. Moeller, Philip. *Helena's Husband.* In his *Five Somewhat Historical Plays.* New York: Knopf, 1918, pp. 9–43.

Helena's Husband is a curious little play set in ancient Greece, depicting Helena's departure with Paris for Troy, leaving her husband Menelaus behind. King Menelaus's librarian, the aged Analytikos, urges Menelaus to vengeance and war in the wake of Helena's faithlessness. The last speech in the play belongs to Analytikos, who rallies the Spartan masses with hatred of the Trojans as the peace-loving Menelaus cringes in a corner at the frenzied cheers of the bloodthirsty crowd. The effect would be greater if the play did not feature lines anticipating television melodrama: "I can't face him every morning at breakfast for the rest of my life," says Helena. "That's even more than a queen can bear."

340. Plater, Alan. *I Thought I Heard a Rustling.* Charlbury, England: Amber Lane, 1991. 88p.

Unpublished "writer"-in-residence and alleged former coal miner Bill Robson is presented at a pitiful press conference in the Eastwood Road branch library on the edge of London. Ellen Scott is head librarian, and she realizes immediately that the poems Robson submitted in his application for the position are plagiarized. Ensuing scenes in the library between Scott and Robson are most amusing. Scott is an ironic quipster and lover of literature who finds Robson's brazen naïveté baffling and outrageous. Robson sloughs off his task of criticizing would-be writers' amateurish bilge onto Scott but lines up solidly with her to defend the library against the town council's plan to sell the building to make room for a supermarket. Robson helps her save the library; if it takes a pack of lies to do the job, it is still a job well done. Scott is a strong character who likes her work and treats it as a calling: "Art and Beauty and Truth are the only things that matter a damn. I try to put it into practice in a tatty little branch library patronised by deaf old women and short-sighted old men." It's a funny and even inspiring play. (The title constitutes a running joke in the work.)

341. Stoppard, Tom. *Travesties.* New York: Grove, 1975. 99p.

"Sssssh!" is the first we hear from Cecily Carruthers, the young librarian in this play featuring Lenin, James Joyce, and the Dadaist Tristan Tzara, living in Zurich during World War I — and who gather here in the Zurich public library. Cecily is shushing Joyce and Lenin. "Cecily does not approve of garrulity in the Reference Section," observes Tzara. He further notes that although Cecily is rather pretty, her views on poetry are old-fashioned and her knowledge of poets eccentric, owing to her habit of reading them in alphabetical order. Cecily assumes major importance in Act II, which she opens with a lecture on Marx and Lenin. She comments that with her reference help, Lenin is writing his book on "Imperialism, the highest stage of capitalism." She has a long argument with another historical character, Henry Carr, about the nature of socialism. Cecily also has an opportunity to recite simple verse, including a lament for the Bolsheviki bound for Petrograd. In the end, she appears as her 80-year-old self, still argumentative after all these years about who did what and when during the old days in Zurich. It's an ingenious, funny, provocative play, and Cecily is definitely a figure to be reckoned with.

342. Volodin, Aleksandr. *The Idealist.* In *White Stones and Fir Trees: An Anthology of Contemporary Slavic Literature.* Edited by Vasa D. Mihailovoch. Rutherford, N.J.: Fairleigh Dickinson, 1977, pp. 433–441. *The Literary Review* 13 (Spring 1970): 387–396.

In a work that reads more like a short story than a play, the narrator, an unnamed Soviet librarian, reflects on her life and work in her small library from the 1920s to the present. To illustrate her durability, both on the job and in her thinking, the author presents her meeting with one of her first patrons at various times in his career, from student to postwar persona non grata with the authorities to present-day prominent scholar. In a nice conclusion, the librarian greets the scholar's adolescent son, who has come to use the library. The boy is "self-confident about what he doesn't understand … and at the same time knows what I don't know and can barely hope to learn." The librarian observes that, in hard times, she could have "lost faith in everything," but she did not; her quotation of Pushkin, "Greetings, young, unknown generation!" suggests why she did not.

343. Welty, Susan. *Library Open Hours.* In *100 Non-Royalty One-Act Plays.* Compiled by William Kozlenko. New York: Greenberg, 1940, pp. 163–169.

One cold winter afternoon during the Great Depression, Mr. Charles, elderly head of the Lebanon Public Library, comes in to work in spite of his recent influenza. Mr. Charles is a kind man and good-humored, although his wife's death is often near the front of his thoughts. Times are hard in Lebanon; Mr. Charles receives only a dollar a day for his work. This brief play's crisis concerns the apparent discovery by the assistant librarian, the shrill Mrs. Jay, that someone has been sleeping overnight in the library basement. It's an effective Depression vignette.

IV. Secondary Sources

Bibliographies and Indexes

In addition to such guides as H. W. Wilson's *Short Story Index* and *The Fiction Catalog*, the following sources also proved useful in identifying works of fiction for potential inclusion in this bibliography. The emphasis must go on "potential" in many cases, for, as noted below, absence of annotations, marginally informative annotations, or ambiguous subject classification limited the utility of a number of these sources (and significantly raised my frustration level!) Various critical studies and feature articles also proved valuable in the task of compiling titles for further investigation; these receive pertinent remarks in the annotations below.

344. Chaintreau, Anne-Marie and Renée Lemaître. *Drôles de Bibliothèques ... Le Thème de la Bibliothèque dans la Littérature et le Cinéma.* Paris: Editions Cercle de la Librairie, 1993. 416p.

Drôles de Bibliothèques is an enjoyable and useful book for readers interested in the depiction of the librarian and the library in French literature and film. It more than justifies digging out the old pocket *Larousse* for those whose French needs oiling. The bibliographic section lists and describes close to 300 works, including some originally published in English and other non–French languages. The authors' scope is broader than that of the present bibliography; their chief focus is on adult fiction, but they also cover comic books, children's literature, and poetry. Their filmography contains over 90 annotated entries. A significant portion of the book is devoted to meaty excerpts from works treated in the bibliography. In a particularly interesting chapter ("Portraits"), the authors discuss the kinds of librarians who appear in the works under consideration. It is well illustrated, with thoughtfully prepared indexes, an all-around agreeable work that enabled this bibliographer to identify some French and other fiction that later proved available in English translation.

345. *Cumulated Fiction Index.* London: Association of Assistant Librarians, 1952–.

This index contains no annotations.

346. Duda, Frederick. *Bib/Triv: Profundities, Banalities, and Trivialities in Libraryland.* Jefferson, N.C.: McFarland, 1992. 119p.

Bib/Triv includes a three-page unannotated list of "Fiction Titles with References to Libraries or Librarians."

347. Ellis, Edward F. *The British Museum in Fiction: A Check-List.* Portland, Maine: Authoensen Press, 1981. 193p.

The British Museum in Fiction is a lengthy annotated list of references to works of fiction including mention of the British Museum. Its strength is its comprehensiveness; its weakness is that it does not make clear the extent of the focus on the British Museum. The focus proves trivial in a great many instances.

348. _____. **"The New York Public Library in Fiction."** In his *The New York Public Library in Fiction, Poetry, and Children's Literature.* New York Public Library, 1956. pp. 9–19.

This list of works, chiefly novels, is annotated.

349. Frylinck, John and Janice Oliver. *Looks in Books: Images of Librarians in Literature, 1945–1990: A Bibliography.* Perth, Australia: The Library, Curtin University of Technology, 1990. 59p.

Looks in Books is a useful if somewhat frustrating guide to fiction involving librarians. It is useful because it lists close to 300 items; frustrating because there is no indication in the unannotated bibliographic entries whether a given work dwells at length or only in brief passing on a librarian character or whether the item is intended for adult or for younger readers. The authors provide some two dozen pages of discussion of librarians' images in various pieces of fiction — amusing, but not very helpful as a door to the bibliographic entries as a whole. Includes a list of 50 "Sources Consulted," from *Short Story Index* to letters to the editors of library journals.

350. Menendez, Albert J. "Quiet Please: Bookshops, Libraries, and Murder." In his *The Subject Is Murder: A Selective Subject Guide to Mystery Fiction.* New York: Garland, 1986, pp. 179–191, 290.

"Quiet Please" Lists 160+ 20th-century books but provides, unfortunately, no annotations or helpful classification breakdown. Is it a "bookshop" mystery? A "library" mystery? There is no way to tell from this bibliography.

351. _____. *The Subject Is Murder: A Selective Subject Guide to Mystery Fiction.* New York: Garland, 1990. 216p.

This sequel to the guide described in Item 350 lists on pages 43–45 approximately three dozen books in which mysteries involve "books and libraries." It has no annotations.

352. Rosenberg, Betty. *The Letter Killeth: Three Bibliographical Essays for Bibliomaniacs.* Los Angeles: Kenneth Karmiole, 1982. 60p.

The Letter Killeth lists mystery and murder fiction involving libraries, librarians, and other book-world entities.

353. Wertsman, Vladimir F. *The Librarian's Companion: A Handbook of Thousands of Facts and Figures on Libraries, Librarians, Books, Newspapers, Publishers, and Booksellers.* New York: Greenwood Press, 1987.

Chapter 4, "Librarian's Belle Lettres: Librarians, Publishers, and Booksellers in Novels and Plays," lists and very briefly annotates some 90+ works, many of which feature librarians.

Theses

354. Kirkpatrick, Mary. "American and Foreign Fictional Librarians: A Comparison." Master's thesis, Western Reserve University, Cleveland, 1958. 58p.

Kirkpatrick attempts a "content analysis" in which she notes fictional librarians' qualities, such as appearance, training, background, intelligence, personality, and so on and then totes the results into percentages of the body of literature she examines. She takes into her tabulation four dozen books about American librarians and some two dozen about foreigners. It is a curious, sociological oriented way of dealing with fiction, and some of the author's categories seem a little questionable. (This bibliographer did not feel terribly superannuated until seeing Kirkpatrick's definition of an "old" librarian as one who is over 50. Would someone please hand him his cane and truss?) She finds in her study that "librarians are generally regarded as intelligent, nice people," even if the two "most important" qualifications for the job, in the public mind, are the ability to read and the ability to sit for long periods doing nothing. Kirkpatrick concludes that "to be fitted for her new role, today's librarian must have a pleasing personality and a somewhat normal outlook on life." Her bibliography is briefly and not very satisfyingly annotated; all but a very few of the books she treats are included in the present bibliography.

355. Long, Lucille E. "The Stereotyped Librarian as Portrayed in Modern American Belles-Lettres." Master's thesis, Kent State University, Kent, Ohio, 1957. 93p.

In this in-depth examination, the author covers close to 100 works of creative writing (fiction, drama, poetry) as well as a number of essays and orations. Long laments that "the general public has been duped into certain erroneous and harmful ideas about the vital tasks of the librarian in our modern educational age" and then shows how the works in question have contributed to the duping. She also attempts to demonstrate how the works illustrate a number of librarian stereotypes she identifies, such as eccentricity, authoritarianism, devotion to duty, and so on.

356. Nation, Margaret A. "The Librarian in the Short Story: An Analysis and Appraisal." Master's thesis, Florida State University, Tallahassee, 1954. 55p.

Nation discusses the sometimes scant roles of librarians in 16 works, including the multiple-tale volumes of Edmund Pearson. Most of the other stories she notes also receive attention in this bibliography. Nation complains about the difficulty of finding stories published after 1920. She finds that the stories "present at best a weak portrayal of the profession in action" and that they are riddled with negative stereotypes.

357. Ross, J. J. "The Personality of the Librarian with Reference to the Librarians Portrayed in Australian Creative Writing and Australian Newspapers." Master's thesis, Monash University, Melbourne, Australia, 1988.

I was unable to obtain Ross's paper for review.

358. Speiden, Virginia M. "Image of the Librarian as Seen in Eight Library Career Novels." Master's thesis, University of North Carolina, Chapel Hill, 1961. 43p.

With one or two exceptions, library career novels do not appear in this bibliography. For those interested in the subgenre, Speiden's paper is a dated but interesting and detailed investigation.

359. Williams, Lisa W. "Libraries and Librarians in Murder-Mystery-Suspense Fiction, 1931–1980: A Content Analysis." Master's thesis, University of North Carolina, Chapel Hill, 1981. 35p.

Williams analyzes 20 novels regarding the roles and descriptions of libraries and librarians. Williams finds that when librarians are major characters, they do not fit a specific stereotype and that stereotyping is more prevalent when librarians serve as secondary characters.

Articles

360. Colquhoun, Jean. "As Others See Us, or Why Don't They?" *Wilson Library Bulletin* 26 (March 1952): 536–537.

"What is it in the make-up of a librarian," asks the author, "which makes him or her a difficult subject for the writer of fiction?" She does not quite answer the question but discusses several fictional librarians and then rephrases the question in her conclusion.

361. Cowell, Penny. "Not All in the Mind: The Virile Profession." *Library Review* 29 (Autumn 1980): 167–175.

Cowell comments on several novels in her discourse on the negative image of librarians she finds proffered to the public. She sets these negative impressions in an historical context, with numerous references to library literature, and finds the image of librarians formed by "an amalgam of ... an unfortunate stereotype, a low-status profession, and an aura of bourgeois respectability." She argues that attitudes toward librarians are rooted in inequalities of the social system, not in librarianship itself.

362. Filstrup, Jane M. "The Shattered Calm: Libraries in Detective Fiction." *Wilson Library Bulletin* 53 (Dec. 1978): 320–327.

Filstrup discusses the tradition of private libraries as settings for detective fiction, from Agathie Christie to Poe. She notes that "most of the [mystery] novels in which librarians play a part place them at the apex of victim," an observation that, she argues, lends substance to "the feminized image of the library." Librarian characters may be "tame," she writes, but they also are "often aggressive in their curiosity to ferret out the explanation for circumstances that puzzle them." It includes remarks on a number of novels, including Gwen Bristow's *The Gutenberg Murders* (Item 24), Charles J. Dutton's *Murder in a Library* (Item 60), and Marion Boyd Havighurst's *Murder in the Stacks* (Item 92), among others.

363. _____. "The Shattered Calm: Libraries in Detective Fiction, Part II: The Librarian as Sleuth." *Wilson Library Bulletin* 53 (Jan. 1979): 392–398.

This commentary on several novels and stories in which librarians do the detecting offers some interesting observations on the nature of the library and its relationship to detective fiction.

364. Glencross, Alan. "Boys in Green." *Assistant Librarian* 48 (Dec. 1955): 189–190.

Glencross complains that librarians are almost totally ignored in British fiction. When they are represented, they are described in a derogatory manner.

"Almost the only 'nice' librarians in British fiction occur in Prudence Summerhayes' *Girls in Green* (Item 201)—and what a boring giggle of girls they are!" Glencross discusses that novel, along with several others presenting librarians in a more-or-less dreary light.

365. Goodrum, Charles A. "Writing the Library Whodunit: Murder and Intrigue Stalk the Werner-Bok Library." *American Libraries* 8 (April 1977): 194–196.

"Writing the Library Whodunit" is an amusing essay in which Goodrum, author of *Dewey Decimated* and other novels about librarians (Items 83–85), tells the reader what it was like to write "*the* library whodunit." He describes *Dewey Decimated* as "a two-evening throw-away while you're recovering from the flu or a bad sunburn."

366. Griffen, Agnes M. "Images of Libraries in Science Fiction." *Library Journal* 112 (Sept. 1, 1987): 137–142.

"Images of Libraries in Science Fiction" is an interesting and thoughtful essay on the title topic in which Griffen identifies various future library cultures, ranging from the barren (in postapocalyptic fiction) to information retrieval systems independent of human mediation. The library future Griffen sees in science fiction is, in fact, one largely devoid of librarians.

367. Gunn, James E. "'Dreams Written Out': Libraries in Science Fiction." *Wilson Library Bulletin* 69 (Feb. 1995): 26–29.

Gunn "examines the concept of *library* in many classic sf texts." His survey lingers briefly on the works themselves; as in Agnes Griffen's essay noted in Item 366, the impression of future librarians gleaned from Gunn's view is not encouraging for anyone who prefers the human touch to the automated.

368. Hutton, Muriel. "Librarians in Literature." *Books* 359 (May/June, 1965): 99–102.

"Librarians in Literature" is another lament on the theme. It ranges over a number of fictional libraries, most discussed in this bibliography; the only attractive female librarian Hutton finds is Eve Halliday in Wodehouse's novel *Leave It to Psmith* (see Item 223). Eve is, of course, a mere amateur. Hutton notes that librarians in fiction seem to do nothing but catalog and charge out books, apparently "the only duties authors have ever heard of in libraries."

369. McReynolds, Rosalee. "A Heritage Dismissed: Librarians in Search of Their Place in American Popular Culture, 1876–1950." *Library Journal* 110 (1965): 25–31.

"A Heritage Dismissed" is a well-researched and thoughtful analysis of the image of librarians during the period indicated, with a strong focus on librarians' perceptions of themselves. McReynolds discusses the development of the popular and notorious spinster image and reflects on the irony of a profession whose ranks are dominated by women but whose administration is disproportionately male. It includes close to four dozen references, as well as a sidebar annotating a number of fictional works.

370. Moynahan, Julian. "Libraries and Librarians: Novels and Novelists." *American Libraries* 5 (Nov. 1974): 550–552; 6 (Feb. 1975): 69.

Moynahan, author of the novel *Pairing Off* (Item 162), identifies two images of libraries and librarians in fiction: "On the one hand, libraries are places of withdrawal and escape, peopled by shy and eccentric individuals of introvert character who have turned away from the noise and bustle of the clamant world outside to make a separate peace. On the other, there is the image of the library as a busy public institution serving society and culture and staffed by energetic, ambitious people who work by the same kind of professional standards as, say, lawyers, architects, and educators do." He hopes that most real libraries have room for both these varieties.

371. Olen, Sandra. "The Image of Librarians in Modern Fiction." *Mousaion* 5(2): 48–57, 1987.

Olen discusses images of librarians found in a handful of recent novels. She wants to know if "the librarian is now seen as a person who can communicate successfully, who can use modern technology to assist him/her in serving users and providing for their various information needs." The answer, paraphrased, is "not really." The question is the wrong one to ask; it is not pertinent to the broad realms of the most meaningful fiction, which concern not narrow professional attributes, much less professional propagandizing, but the entire range of human experience.

372. Pankin, Mary F. P. "Librarians in Mystery Stories." *West Virginia Libraries* 31 (Winter 1978): 11–18.

Pankin examines a number of mystery novels featuring librarians and comments on the stereotyped depictions of both male and female members of the profession. She notes, accurately, that the authors show poor understanding of the profession's educational requirements.

373. Tannenbaum, Earl. "The Librarian in the College Novel." *College & Research Libraries* 24 (May 1963): 248–250.

Tannenbaum attempts to determine librarians' status in the academic novel, using as his basic texts 15 post–1950 novels cited in John O. Lyons's *The College Novel in America* (Southern Illinois Univ., 1962). "Out of some 55 hundred pages in the 15 novels only about 40 short quotations refer in any way to the library or the librarian.... Librarians themselves are rarely mentioned; if they are, it is usually within the pejorative framework of a current cliche." He advances but does not elaborate on a few tentative explanations for this shabby treatment. "Perhaps," he concludes, "the 'library explosion' has not yet sounded in fiction."

374. Walsh, Daniel P. "'On Fire or On Ice': Prefatory Remarks on the Library in Literature." *Reference Librarian* 18 (Summer 1987): 211–238.

Walsh discusses various works of creative writing with a focus on librarians. Walsh states that his "paper hopefully revealed the potential richness of the enormous amount of material regarding the Library as symbol/sign and the implications of such an interpretation." It's a tad heavy on critical jargon but also contains worthwhile insights on the works in question.

V. Bibliographer's Choice: Works Not to Miss

Novels

Amis, Kingsley. *That Uncertain Feeling*. (Item 4)
Anderson, Sherwood. *Beyond Desire*. (Item 5)
Astley, Thea. *Reaching Tin River*. (Item 6)
Bowes, Barry. *Between the Stacks*. (Item 16)
De Bruyn, Gunter. *Buridan's Ass*. (Item 44)
Eco, Umberto. *The Name of the Rose*. (Item 61)
Guilloux, Louis. *Bitter Victory*. (Item 88)
Hayes, Marjorie. *Homer's Hill*. (Item 94)
Lewis, Sinclair. *Main Street*. (Item 133)
Lively, Penelope. *Passing On*. (Item 136)
McCracken, Elizabeth. *The Giant's House*. (Item 140)
Mac Laverty, Bernard. *Cal*. (Item 145)
Mallea, Eduardo. *The Bay of Silence*. (Item 150)
Mojtabai, A.G. *Mundome*. (Item 152)
Moynahan, Julian. *Pairing Off*. (Item 162)
Pirandello, Luigi. *The Late Mattia Pascal*. (Item 177)
Rio, Michel. *Archipelago*. (Item 183)
Sallenave, Daniele. *The Phantom Life*. (Item 186)
Smiley, Jane. *Duplicate Keys*. (Item 195)
Torday, Ursula. *Dewey Death*. (Item 207)
Wiesel, Elie. *The Fifth Son*. (Item 220)

Short Stories

Borges, Jorge Luis. "The Library of Babel." (Item 242)
Chappell, Fred. "The Lodger." (Item 254)

Dabrowska, Maria. "Miss Vincent." (Item 257)
Kees, Weldon. "The Sign." (Item 283)
Koger, Lisa. "The Retirement Party." (Item 284)
Moore, Lorrie. "Community Life." (Item 299)
Munro, Alice. "Carried Away." (Item 300)
Painter, Pamela. "Something to Do." (Item 305)
Phillips, Robert. "Peckerman." (Item 310)
Shibaki, Yoshiko. "Ripples." (Item 316)
Walker, Augusta. "The Day of the Cipher." (Item 324)

Plays

Gagliano, Frank. *Night of the Dunce.* (Item 333)
Maggi, Carlos. *The Library.* (Item 337)

Index

References are to entry numbers. Novels and short story collections are in italics,
short stories in " " and plays in SMALL CAPS; *authors and secondary works are in roman*